Problems of Metaphysics and Psychology

Jay N. Eacker

Problems of Metaphysics and Psychology

Nelson-Hall nh Chicago

LIBRARY OF CONGRESS CATALOGING IN PUBLICATION DATA

Eacker, Jay N.
Problems of metaphysics and psychology.

Includes bibliographical references and index.
1. Psychology—Philosophy. I. Title.
BF38.E128 1983 150'.1 82-8053
ISBN 0-88229-685-X (cloth) AACR2
ISBN 0-88229-814-3 (paper)

Manufactured in the United States of America

10 9 8 7 6 5 4 3 2 1

The paper in this book is pH neutral (acid-free).

In Memory of Anna
1937–1975

Contents

Preface

Many of those who develop an interest in psychology, or any other subject for that matter, may assume that there must be experts somewhere who can tell them what it is. In addition, they may suppose that colleges and universities employ people with expertise of the kind required to inform them or to teach them what psychology is. As a result, they may read books written by those experts, or take courses taught by them, in an effort to find out what it is.

Unfortunately, most of these students probably are disappointed by what they read or are taught. They are disappointed because they find that, if they read more than one book or take more than one course, the experts do not all agree on what the subject is; there may also be just plain disagreement over other matters as well.

The lack of agreement, and outright disagreement, may come from a number of sources. One is that those who profess an expertise in psychology are not as expert as they profess to be. Another is that they are sufficiently expert but interpret their data differently. A third is that the student of the subject has asked the wrong kind of question about it.

With some too notable exceptions, it is probably not the case that the colleges and universities have been misled; most professors are experts in what they profess. In addition, experts may quite honestly and sincerely disagree on what their data mean. Consequently, if these are the only three sources for the lack of agreement and disagreement, then the fault may be in the question.

However, to most of us, it may seem absurd to fault the question. After all, most of us spend most of our lives trying to find out what things are and, for the most part, are rather successful at it. Nevertheless, the fault still may be in the question.

The question may be at fault for a number of reasons. One is that most questions seem to be based on the supposition that, since they can be asked, there must be answers for them. We seldom, if ever, consider the possibility that there might be some questions for which there are no answers and find it laughable to suggest that there might be some answers for which there are no questions. However, there may be a good many questions for which there are no answers. One example may be "How many angels can dance on the head of a pin?" Another may be "What is the meaning of life?" A third may be "Why did a loved one have to die?"

A second reason that the question may be at fault is that it assumes (1) there is a subject of the question which (2) has essential characteristics, an essential nature, or an essence that (3) can be known as well as stated in the form of an answer. Those assumptions may be impossible to defend. They may be impossible to defend because, even if there were things and they in turn had essential characteristics, an essential nature, or an essence, we would never know whether we had discovered them or simply invented them. Our lack of certainty is related to our assumptions about what there is and our methods for knowing what there is or our metaphysics.

This book examines the basis for questions of this kind in somewhat greater detail. It then considers several of these questions as they might be raised by students of psychology and offers answers to them based either on what appears to be consensus or on a behavioral perspective within psychology, most often the latter. Finally, it attempts to draw some conclusions about the questions, as well as the answers, as they might relate to contemporary psychology.

This book might be thought of as a sequel to *Problems of Philosophy and Psychology* (Chicago: Nelson-Hall, 1975). That book was an attempt to present, in a somewhat systematic way, thirteen problems encountered in psychology that did not appear to be solvable with the methods of science as they are currently understood; they were therefore said to be problems of philosophy as well as psychology. This book is similar to that first one, except that the problems considered are somewhat different. The problems examined this time are once again not likely to be solved with the methods of science, but they seem to be more appropriately classified as specifically metaphysical rather than just generally philosophical.

To be still more specific, the problems considered here are ontological problems of psychology because they appear to arise from assumptions psychologists and students of psychology make about the nature of reality, whether they do so by accident or by design. Ontology, or the study of being, and epistemology, or the study of knowing, combine as metaphysics for many contemporary philosophers. In somewhat different terms, ontology has to do with what there is, while epistemology has to do with how we know what there is; both are aspects of metaphysics in philosophy.

The word *metaphysics,* however, probably is more familiar to most people than either *ontology* or *epistemology,* and so it has been chosen for the title.

All of the problems examined at this time seem to presuppose what exists, as well as how we know what exists, when neither can be known with the methodology of science. The first cannot be known because the methods of science are based on observation, and, so far as we know, observations are never complete. The second cannot be known because the method for knowing the methodology of science cannot be the methodology of science. With statements such as these, it now may be more clear why what follows are considered problems of metaphysics and psychology.

Mentors, colleagues, students, friends, casual acquaintances, mystery persons, and two special loved ones have made their differential contributions to these efforts, although none is responsible for the final product. Mentors include especially Ed Moore, Frank Seaman, and Dud Klopfer. Colleagues include Joe Maier and Steve Rubin; it was the latter who informed students they had been "Eacker'd" when they were overheard discussing some of the issues examined here. Students are Wayne Norman and Jim Dougan. Friends and acquaintances are too numerous to mention. One mystery person is B. The special loved ones are Anne and Jane; the book is dedicated to the memory of their mother.

Chapter One

Introduction

Several years ago, I wrote and was able to publish a small book entitled *Problems of Philosophy and Psychology* (1975). In the conclusion, it was stated that, based simply on the length of the chapter in which it was presented, the discussion on the problem of metaphysics appeared to be very short. However, since nearly all of the problems discussed in the book were in some way related to the problem of metaphysics, the entire work might conceivably have been regarded as a discussion of metaphysics. In somewhat different terms, the title of that book might just as well have been the same as the title for this one. However, since that time, some additional problems have become apparent to me, and they seem to stem more directly from the assumptions that psychologists and other students of psychology have been willing to make about the nature of reality; it is assumptions of this kind which make the problems metaphysical, or, more precisely, ontological. And, since it is problems of this sort which are examined here, the title for this book is particularly apt.

To summarize the discussion of the problem of metaphysics

in the earlier book (Eacker, 1975, pp. 25–32), there appear to be at least two metaphysical positions that are possible and defensible in science; the problem is which to adopt. One of them is realism; the other is phenomenalism. Realism is the commonly accepted view that a real, objective world exists independently of any observer; it is a world with real objects and events existent in it. Phenomenalism is the not so commonly accepted view that the world is constructed by an observer out of his own sense experience and that of others as they report it; the objects and events in this world, to the extent that they are in a world, are constructions of logic and sense experience. The problems examined in what follows seem to arise from a realistic metaphysics or ontology, and it is in that sense that they are considered problems of metaphysics and psychology.

They may, perhaps, most easily be stated in the form of questions, such as: What is psychology? What is behavior? What is a stimulus? What is learning? or What is reinforcement? Each of these questions contains some form of the verb *to be* which might suggest, at least to a realist, that either the subject or the object of the verb, or some characteristic of both, exists and can be known. In addition, each of the questions appears to require not simply one from among various possible answers but a definitive one. For example, the first question seems to imply, What is psychology (really)? Similarly, an implication of the fifth question is, What is reinforcement (really)? Definitive answers probably are pursued more diligently in metaphysics than they are in the sciences.

When posed in the form of questions, each of these problems appears to be a simple matter of definition; as students are fond of saying, "It's all a matter of semantics." That is, it would seem that all that must be done to answer the first question is to define psychology. However, although a term may be defined, it might not refer to anything, or at least anything observable. For example, the definition of a centaur is that it is a four-legged creature with the head and trunk of a man but the fore- and hind-quarters of a horse. Thus, the word *centaur* can be given a definition. But no one has ever supported the claim that they had observed a centaur, except perhaps in imaginative pictures, alcoholic delirium, or psychotic illusions. So far as is known, the word has no empirical referent, in the sense that it refers to something that has been observed. It is assumed that most psychologists and other students of psychology would require, as answers to these questions, definitions with empirical referents. Otherwise, the definition would be empty; it would be nonsense or nonsensible to the extent that it would not be related to sense experience. That requirement requires further discussion of definition itself and particularly of the distinction between formal, as opposed to operational, definitions.

A formal definition states the class that includes the object defined and the characteristics by means of which it may be distinguished from other objects in that class; it is sometimes referred to as definition by genus and species. On the other hand, an operational definition states the operations or procedures, frequently measurements, used to distinguish the objects referred to from other objects. Neither definition guarantees the existence of the thing defined; they merely give the thing defined meaning. There are many other types of definitions, and, since the subject of definition is so closely related to all of these problems, it seems necessary at this point to assert that they are not simply problems of definition. Support for this assertion may become more evident as the discussion proceeds.

It might also be observed that, when definitive answers to questions about the nature of things are not immediately and directly given, beginning students of psychology may conclude that the psychologist to whom they are addressed does not know what he is talking about or the discipline is so obscure that it is not worth the trouble to study it further. A good many psychologists may have found themselves defending answers they have given to these questions when bright and perceptive students have pointed out exceptions. This discussion will not necessarily eliminate such exchanges, but it may indicate how it happens that definitive answers to these questions remain so elusive.

While in general the problems examined here may be considered problems of metaphysics and psychology, it appears that their source is, more specifically, essentialism, which is in itself regarded by some philosophers as a metaphysical problem. Essentialism is not a school of psychology, such as behaviorism. Moreover, while it is a term familiar to many philosophers, it is not a school of philosophy, such as positivism. It is, rather, a search for "essences."

Each of the above questions seems to require a statement of the "essence" of the subject of the question, whether the subject is psychology or some other matter commonly included within psychology. For example, the question "What is psychology?" suggests for many of those who ask it that there is one and only one thing that psychology is and that the answer to the question must state what that thing is. Consequently, when they read that "psychology is the science of behavior" in one textbook and that it is the "science of mind" in another, they may conclude that one or the other is in error or that the authors of both do not know what they are talking about. Another conclusion they may reach is that their search for an answer to the question must be continued until the "essence" of psychology has been found and stated. That quest assumes, of course, that the term *psychology* has a referent; that is, it assumes there is one thing that is psychology, to which the term *psychology* refers. It is because of this assumption that the question is philosophical or, more accurately, metaphysical. It is philosophical because there does not appear to be any way that the experimental methods of science can be used to establish the existence of a thing. An experiment to determine what it is to which the term *psychology* refers does not appear possible since, for one thing, such an experiment seems to require that psychology be identified before it can be identified.

The question is more specifically metaphysical because it assumes the existence of some thing to which the term *psychology* refers, and assumptions about the existence of a thing are metaphysical. To be still more precise, they are ontological; that is, they are concerned with the nature of being or existence. Ontology and epistemology, or theory of knowledge, are combined as metaphysics by many contemporary philosophers (cf. Margenau, 1950, p. 80).

As will be seen with regard to these and other matters, the "essence" of essentialism probably cannot be stated. Nevertheless, an attempt at least to characterize it has been made by Sir Karl Popper, who is among the most eminent and influential of contemporary philosophers. In a footnote to his intellectual autobiography, Popper (1974, pp. 11–23) stated that he first used the term *essentialism* in *The Poverty of Historicism* (1957) as well as the two volumes of *The Open Society and Its Enemies* (1952); he also indicated that the problem of essentialism was his first philosophical failure or at least contributed to it. This discussion of essentialism is based largely on these two works.

In the opening passages to section ten of *The Poverty of Historicism* (1957, pp. 26–34) entitled "Essentialism versus Nominalism," Popper asserted that the problem of essentialism, or the problem of universals, was "one of the oldest and most fundamental problems of philosophy" and that it was "rooted in the philosophies of Plato and Aristotle." In addition, "it is usually considered as a purely metaphysical problem"; although, for him, "like most metaphysical problems it can be reformulated so as to become a problem of scientific method" (Popper, 1957, p. 27); the problems examined in the chapters that follow cannot.

He continued in the next paragraph with the statement that "every science uses terms which are called universal terms, such as 'energy,' 'velocity,' 'carbon,' 'whiteness,' 'evolution,' 'justice,' 'state,' 'humanity.' These are distinct from the sort of terms which we call singular terms or individual concepts, like 'Alexander the Great,' 'Halley's Comet,' 'The First World War' " (Popper, 1957, p. 27). The former are universals, and the latter are particulars. There does not appear to be much doubt about the existence of things denoted by particulars (although, after a first course in philosophy, most college freshmen come to realize that almost everything can be doubted). But, the same cannot be said for universals, which, of course, reveals the metaphysical, or ontological, aspect of the problem. That is, there is less doubt about the existence of particulars than there is about the existence of universals. In somewhat different terms, the problem of essentialism, or universals, is whether there are any universals, or essences.

This interpretation of the problem was further developed by Popper (1957, pp. 27–28) in his next paragraph, where he remarked that

> over the nature of universal terms a long and sometimes bitter dispute raged between two parties. One held that universals differ from proper names only in being attached to the members of a set or class of single things, rather than to just one single thing. The universal term 'white', for instance, seemed to this party to be nothing but a label attached to a set of many different things —snowflakes, tablecloths, and swans, for instance. This is the doctrine of the *nominalist* party. It is opposed by a doctrine

> traditionally called *'realism'*—a somewhat misleading name, as seen by the fact that this 'realist' theory has also been called 'idealist'. I therefore propose to re-name this anti-nominalistic theory *'essentialism'*. Essentialists deny that we first collect a group of single things and then label them 'white'; rather, they say, we call each single white thing 'white' on account of a certain intrinsic property that it shares with other white things, namely 'whiteness'. This property, denoted by the universal term, is regarded as an object which deserves investigation just as much as the individual things themselves. (The name 'realism' derives from the assertion that universal objects, for instance, whiteness, 'really' exist, over and above single things and sets or groups of single things). Thus universal terms are held to denote universal objects, just as singular terms denote individual things. These universal objects (called by Plato 'Forms' or 'Ideas') which are designated by the universal terms were also called 'essences'.

Essentialists believe "in the existence of universals (i.e., of universal objects)"; they also stress the importance of universals for science. For them, science must "penetrate to the essence of things. But the essence of anything is always something universal" (Popper, 1957, p. 28).

For Popper, "these last remarks indicate some of the methodological implications of this metaphysical problem." However, there are methodological issues related to essentialism that may be "considered independently of the metaphysical issue," one of which "avoids the question of the existence of universal and singular objects, and of their differences" (Popper, 1957, p. 28); this way of considering the problem is undoubtedly what he meant by his assertion that most metaphysical problems can be reformulated so as to become problems of scientific method. Obviously, if the question of existence is ignored, the problem is no longer metaphysical.

He began the examination of the metaphysical issue with the statement:

> The school of thinkers whom I propose to call *methodological* essentialists was founded by Aristotle, who taught that scientific research must penetrate to the essence of things in order to explain them. Methodological essentialists are inclined to formulate scientific questions in such terms as 'what is matter?' or 'what is force?' or 'what is justice?' and they believe that a penetrating answer to such questions, revealing the real or essential meaning of these terms and thereby the real or true nature of the essences denoted by them, is at least a necessary prerequisite of scientific research, if not its main task. [Popper, 1957, pp. 28–29]

This quotation provides at least some evidence for the thesis that essentialism is the source of questions like "What is psychology?" and "What is science?" It also reveals the essentialist view of scientific explanation, which differs rather substantially from the various discernible types of explanation in contemporary psychology (cf. Eacker, 1975, pp. 41–54).

Popper gave a somewhat different account of essentialism in *The Open Society and Its Enemies* (1952a, p. 31).

> I use the name methodological essentialism to characterize the view, held by Plato and many of his followers, that it is the task of pure knowledge or 'science' to discover and to describe the true nature of things, i.e., their hidden reality or essence. It was Plato's peculiar belief that the essence of sensible things can be found in other and more real things—in their primogenitors or Forms. Many of the later methodological essentialists, for instance Aristotle, did not altogether follow him in this; but they all agreed with him in determining the task of pure knowledge as the discovery of the hidden nature or Form or essence of things. All these methodological essentialists also agreed with Plato in holding that these essences may be discovered and discerned with the help of intellectual intuition; that every essence has a name proper to it, the name after which the sensible things are called; and that it may be described in words. And a description of the essence of a thing they all called a 'definition'.

Thus, according to this account and Popper's understanding of Plato and Aristotle, they were (1) methodological essentialists who (2) viewed the task of science as the discovery of the true nature of things through the use of (3) intellectual intuition and (4) expressed their intuitions in the form of definitions.

However, it was not clear to Popper (1952 b, p. 11) how intellectual intuition unerringly arrived at the essences of things.

> Although Aristotle is not very clear on this point, there can be little doubt that, in the main, he again follows Plato. Plato taught that we can grasp the Ideas with the help of some kind of unerring *intellectual intuition;* that is to say, we visualize or look at them with our 'mental eye', a process which he conceived as analogous to seeing, but dependent purely upon our intellect, and excluding any element that depends upon our senses. Aristotle's view is less radical and less inspired than Plato's, but in the end it amounts to the same. For although he teaches that we arrive at the definition only after we have made many observations, he admits that sense-experience does not in itself grasp the universal essence, and that it cannot, therefore, fully determine a definition. Eventually he simply postulates that we possess an intellectual intuition, a mental or intellectual faculty which enables us unerringly to grasp the essences of things, and to know them. And he further assumes that if we know an essence intuitively, we must be capable of describing it and therefore of defining it.

Thus, it appears that for both Plato and Aristotle we know the essence of a thing by means of intellectual intuition rather than sense experience because, to show the circularity of the position, we know the essences of things by means of intellectual intuition rather than sense experience; presumably, both of them knew that by means of intellectual intuition!

Another way to view methodological essentialism, according to Popper (1952a, p. 32), is to contrast it with methodological nominalism.

> Instead of aiming at finding out what a thing really is, and at defining its true nature, methodological nominalism aims at describing how a thing behaves in various circumstances, and especially, whether there are any regularities in its behaviour. In other words, methodological nominalism sees the aim of science in the description of the things and events of our experience, and in an 'explanation' of these events, i.e. their description with the help of universal laws. And it sees in our language, and especially in those of its rules which distinguish properly constructed sentences and inferences from a mere heap of words, the great instrument of scientific description; words it considers rather as subsidiary tools for this task, and not as names of essences. The methodological nominalist will never think that a question like '*What is* energy?' or '*What is* movement?' or '*What is* an atom?' is an important question for physics; but he will attach importance to a question like: 'How can the energy of the sun be made useful?' or 'How does a planet move?' or 'Under what condition does an atom radiate light?' And to those philosophers who tell him that before having answered the 'what is' question he cannot hope to give exact answers to any of the 'how' questions, he will reply, if at all, by pointing out that he much prefers that modest degree of exactness which he can achieve by his methods to the pretentious muddle which they have achieved by theirs.

According to this account and Popper's understanding of modern science, scientists apparently are (1) methodological nominalists who (2) view the task of science as the description of how things behave under various circumstances through the use of (3) observation and (4) express their findings in the form of universal laws. Otherwise stated, methodological nominalism not only contrasts with methodological essentialism but it also appears to represent current practices in the natural sciences. Nominalists do not ask what things are but how they function or behave, which, of course, is the practice of the behaviorists in psychology at the present time.

As indicated by the conclusion of the preceding paragraph, there is opposition to essentialism in science and, therefore, in psychology. Popper very clearly opposed it. For example, in the paragraph following the remarks quoted above, Popper (1952a, pp. 32–33) stated that

> methodological nominalism is nowadays fairly generally accepted in the natural sciences. The problems of the social sciences, on the other hand, are still for the most part treated by essentialist methods. This is, in my opinion, one of the main reasons for their backwardness. But many who have noticed this situation judge it differently. They believe that the difference in method is necessary, and that it reflects an 'essential' difference between the 'natures' of these two fields of research.

Obviously, those who "judge it differently" are methodological essentialists.

Later, in a somewhat different context, Popper (1952b, p. 9) remarked that

> the development of thought since Aristotle could, I think, be summed up by saying that every discipline, as long as it used the Aristotelian method of definition, has remained arrested in a state of empty verbiage and barren scholasticism, and that the degree to which the various sciences have been able to make any progress depended on the degree to which they have been able to get rid of this essentialist method. (This is why so much of our 'social science' still belongs to the Middle Ages.)

The "social science" to which he referred did not necessarily include psychology, but to the extent that there are those who still classify psychology as a social science his remarks do apply. Furthermore, these two quotations may be more applicable to a stage through which the social sciences already have evolved. But, while that may be true of those sciences, it does not appear to be true for many of those scientists and especially their students. Many of them still ask essentialist, or "What is" questions, which, of course, it is the purpose of this discussion to dispel or at least to modify.

In general, Popper's (1952b, pp. 12–13) reasons for opposing the practices of essentialism were that they stand "in the strongest possible contrast to the methods of modern science." More specifically, he argued that essentialism requires a certainty, or finality, in human knowledge which the methods of science cannot supply. Scientific knowledge is never, so far as can be discerned, certain; it is only more or less probable. Furthermore, there are no "proofs" in the empirical sciences, if a proof "establishes once and forever the truth of a theory."

A second more specific reason for his opposition to essentialism is related to the function of definition in modern science. The essentialists, especially Aristotle, hold to the view that a definition first points to the essence of the thing in question and, by describing its essence, then determines or explains the meaning of the term so defined. By contrast, the methods of modern science use words as shorthand expressions for longer descriptions; they help to summarize those descriptions. This distinction between the two types of definitions may be what some scientists and philosophers of science refer to as the difference between formal and operational definitions; although that is not the language used by Popper. Rather, he refers to the latter type of definition as nominalist and the former as essentialist.

After making this distinction, Popper (1952b, pp. 15–17) went on to argue that the essentialist view of definition is, as it stands, untenable because it is based on the doctrine of intellectual intuition, as well as the more popular doctrine that precision in discourse requires definition of terms. With regard to the first doctrine, the problem of how to decide between two opposing intellectual intuitions of the same phenomenon immediately arises. And, with regard to the second doctrine, if terms must be defined for purposes of precision in discourse, it is not clear when to stop defining terms; for that matter, it is not clear how to start. The second doctrine leads to an infinite regression. Thus, aside from the fact that essentialism strongly contrasts with the methods of modern science, it is also logically untenable according to Popper.

Another philosopher, Ludwig Wittgenstein, was also opposed to essentialism (and on occasion opposed, and was opposed by, Karl Popper). For example, in a chapter entitled "The Attack on Essentialism," from his book *The Philosophy of Wittgenstein*, George Pitcher (1964, p. 217) remarked that

> Wittgenstein sets out to show that the belief in essences, although widespread and entirely natural, is mistaken. Whereas philosophers have traditionally looked for sameness and unity, Wittgenstein looks for difference and multiplicity; indeed, he once remarked to a friend that he had considered using as a motto for the *Investigations* a line from *King Lear*—"I'll teach you differences". According to Wittgenstein, one has only to examine, for example, the various individuals to which a given general term applies, to see that there is nothing which they all have in common. As a plain matter of fact, they do not share a common essence. Wittgenstein cites the example of games: If we look at all the things called 'games', we will not find some characteristic(s) that they all have, in virtue of which we call them by that name.

Pitcher supported this conclusion with a quotation from Wittgenstein's *Philosophical Investigations* (1953, pp. 31–32).

> Consider for example the proceedings that we call 'games'. I mean board-games, card-games, ball-games, Olympic games, and so on. What is common to them all?—Don't say: "There must be something common, or they would not be called 'games' "—but *look and see* whether there is anything common to all.—For if you look at them you will not see something that is common to *all*, but

> similarities, relationships, and a whole series of them at that. To repeat: don't think, but look!—Look for example at board-games, with their multifarious relationships. Now pass to card-games; here you find many correspondences with the first group, but many common features drop out, and others appear. When we pass next to ball games, much that is common is retained, but much is lost.—Are they all 'amusing'? Compare chess with noughts and crosses. Or is there always winning and losing, or competition between players? Think of patience. In ball games there is winning and losing; but when a child throws his ball at the wall and catches it again, this feature has disappeared. Look at the parts played by skill and luck; and at the differences between skill in chess and skill in tennis. Think now of games like ring-a-ring-a-roses; here is the element of amusement, but how many other characteristic features have disappeared! And we can go through the many, many other groups of games in the same way; can see how similarities crop up and disappear.

Pitcher pointed out, however, that this "insight was not original with Wittgenstein." William James (1902, pp. 26–27) had earlier made a similar observation about "religion" and "government."

> Most books on the philosophy of religion try to begin with a precise definition of what its essence consists of. Some of these would-be definitions may possibly come before us in later portions of this course, and I shall not be pedantic enough to enumerate any of them to you now. Meanwhile the very fact that they are so many and so different from one another is enough to prove that the word 'religion' cannot stand for any single principle or essence, but is rather a collective name. The theorizing mind tends always to the over-simplification of its materials. This is the root of all the absolutism and one-sided dogmatism by which both philosophy and religion have been infested. Let us not fall immediately into a one-sided view of our subject, but let us rather admit freely at the outset that we may very likely find no one essence, but many characters which may alternately be equally important in religion. If we should inquire for the essence of 'government', for example,

> one man might tell us it was authority, another submission, another police, another an army, another an assembly, another a system of laws; yet all the while it would be true that no concrete government can exist without all these things, one of which is more important at one moment and others at another. The man who knows governments most completely is he who troubles himself least about a definition which shall give their essence. Enjoying an intimate acquaintance with all their particularities in turn, he would naturally regard an abstract conception in which these were unified as a thing more misleading than enlightening. And why may not religion be a conception equally complex?

Thus, for James, the more a subject is understood, the less there is need for a definition which states its essence, if one could ever be stated, or, for that matter, even known. It may very well be the case that the extent to which students, especially students of psychology, ask essentialist questions is a measure of how much they understand the subject; as they learn more about it, these questions gradually may disappear or perhaps be extinguished since they receive so little reinforcement. On the other hand, essentialist questions and answers may have evolved as pedagogical devices from which students (and a good number of their mentors) must be weaned; this discussion may help to hasten that process if it is true that such questions have evolved as pedagogical devices.

To return to Pitcher's analysis of Wittgenstein's philosophy and his opposition to essentialism, the traditional view of essentialism is that the characteristics of a thing can be divided into two different categories. The first is a small number of essential characteristics; they are characteristics a thing must necessarily have in order to be classified as what it is. The second is a somewhat larger number of nonessential, or accidental, characteristics; they are characteristics a thing may have, but not of necessity, in order to be classified as what it is.

According to Pitcher (1964, pp. 221–22), Wittgenstein does

away with this distinction. He argues against essential and accidental characteristics for a single set of characteristics, "some sub-set of which, and not the *same* sub-set in every case, a thing must have in order to be" what it is or at least be classified and called what it is.

In addition, Wittgenstein observed "that many terms not only fail to have a unitary meaning, but also fail to have a fixed meaning—the cluster of characteristics associated with the term is always subject to change." As an example of this defect in the assumptions of essentialism, Pitcher (1964, p. 222) cited the possibility of blue sugar, which probably still would be called sugar.

A lesson about essentialism for psychologists and students of psychology was contained in a statement that immediately followed Pitcher's reference to sugar.

> If, however, we shift from everyday practical life to a discipline where a certain amount of rigor is required—to science, for example—essentialism might seem to regain its foothold. It often happens in science that certain characteristics of a substance or phenomenon are considered to be so central as to be treated as absolutely essential, as defining, characteristics of it. Wittgenstein would not want to deny this. He would not deny that for certain special purposes, such as those of a scientist, terms can and sometimes should be *given* a circumscribed, unitary meaning. But even in these cases, the unitary meaning cannot and should not be considered final and unalterable. As science advances, and new theories are propounded, new facts and procedures discovered, some formerly privileged characteristics will be dropped from the inner circle and others take their place. So in science as in everyday life, terms often, and perhaps always, have no fixed meaning. [Pitcher, 1964, pp. 222–23]

The lesson for psychologists and students of psychology is that questions like "What is psychology?" or "What is learning?" may never receive definitive answers, if they receive any answers at all, since words may not have fixed meanings.

Pitcher (1964, p. 223) went on to observe that, apparently, Wittgenstein

> held that all words which are involved in philosophical puzzlement, all words which are philosophically interesting, have no unitary, fixed meaning. They do not, in other words, designate essences. And once we free ourselves from the belief in an essence corresponding to each word, we shall be well on the way towards freeing ourselves from at least some kinds of philosophical bewilderment.

The same may be true for words that are not philosophically, but rather scientifically, interesting.

Still another philosopher and early psychologist who opposed essentialism, although not all forms of it, was John Dewey. For example, in *Experience and Nature,* he stated that

> "essence", as it figures in Greek theory, represents the mysterious potency of earlier "symbols" emancipated from their superstitious context and envisaged in a dialectic and reflective context. The essences of Greek-medieval science were in short poetic objects, treated as objects of demonstrative science, used to explain and understand the inner and ultimate constitution of things. While Greek thought was sufficiently emancipated from magic to deny "efficient" causality to formal and final essences, yet the latter were conceived of as making particular things to be *what* they are, members of natural kinds. Moreover, by a reversal of causal residence, intrinsic seeking for such forms was imputed to changing events. Thus the ground was prepared for the later frank return of patristic and scholastic thought to a frank animistic supernaturalism. The philosophic theory erred, as did magic and myth, regarding the nature of the efficacy involved in ends; and the error was due to the same causes, namely, failure of analysis into elements. It could not have occurred, were there that sharp division

> between means and ends, fruitions and instrumentalities, assumed by current thought. [Dewey, 1925, pp. 387–88]

Regardless of whether his explanation of the error is correct, the fact remains that he considered the search for essences by the early Greek philosophers an error.

His own view of essentialism is perhaps best expressed in the following quotations:

> The counterpart of classic thought which took ends, enjoyments, uses, not simply as genuine termini of natural events (which they are), but as the essence and form of things independent of human experience, is a modern philosophy which makes reality purely mechanical and which regards the consequences of things in human experience as accidental or phenomenal by-products. In truth, abstraction from human experience is but a liberation from familiar and specific enjoyments, it provides means for detecting hitherto untried consequences, for invention, for the creation of new wants, and new modes of good and evil. In any sense in which the conception of essence is legitimate, these human consequences are the essences of natural events. Water still has the meanings of water of everyday experience when it becomes the essence H_2O, or else H_2O would be totally meaningless, a mere sound, not an intelligible name. [Dewey, 1925, pp. 193–94]
>
> This capacity of essences to enter readily into any number of new combinations, and thereby generate further meanings more profound and far reaching than those from which they sprang, gives them a semblance of independent life and career, a semblance which is responsible for their elevation by some thinkers into a realm separate from that of existence and superior to it. Consider the interpretations that have been based upon such essences as four, plus, the square root of minus one. These are at once so manipulable and so fertile in consequences when conjoined with others that thinkers who are primarily interested in their performances treat them not as significant terms of discourse, but as an order of entities independent of human invention and use. The fact that we can watch them and register what

> happens when they come together, and that the things that happen are as independent of our volition and expectation as are the discoveries of a geographic exploration, is taken as evidence that they constitute entities having subsistent Being independently not only of us but of all natural events whatever.
>
> Alternatives are too narrowly conceived. Because meanings and essences are not states of mind, because they are as independent of immediate sensation and imagery as are physical things, and because nevertheless they are not physical things, it is assumed that they are a peculiar kind of thing, termed metaphysical, or "logical" in a style which separates logic from nature. But there are many other things which are neither physical nor psychical existences, and which are demonstrably dependent upon human association and interaction. Such things function moreover in liberating and regulating subsequent human intercourse; their essence is their contribution to making that intercourse more significant and more immediately rewarding. [Dewey, 1925, pp. 195–96]

Thus, for Dewey, to the extent that essences are anything at all, they are interactions, or relations, between the knower and the known, if, in fact, there is a difference between the knower and the known.

There may well be other first rank philosophers and psychologists opposed to essentialism, just as there may be some who defend it. However, perhaps enough of those who oppose it have been mentioned that a few conclusions may be drawn from the views of essentialism and the opposition to it that are of relevance for the discussions of essentialist-type questions that occur in subsequent chapters.

The first and most obvious conclusion from the above discussion is that essentialism has not been refuted by any of the authors to which reference has been made; it simply has been rejected. For example, Popper did not provide evidence against essences; he simply asserted that the methods of science cannot be used to provide such evidence (if there is such a thing as negative evidence, it may not be very easy to provide anyway). Similarly, Wittgenstein was not able to discover any essences in games, but others may, especially if they find the concept of essence useful in their respective areas of inquiry. James's contention that there is no single definition for either religion or government does not prove that they have no essences or that essences do not exist. Proof is not possible in science, as pointed out by Popper; although there may appear to be exceptions in the case of logic and mathematics. However, the conclusions of logic and mathematics may have little to do with what is observed, as those who have arrived at untested, and untestable, conclusions about human nature in the history of psychology more than amply attest. Finally, Dewey simply treated essences as poetic objects rather than as objects of demonstrative science.

There appears to be no more evidence against essences than there is evidence for them, which suggests that the search for essences is a philosophic matter rather than a scientific one. That is, essentialism may not be an issue that can be resolved with the methods of science; therefore, it is a matter to be dealt with by philosophy, or metaphysics, or ontology. If so, then questions like "What is psychology, or science, or behavior?" cannot be answered by psychologists as scientists; they can be answered only by psychologists as philosophers. However, the answers psychologists give as philosophers may be as various as the psychologists themselves, since apparently none of the answers can be subjected to an empirical test under controlled conditions of observation, except perhaps that of consensus. If the questions are a matter of consensus, then obviously the answers given to them at one point in time may not be the same as those given at another; more will be said about the subject of consensus and how it might relate to essentialist questions toward the close of this chapter.

A second conclusion that may be drawn from the opposition to essentialism is that it appears to conflict with current practices in the natural sciences, which many contend include psychology. Essentialism requires certainty or proof, but the truths of the natural sciences are only probable. It presupposes the veracity of intellectual intuition, but the natural sciences accept the products of intellectual intuition, to the extent that they accept them at all, as hypotheses to be tested. Essentialism asks "What is a thing?" rather than "How does it function?" And, finally, essentialism attempts to determine the true, or ultimate, nature of a thing rather than its laws.

A third conclusion that may be drawn from the opposition to essentialism, very closely related to the second, is that essentialist explanation differs from explanation in the natural sciences. According to the essentialists, a thing, object, or event is explained by its essence, essential characteristics, or ultimate nature. By contrast, it appears that a thing, object, or event in the natural sciences is explained by its laws or, in the case of behavioral events, by the variables related to it. To say that something is explained by its essence, essential characteristics, or ultimate nature is very much like saying that a thing is what it is because it is what it is, which, of course, is a tautology. On the other hand, to say that something is explained by its laws is to make reference to the things that affect it, which takes the thing as it is, whatever it is, and inquires about it from that point. What the thing is may then, perhaps, emerge from the inquiry, although it was not necessarily there before the inquiry began, and it may not be there, i.e., an existing thing, when the inquiry terminates.

A fourth conclusion that may be drawn from the opposition to essentialism is that it may have retarded, and still may be retarding, the evolution of psychology as a natural science. The remarks of Popper and Pitcher relevant to this point are, of course, simply their assessment of the situation in the social sciences. Nevertheless, it may well be that giving up the essentialist approach to subject matter areas in psychology, such as learning and motivation, might lead to some new ways of formulating some old problems. For example, psychologists and other students of psychology might no longer concern themselves with the ultimate nature of learning and motivation but instead with the laws of learning and motivation. And, this alternative approach might lead to less "pretentious muddles" than the theories of learning and motivation, as well as personality and psychopathology, that have been proposed so far; this subject will receive further discussion in the chapters on learning and motivation.

A fifth, and final, conclusion that may be drawn from the opposition to essentialism and the discussion up to this point is that a concern for "What is psychology, or learning, or motivation?" may represent a misunderstanding of what a science of behavior is about. A preoccupation with such questions may lead psychologists and other students of psychology away from questions that the methods of science are able to answer and for which they were especially developed. Nevertheless, some concern for essentialist questions may be justified, to the extent that justification is required, if it leads psychologists back to the laboratory rather than away from it (cf. Skinner, 1961). It also is justified if it leads other students of psychology to the laboratory for the first time. Finally, it is justified if it only reminds those who ask such questions how it happens that they have not been answered; these considerations provide some rationale for continuing to discuss these questions in the chapters that follow.

It was indicated a bit earlier that the subject of consensus and how it might relate to essentialist questions would receive further discussion toward the close of this chapter. If, as suggested by Popper and others, things, objects, or events do not have essences, then essentialist-type questions, "What is" questions, either must not be answered at all or must be answered in some way other than by stating the essence of the thing being inquired about. Since they are asked, and those who ask them seem to expect an answer, an answer of some sort seems to be required. As suggested by Dewey, alternatives to essentialism may be too narrowly conceived, but one possibility with respect to how essentialist questions might be answered is consensus. That is, answers to essentialist questions are simply conventions that have been adopted, whether inadvertently or by design, with respect to them. Thus, for example, it was true that, early in its history, psychology was the study of the psyche. Those concerned with the question "What is psychology?" could agree with that answer to the question; there was some consensus about it. That was the conventional view of psychology, although there might not have been universal agreement.

Conventions may be thought of as the customary ways in which things are done or, in this instance, the ways in which terms are used. It is conceivable that the way in which a term is used may have very little, if anything, to do with the "essence" of the thing to which it refers. Even if it does, it is not entirely clear how we can know that it does, since to know the "essence" of a thing seems to require that we know it as it is, and, so far as we know, human knowledge is always related to ourselves; the "thing in itself" seems to be unknowable.

If consensus is the basis for conventions, and if conventions are the customary ways in which things are done, and if they include the ways in which terms are used, they are subject to change. Thus, it may have been true that, at one time, psychology was the study of the psyche. It also may be true that, at one time, it was the study of mind, which may be different than psyche. It also may be true that it is now the science of behavior. What it will be in the future remains to be seen.

Nevertheless, the question can be given an answer in psychology, at the present time, and it is the purpose of this work to examine that answer in greater detail. A number of other persistent essentialist questions in psychology will receive that same scrutiny. In the process of doing so, an effort will be made to indicate what the current conventions are with regard to these questions; however, since the book is written from a behavioral perspective, the "conventions" stated may be simple extrapolations from that perspective.

No attempt will be made to be exhaustive. In psychology, there are many more questions of this type than will be examined here. Nevertheless, those selected and discussed may provide some clue as to how the others that could have been asked might have been answered. The questions that seem especially significant from a behavioral perspective, and based on a casual assessment of the frequency with which they occur, are: What is psychology? What is behaviorism? What is science? What is behavior? What is a stimulus? What is learning? What is reinforcement? What is motivation? What is emotion? What is instinct? and What is human nature? These are the questions that will be examined in the chapters that follow.

Chapter Two

What Is Psychology?

This question is perhaps the one most frequently asked by beginning students of psychology, but it also may challenge more advanced students, as well as recognized psychologists, from time to time. Efforts to answer the question abound. The difficulty in doing so is illustrated by the often repeated, and perhaps apocryphal, story about the professor of psychology who found it necessary to be absent during the first several weeks of an introductory course she had agreed to teach. As a result, a graduate teaching assistant was left in charge. The teaching assistant, who was a rather conscientious fellow, decided that the only way to begin such a course was with a definition of psychology; after all, he reasoned, you cannot talk about something unless you can say what it is. When the professor returned some three or four weeks later, she found the graduate assistant still struggling with the definition.

The graduate assistant's reasoning helps to illustrate the essentialist, or, to be more precise, methodological essentialist, view of science discussed in the first chapter. That is, essentialists tend to formulate scientific questions, or what appear to them to be scientific questions, in the same way as the graduate assistant; they want to know what something is—its true nature, hidden reality, or "essence." In addition, they may expect every answer to reveal the real or essential meaning of the major terms in its question, for example, "What is psychology?" which in turn would reveal "the real or true nature of the essences denoted by" those terms (Popper, 1957, pp. 28–29).

However, contrary to the essentialist view of things, it is possible to say something about a subject before we are able to say what it is. Indeed, most of what we say may take that form. It takes that form because human knowledge, and especially scientific knowledge, can never be known to be complete. That is, to the extent that scientific knowledge is based on observation, it is always possible to make one more observation immediately after the last one has been made, so long as there are people around to observe. Consequently, scientific knowledge, in particular, and human knowledge, in general, cannot be complete. Stated differently, if our basis for knowing is observational, we cannot know, observationally, when it is that we are through making observations. These considerations aside, reasoning such as that displayed by the graduate assistant leads to a logical absurdity: if we must be able to say what a thing is before we can talk about it, then we must know everything about something before we can begin to investigate it; if we don't, we will not know what we are investigating. Considerations of this kind help to illustrate some of the philosophical, if not metaphysical, aspects of these questions.

The history of psychology demonstrates, contrary to essentialist reasoning, that we can talk about a subject, such as psychology, before we can say what it is. Many psychologists have talked about psychology and have tried to say what it is. Furthermore, they have all met with some success, although not the kind that abides. For example, in the first paragraph of *A Primer of Psychology,* the structuralist Edward Bradford Titchener (1898, p. 1) remarked:

> The word 'psychology' comes from the two Greek words *psyche,* 'mind', and *logos,* 'word'. Psychology therefore means, by derivation, 'words' or 'talk about mind'. But it is understood among scientific men that when the word *logos* forms the last part of a compound English word it shall mean not simply 'talk about' a subject, but the *science* of that subject. Hence we sometimes speak of the sciences as the 'ologies'. Biology, for instance, which is derived from the Greek *bios,* 'life', and *logos,* means the *science* of life; and oölogy, which comes from *oon,* 'egg', and *logos,* is the *science* of birds' eggs. It would not be quite true to say, then, that psychology means 'talk about mind'; it rather means 'science of mind' or 'mental science'.

Titchener does not appear to have been naive about issues that might be considered philosophical or even metaphysical. For example, in the preface to the *Primer of Psychology,* he expressed a concern for how psychology was related to ontology and epistemology, or metaphysics. In other words, he probably realized he had not stated the "essence" of psychology or determined with certainty what its essential characteristics were. However, the same may not have been true of those for whom his book was intended; it was a primer, and, therefore, may have oversimplified many complex topics, including the definition of psychology. In addition, while the linguistic derivations of the name of a subject may indicate that the name means one thing, other considerations may make the name mean something quite different than what was intended. Nevertheless, those who read Titchener's book might rather easily have reached the conclusion that his definition corresponded to what psychology really is; many people today still regard psychology as the study of mind, if not the science of mind, and they have never read the *Primer of Psychology* or even heard of Titchener. Furthermore, the above conclusion, drawn by those who read the book, might have been strengthened by the systematic and coherent way in which Titchener subsequently developed his views on psychology. A rudimentary correspondence and/or coherence theory of knowledge, or epistemology, combined with a realistic ontology could easily have led to the conclusion; a good many views in academic psychology probably have been accepted on the basis of assumptions about how we know something no different than the assumptions of Titchener's readers.

A correspondence theory of knowledge is that what we know corresponds to what is known, that is, what is in our heads corresponds to what it is about. A coherence theory of knowledge is that we know something when what we know is coherent, "hangs together," is internally consistent, or does not contradict itself. A realistic ontology (cf. Eacker, 1975, p. 28) is that a world really exists independently of ourselves. Thus, a correspondence and/or coherence theory of knowledge combined with a realistic ontology is that what is known is coherent and corresponds to what there is.

There have been many other statements made about what psychology is, and they do not all agree with the one made by Titchener. For example, in a little book entitled *The Definition of Psychology,* the distinguished psychologist Fred S. Keller (1937, p. 106) stated that a system of psychology "is an attempt to say just what psychology is, what it is the science of, what the whole enterprise is about—to define a subject matter and hence to direct research." In one sense, a system of psychology is

> ". . . nothing more than a logical framework into which may be fitted the findings of the science." In another sense a system is nothing more than an elaborate *definition* of psychology. Every textbook is a step-by-step vindication of a point of view announced, if the author is truly "systematic," in an introductory chapter, paragraph, or sentence. Only when we have carefully examined the system, through reading of the text, are we able to grasp the substance of the definition. [Keller, 1937, p. 99]

Thus, for Keller, a system of psychology is a definition of psychology; it is a statement of what psychology is. However, it is a bit more than a definition, to the extent that it gives a systematic view of what psychology is.

It is of some interest to speculate about how the word *system* came to be applied to these different views of psychology. One possibility is that the views were, or attempted to be, systematic in the sense that they had something to say about most of the topics that were included within psychology at the time they were written. Another possibility is that they were, or attempted to be, comprehensive views of psychology, very much like the comprehensive views of philosophy that had preceded them. Most college graduates have encountered, at one time or another, the systems of philosophy proposed either by rationalists, such as Descartes, Spinoza, and Leibniz, or by empiricists, such as Locke, Berkeley, and Hume. Indeed, the system builders in psychology might simply have been continuing the tradition of the system builders in philosophy but on a somewhat smaller scale. Similarly, the learning theorists in psychology may have continued on a still smaller scale.

The system building tradition may have been abandoned when it became clear, though not made explicit, that all efforts to give a comprehensive and/or systematic view on some area of inquiry are futile. They are futile because even if they are true we are never quite certain that they are true, since someone else can present another, and very different, view, and our efforts to decide between them, if based on observation, will not be complete until the last observer has perished. Furthermore, if that tradition is simply a slightly different form of the search for essences, which it very well might be, then what has been said in these last two paragraphs is that the essentialist tradition was abandoned by the system builders in psychology when it was found to be unfruitful.

Such speculation aside, there were four systems of psychology examined by Keller in the first edition of his book. They were: structuralism, functionalism, gestalt psychology, and behaviorism. It was stated somewhat earlier in this chapter that structuralism was the psychology of Titchener. He defined psychology as the science of mind. Consequently, his answer to the question "What is psychology?" was that "Psychology is the science of mind."

No one has ever been entirely clear about what mind is, but Titchener defined it as the sum total of mental processes that occur in the lifetime of each one of us. It seems, therefore, that the concept of greater importance than mind in his system is mental process.

A process occurs; it is ongoing; it happens. For Titchener, mental process goes on inside of us. It goes on inside each one of us and so can be known by only one person. However, it can embrace the whole world, since every object dealt with by the sciences can be changed into a mental process, regardless of whether it is a thing or a process and inside or outside of the body. Objects of science can be changed because they can be looked at in two ways. One way is to consider them as they are in the world, the other is to consider them as they are in someone's experience. In the first, they are physical things or chemical processes or physiological processes. In the second, they are mental processes. Thus, it appears that for Titchener everything has a double aspect, a physical aspect and a mental aspect; it is the latter, of course, that is of importance for psychology. However, since it is we who consider objects as they are in the world, or as they are in our experience, they are still in our experience. Hence, it might be argued that both aspects are mental processes, although Titchener did not do so.

Regardless of that argument, psychology was the science of mind for Titchener. The major method by which mind was to be investigated was introspection, the "looking within" on the content of consciousness by trained observers. Introspectionists were trained to report the content of consciousness. They were observers of consciousness, although it was never made entirely clear what sensory system was used when they observed consciousness. Nevertheless, the claim was that they observed the content of consciousness and did so without committing the "stimulus error," which occurred when they reported characteristics of the stimulus rather than the sensation.

The problem for psychology was the analysis of mental phenomena into their elements, how they were synthesized or connected, and the explanation of mind by reference to the nervous system; these three features of the problem are sometimes referred to as the "What?" "How?" and "Why?" of mind. The structure of mind that resulted from such inquiry consisted of such things as sensations, images, affective processes, and attention.

Titchener's concept of process deserves some additional comment. Processes occur; they are ongoing; they happen. Similarly, the behavior in which contemporary behavioral psychology claims to be interested occurs, is ongoing, or happens. The chief difference between the processes in which Titchener was interested and the behavior in which contemporary behavioral psychology is interested may be that the former are internal, or covert, whereas the latter is external, or overt, although at least one contemporary behavioral psychologist has displayed an interest in both overt and covert behavior (cf. Skinner, 1963). Whether covert or overt, behavior appears to us to be either internal or external, just as Titchener's objects and processes may appear to us to be either inside or outside of us.

Furthermore, just as processes and behavior occur, are ongoing, or happen, so do events occur, go on, or happen, and the latter may be more general cases of both processes and behavior. If so, then perhaps Titchener was interested in internal events rather than mental processes; and contemporary behavioral psychology is interested, with the exception noted, in external events rather than behavior. If that is so, then perhaps psychology was always concerned, as it is now, with internal and external events but conceptualized them as mental processes on the one hand and behavior on the other.

The major implication of these considerations may be that an emphasis on events, observed events, rather than mental processes or behavior, might help to relate the various systems of psychology more closely to one another and thereby provide a more unified view of the discipline. What may emerge from such an emphasis is a new system of psychology that is more inclusive than the previous systems.

The second system of psychology examined by Keller was functionalism. The functionalists generally held to the view that the subject matter of psychology was "mental activity." Hence, they can be said to have defined psychology as the science of mental activity. Mental activity included such things as thinking, feeling, imagining, and perceiving. These were "functions" of the human organism and other animals—the things that they did. In addition, mental activity was psychophysical in the sense that there was no difference between the mental and physical aspects of experience in psychology.

Elsewhere (cf. Marx and Hillix, 1973, p. 152), mental activity was equated with adaptive behavior. An adaptive act was said to involve a motivating stimulus, a sensory situation, and a response that changed things in such a way that the motivating conditions were satisfied. The motive was considered a stimulus that dominated the behavior of a particular organism until it reacted in such a way that the stimulus was removed or, at least, was no longer effective; thus, motive was not necessary for behavior to occur but was a directive force that functioned in a general way to determine what would take place.

Motives could be resolved by an adaptive act in three ways. In the first, the act might simply remove the stimulus. In the second, the act might disrupt the stimulus by the introduction of a stronger one. In the third, the act might make the stimulus less effective through sensory adaptation. The methods by which these acts were studied were introspection, or subjective observation, and experimentation, or objective observation, and they were used mainly in the areas of perception, learning, and mental activity.

The problem for functional psychology was similar to that for structural psychology. That is, it too was interested in the "What?" "How?" and "Why?" of mental activity. However, the functionalists seemed more interested in what is accomplished by it, how it occurs, and why it takes place.

A third system discussed by Keller in the first edition of *The Definition of Psychology* (1937) was gestalt psychology. Gestalt psychology, as might be expected, originated in Germany. It defined psychology as the study of behavior in its causal connection with the psychophysical field.

The subject matter of psychology was behavior as determined by psychophysical processes. Psychophysical processes were psychological and physical to the extent that, for example, behavior took place in a behavioral environment where the behavioral environment was the geographical environment as viewed by the organism. The geographical environment as viewed by the organism apparently was a gestalt, a form quality of perception or experience. Consequently, and in somewhat different terms, the subject matter of psychology was gestaltqualität, or form qualities, of experience.

The methods for investigating gestalt were on some occasions direct observation and on others introspection; although it was not the introspection advocated by Titchener. Rather, it was the introspection of untrained observers, or, as it has sometimes been called, phenomenological observation. Phenomenological observation meant a naive and full description of direct and immediate experience by an observer who had no training in the technique of doing so; the method was known as phenomenology and is to be distinguished from phenomenalism (cf. Eacker, 1975, p. 29).

The problem for gestalt psychology was to comprehend the intrinsic nature and organization of the psychophysical field and how it was related to the geographical environment, as well as to comprehend the behavior that resulted from the organization of the field. Furthermore, it attempted to account for direct experience by referring to the underlying field, which was considered to be almost entirely physiological.

The fourth system of psychology examined by Keller in the first edition of *The Definition of Psychology* (1937) was behaviorism. According to the early or classical behaviorists, psychology was the science of behavior. The subject matter was the behavior of organisms. Its methodology was the objective method of science. The problem for psychology was the same as that for all of the sciences, namely, prediction and control. However, in contrast to the other systems, John B. Watson, the founder of classical behaviorism, claimed to find no evidence for the existence of mental phenomena or, for that matter, processes that could be called mental.

The term *behavior* referred to "responses," "reactions," or "adjustments" of the organism to particular antecedent conditions called "stimuli" or "stimulus-situations." The use of the words *stimulus* and *response* appears to have originated in physiology, but Watson extended their meanings to include more complex and integrated events than those usually dealt with by physiologists. Thus, for example, a "stimulus-situation" could be resolved into a complex group of stimuli, and an "adjustment" included a group of responses which were integrated in such a way that an organism did something which could be given a name.

For Watson, there were two ways of subdividing the response factor, physiological and psychological. With regard to the former, responses occur through the action of muscles and glands, otherwise known as "effectors." All external movements of an organism in space are accomplished by the striped, or skeletal, muscles; internal adjustments are brought about by the unstriped, or smooth, muscles. Glandular responses involve the secretion of such things as saliva, sweat, and tears under the appropriate circumstances; not much was said about the "blood, sweat, and tears" commonly encountered in daily living by most of us.

With regard to the latter subdivision, there were four main classes of responses exhibited by the muscles and glands. They were: explicit habit responses, implicit habit responses, explicit hereditary responses, and implicit hereditary responses. This category for subdividing the response factor was psychological rather than physiological and apparently referred to the learned and unlearned features of behavior. In addition, the words *explicit* and *implicit* appear to correspond, respectively, with "external" and "internal" behaviors, "overt" and "covert" behaviors, or "observable" and "non-observable" behaviors; more will be said about these distinctions in subsequent chapters, since, as suggested by the digression on events in this one, a detailed examination of them may lead to a new view or integration or system of psychology.

The general method of psychology for the classical behaviorists was objective observation. Specific types of objective observation included: naturalistic and laboratory investigations, Pavlovian conditioning, verbal reports, and tests.

The problem for psychology was the prediction and control of human behavior. Stated in somewhat different terms, the problem was to delineate the stimulus given the response or to predict the response given the stimulus.

There are other definitions, statements, or systems explaining what psychology is. For example, Edna Heidbreder (1933) examined seven of them in a book with that title, *Seven Psychologies.* Aside from those mentioned above and based on chapter headings, they were: the Psychology of William James, Dynamic Psychology and Columbia University, and Freud and the Psychoanalytic Movement. On the other hand, Marx and Hillix (1973) listed six systems of psychology. Again based on chapter headings and including the "classical" four systems, they were: associationism and psychoanalysis. Finally, but not exhaustively, Chaplin and Krawiec (1974, pp. 684–85) discussed eight systems of psychology. Aside from the first four and psychoanalysis, they were: associationism, psychophysics and quantitative psychology, and humanistic and existential psychology.

Regardless of the number of systems that might be examined, all apparently were attempts to state what psychology is, and none of them appears to have been definitive; this state of affairs may serve as additional evidence for the failure of essentialism. Nevertheless, there does appear to be some consensus that psychology is the science of behavior. For example, Keller (1973), in a more recent edition of *The Definition of Psychology,* stated that radical behaviorism "is in fact our only thriving system of behavior at the present time. Indeed, it is perhaps the only system of psychology presently supported by any appreciable number of natural-science workers in our field" (Keller, 1973, p. 143). Similarly, Marx and Hillix (1973, p. 165) stated that behaviorism "is by far the most influential and most controversial of all the American schools." Finally, Chaplin and Krawiec (1974, p. 683) have argued that "broadly speaking American experimental psychology is a functionalistic behaviorism" which seems to combine both functionalism and behaviorism.

They meant that, "while the *definition* of psychology has become more behavioristic, its *spirit* has remained functionalistic" (Chaplin and Krawiec, 1974, p. 683). Thus, a good many psychologists define psychology as the science of behavior. However, they are still concerned with why organisms behave as they do, or motivation, which appears to be the spirit of functionalism.

Another meaning, if not an implication, of the statement by Chaplin and Krawiec is that American experimental psychologists, and especially those committed to an experimental analysis of behavior, are increasingly more interested in functional relationships between the environment and behavior; they are more and more concerned with a functional analysis of behavior, although that sometimes may become quite theoretical. Nevertheless, they seem less interested in why organisms behave as they do and more interested in the conditions under which they behave as they do. Stated somewhat differently, the emphasis in American psychology has shifted away from the causes of behavior toward the variables of which behavior is a function, although there are those who might argue that there is no appreciable difference between these two approaches.

However, there are those who might argue differently. For example, Bolles (1975, pp. 5–10) suggests that the search for the causes of behavior is based on the doctrine of mechanism, whereas the search for the variables of which behavior is a function appears to be based on the doctrine of empirical determinism. Briefly, the difference between the two doctrines is that mechanical determinism seeks the physical agents, forces, or things that make organisms do what they do, while empirical determinism seeks only to state the relationship between what organisms are doing and what is happening in their environments. Psychology, since it is a behavioral rather than a physical science, may have to set aside the doctrine of mechanistic determinism for the doctrine of empirical determinism; more will be said about this subject in later chapters. Whatever the outcome, this second interpretation may more accurately reflect what is meant by functionalistic behaviorism.

Regardless of these considerations, it seems reasonable to conclude that, for now at least, psychology is the science of behavior. But this answer to the question of "What is psychology?" comes from one of its systems and perhaps now is the time to examine what that system has become since it was first formulated by Watson. Consequently, the next chapter will attempt to answer the question "What is behaviorism?"

Chapter Three

What Is Behaviorism?

It very probably appears to most of those who have read this far that the question for this chapter was answered in the previous one. However, the account of behaviorism given there has often been referred to as "classical behaviorism," and there are at least two other versions. One is neobehaviorism, and the other is neo-neobehaviorism, at least according to Koch (1964, pp. 7–21).

He argued that "classical behaviorism" was characterized by objectivism, an S-R orientation, peripheralism, an emphasis on learning and S-R associationism, and environmentalism. Objectivism refers to an insistence on observation as the basis for statements of fact in psychology. The second characteristic is that such statements are to be expressed in the language of stimulus and response. The third is that receptors, effectors, and their direct nerve connections are held responsible for most psychological phenomena. The fourth is that learning and not perception is of central importance in psychology and is to be understood in terms of some form of classical conditioning principles. Finally, environmentalism refers to the emphasis that is placed on environmental determinants of behavior as opposed to genetic, or nativistic, determinants.

Neobehaviorism was a fusion of the characteristics of classical behaviorism and a "new view" of science current at the time of its influence. This view was positivistic, pragmatic, and operational in the sense that it emphasized the hypothetico-deductive aspects of science as it was then understood. That is, the construction of a theory was simply a matter of deducing hypotheses from its postulates or theorems, giving them operational meaning, usually in the form of measurement, and then testing or confirming them under controlled conditions of observation.

Neo-neobehaviorism was a modification and liberalization of the neobehaviorist position. More specifically, this form of behaviorism displayed an interest in research areas that were legislated out of existence by the other two. The areas were: perception, language behavior, thinking, and what are in general called mediational processes; the latter are those processes that might "mediate" between the stimulus and the response.

More could be said about each of these forms of behaviorism as explicated by Koch (1964). However, perhaps enough has been said to suggest that behaviorism has not remained static over the years and, indeed, that it may have become, or may be becoming, something else. To develop this point of view, it is somewhat instructive to examine statements made about behaviorism by two of its leading spokesmen: John B. Watson and B. F. Skinner.

In the opening paragraph to his "behaviorist manifesto," Watson (1913, p. 158) stated that

> psychology as the behaviorist views it is a purely objective experimental branch of natural science. Its theoretical goal is the prediction and control of behavior. Introspection forms no essential part of its methods, nor is the scientific value of its data dependent upon the readiness with which they lend themselves to interpreta-

> tion in terms of consciousness. The behaviorist, in his efforts to get a unitary scheme of animal response, recognizes no dividing line between man and brute. The behavior of man, with all of its refinement and complexity, forms only a part of the behaviorist's total scheme of investigation.

In other words, psychology is the science of behavior; its subject matter is behavior; its methods are those of the natural sciences; and its major area of concern is the behavior of all organisms.

In the opening paragraph of *Behaviorism at Fifty,* Skinner stated that

> behaviorism, with an accent on the last syllable, is not the scientific study of behavior but a philosophy of science concerned with the subject matter and methods of psychology. If psychology is a science of mental life—of the mind, of conscious experience—then it must develop and defend a special methodology, which it has not yet done successfully. If it is, on the other hand, a science of the behavior of organisms, human or otherwise, then it is part of biology, a natural science for which tested and highly successful methods are available. The basic issue is not the nature of the stuff of which the world is made or whether it is made of one stuff or two but rather the dimensions of the things studied by psychology and the methods relevant to them. [1963, p. 951]

Thus, for Skinner, behaviorism is not metaphysics or ontology. Furthermore, behaviorism is not psychology; it is a philosophy of psychology or a philosophy of the science of psychology. He agrees with Watson on the definition of psychology, its subject matter, its methods, and its major area of interest, although Watson may be less clear than Skinner that behaviorism is a philosophy of the science of psychology and not the science itself.

Surprisingly, some suggestions have been made that behaviorism is dead (cf. Wann, 1964, p. 97). What appears to be meant by that statement is that behaviorism as a system of psychology, philosophy of psychology, or philosophy of the science of psychology no longer needs to be defended; it is a dead issue. It has already become, or is becoming, a science of behavior (cf. Skinner, 1969, pp. 267–68). Like the Phoenix, a science of behavior has emerged, or is emerging, from the ashes of behaviorism. Thus, it may be said to have undergone a transformation or, at the least, an evolution. What remains of this chapter will attempt to explicate some of the major features of this emerging science on the assumption that this transformation or evolution has taken place. If it has, then the answer to the question "What is behaviorism?" is, "Behaviorism is the science of behavior," or, taking the discussion in the last chapter into consideration, "Behaviorism is psychology."

The science that is emerging from the ashes of behaviorism is not physics applied to psychology or "physicology," to coin a term, but a science that eventually may be found to be very different from physics and the other existing sciences. Psychologists are not engaged in the task of determining how physical principles or the principles of physics can be used to explain the behavior of organisms. Rather, they are attempting to determine what the principles of behavior are with the same methods as those used by physicists and other scientists. In somewhat different terms, they are using the methods of science to find out whatever they can about the behavior of organisms.

Philosophers of science have informed us that "the scientific method" consists of four or five steps. They are: the statement of a problem; the collection of published information about the problem; the formulation of an hypothesis to resolve it; the test of that hypothesis; and, finally, the relation of the tested hypothesis to whatever theory may have been developed in the process. However, this conception of "the scientific method" does not appear to have been based on an experimental analysis of the behavior of scientists. Instead, it appears to have emerged from a logical analysis of what scientists must do, if they are rational, in order to do science; scientists may not always be rational about what they do.

An alternative view of the method is that, at some point, it involves the test of a scientist's conjectures or hypotheses under controlled conditions of observation, but even that statement may not be descriptive of the behavior of scientists. For example, B. F. Skinner (1961, pp. 78–79) has reminded us that

> if we are interested in perpetuating the practices responsible for the present corpus of scientific knowledge, we must keep in mind that some very important parts of the scientific process do not now lend themselves to mathematical, logical, or any other formal treatment. We do not know enough about human behavior to know how the scientist does what he does. Although statisticians and methodologists may seem to tell us, or at least imply, how the mind works—how problems arise, how hypotheses are formed, deductions made, and crucial experiments designed—we as psychologists are in a position to remind them that they do not have methods appropriate to the empirical observation or the functional analysis of such data. These are aspects of human behavior, and no one knows better than we how little can at the moment be said about them.

This reminder can be found in an article entitled "A Case History in Scientific Method." The complexity of the problem is illustrated further when we consider by what method it is that we are to know the methodology of science.

Whatever the "essence" of the method may ultimately turn out to be, if it has one, its application to human affairs has given us laws and principles of behavior. Laws of behavior are functional relationships between variables. A variable is something that changes, such as the rate at which we depress the handle of a slot machine in Las Vegas, Nevada, or the amount of payoff when we hit a jackpot. The rate at which we depress the handle of the slot machine is otherwise known in psychology as a dependent variable; it is a measure of behavior. The amount of the payoff, or jackpot, is otherwise known as an independent variable; it is an environmental event. If we were to show how the rate of depressing the handle varies, and it probably does, with the size of the jackpot, we would demonstrate a functional relationship between those two variables; otherwise stated, we would have a law of behavior.

There are two basic types of behavioral laws in psychology. One is the relationship between an independent and a dependent variable, such as that between the amount of the jackpot and the rate of depressing a slot-machine handle, if that had been demonstrated. Such a relationship is also referred to as an S-R, or functional, law. The other is a relationship between two dependent variables, such as that between the amount of previous gambling behavior and the length of time one plays slot machines, if that had been demonstrated. This second type of relationship is also referred to as an R-R, or correlational, law.

These two types of laws have products. They are: prediction and control. An S-R law gives us both prediction and control. It gives us prediction because, knowing the relationship between rate of depressing the slot-machine handle and the size of payoff, we can calculate the rate of pressing from the size of payoff or size of payoff from rate of pressing. It gives us control because we can change the size of payoff and thereby change the rate of depressing the handle.

An R-R law gives us only prediction as a product. That is, knowing the relationship between the amount of previous gambling behavior and the length of time one plays slot machines, we can calculate outcomes in either direction. We can calculate previous gambling behavior from the length of time one plays slot machines, or the length of time one will play slot machines from previous gambling behavior. However, we do not have control; we cannot change the amount of previous gambling behavior or the length of time one plays slot machines directly except, perhaps, by force, which is a different kind of control than that given by behavioral laws (although it, too, may be lawful).

The prediction of behavior and the control of behavior require further discussion and development because of what appear to be some common misconceptions related to them. To predict behavior, we must know the extent to which variations in one of the variables in the law used to make the prediction are accompanied by variations in the other variable. That is, whether the law is an S-R or an R-R law, the correlation between the two variables that make up the law must be known in order to make a prediction from it. That correlation is normally expressed in the form of a number, or a correlation coefficient; it states the extent to which variations in one of the variables are accompanied by variations in the other.

Depending on the level of measurement achieved and the type of correlation coefficient that is involved, the correlation coefficient can be used to write a regression equation, which, in turn, can be used to calculate unknown values for one of the variables, from known values for the other. However, since correlations in psychology are seldom if ever perfect, the predicted values for one or the other of the variables are always accompanied by an estimate of the error involved in the prediction. In somewhat different terms, the predictions are never precise or certain, and, of course, they do not make the predicted events take place; because a behavioral event can be predicted from a law of behavior does not mean that it will occur. Behavior can be predicted from laws of behavior, but predictions are not certainties; a good many people seem to think otherwise.

A similar misconception may happen with the subject of

control. It appears that in the American culture the control of behavior is most often achieved by force. We control people by restraining them in some way, or we control them by making them do things they might not do otherwise; we control them by an application of a simple principle of physics, namely, force. However, the control over behavior that is conferred by an S-R type of law is not control by force.

Rather, it is the control conferred by being able to manipulate one of the variables in the law and, specifically, the independent variable of the law. An independent variable is some environmental event which can be assigned different values by someone. The power to assign different values to it yields some control over the dependent variable to which the independent variable is related. Hence, the control achieved by knowing an S-R law is the indirect control of the dependent variable by the direct control of the independent variable. Contrary to common conceptions, organisms are not made to do things by force when a law of behavior is applied; they do things because what they do is related to what is going on in the environment.

Generalizations across laws of behavior are referred to as principles of behavior. There are a number of principles of behavior in psychology that have been established by means of experimental analysis, and, of course, they are a major feature of the science. Four of them are: operant conditioning, reinforcement, extinction, and differentiation, or, shaping. Some others include: discrimination, generalization, schedules of reinforcement, punishment, and motivation. The last five principles will not be examined further at this time; the first four will be discussed in slightly more detail in order to illustrate the direction the science of behavior has taken.

The principle of operant conditioning states that the rate of a response increases when it produces positive reinforcement or eliminates negative reinforcement. Consequently, there are actually two principles of reinforcement. Positive reinforcement is something an organism works to produce or bring about, while negative reinforcement is something an organism works to eliminate or remove. Both types of reinforcement are the consequences of an organism's behavior. Thus, the organism must be active if a change in behavior is to take place.

The principle of extinction states that the rate of a response decreases when it no longer produces positive reinforcement or eliminates negative reinforcement. Finally, the principle of differentiation, or shaping, states that when either positive or negative reinforcement is made contingent upon responses that more closely approximate the response to be established, the response to be established gradually increases in rate.

These statements apply to different operant responses, from lever pressing by rats, to key pecking by pigeons, to talking by humans. They also are applicable to different kinds of reinforcers, including food pellets, grain, M&M's, and "mmhmm's," as well as electric shocks, loud noises, and intense heat. However, none of the above statements refer to these particulars; laws make reference to particulars. It is in that sense that the above statements are generalizations across laws, or, principles.

Another interesting feature of these laws—or, depending upon their generality, principles—may be that they can only be directional in their predictions. That is, the principle of operant conditioning states that the rate of a response increases when it produces positive reinforcement or eliminates negative reinforcement, but the principle does not state how much the response rate increases. Similarly, the principle of extinction states that the rate of a response decreases when it no longer produces positive reinforcement or eliminates negative reinforcement, but the principle does not state how much the response rate decreases. It may be that behavioral laws or principles can only be stated in directional terms and that it is simply not possible for them to be stated otherwise. The attempt to make them more quantitative might very well excessively reduce their generality or perhaps make them so particular that they would explain the behavior only of the subjects on which they were based and the conditions under which those subjects were observed. In somewhat different terms, one of the things that may distinguish laws of behavior from laws in the other sciences is that the former can never be more than directional. Nevertheless, directional laws are still useful laws; they can still be used for the prediction and control of behavior.

The laws and/or principles of behavior also are used to explain behavior. There are several different kinds of explanations in psychology, but the one emerging as the major means of explaining behavior is the functional, or empirical, type of explanation. A functional, or empirical, type of explanation asserts that a behavioral event is explained by its laws or by the variables of which it is a function. An explanation of this type simply states the conditions under which a behavior occurs or the conditions related to the occurrence of that behavior; it takes as given the occurrence of the behavior and attempts to state what other events are related to the occurrence. In that sense, the approach is correlational rather than causal, but, then, attempts to explain things by their causes largely have been abandoned in all of the sciences.

This last statement and the topic of explanation in general may require some further development. In the chapter "Why Organisms Behave," from his book *Science and Human Behavior,* B. F. Skinner (1953, p. 23) stated that

> the terms "cause" and "effect" are no longer widely used in science. They have been associated with so many theories of the

> structure and operation of the universe that they mean more than scientists want to say. The terms which replace them, however, refer to the same factual core. A "cause" becomes a "change in an independent variable" and an "effect" a "change in a dependent variable." The old "cause-and-effect connection" becomes a "functional relation." The new terms do not suggest *how* a cause causes its effect; they merely assert that different events tend to occur together in a certain order. This is important, but it is not crucial. There is no particular danger in using "cause" and "effect" in an informal discussion if we are always ready to substitute their more exact counterparts.

This passage lends further support to the view expressed in the last chapter with respect to an interpretation of how American experimental psychology might be thought of as a functionalistic behaviorism; Skinner, a behaviorist, quite obviously is interested in a functional analysis of behavior. For him, psychology as the science of behavior comes closest to causal laws in the form of the functional laws discussed earlier as S-R laws, or the relationship between an independent and a dependent variable; the other sciences may fare no better.

A somewhat different perspective on the issue of explanation and causality in psychology can be found in *Theory of Motivation*, by Robert Bolles.* He asserted that

> the traditional difference of opinion regarding what constitutes an adequate explanation of any natural phenomenon has centered on purpose and teleology. The scientist has always been reluctant to admit that there are purposes operating in nature, preferring to rely upon what he views as the "real" or physical causes of things. On the other hand, rationalists, humanists, the clergy, and most thoughtful laymen have felt most at ease with, or even insisted

---

*Quoted material on pages 49 to 54 abridged from pp. 6–10 in *Theory of Motivation*, Second Edition, by Robert C. Bolles. Copyright © 1967, 1975 by Robert C. Bolles. Reprinted by permission of Harper & Row, Publishers, Inc.

upon, teleological accounts of certain natural phenomena, such as human behavior. The question at issue has traditionally been whether physical causes provide a total explanation or whether teleological principles had to be added for some phenomena. Before David Hume (1739) did so, no one seemed to question whether physical causes were necessary but only whether they were sufficient. Hume asked: How can we know the nature of causation? How can we know if causes really produce their effects? Hume's skeptical epistemology led him to the realization that the best evidence we can ever obtain is that two events invariably occur together, one preceding the other, always in the same order, and neither occurring alone. The imputation of causation, the abstract conception that the prior event necessitates the subsequent event, is an inference that goes beyond the evidence. There may be physical or material causation, of course, but we can never be sure whether nature operates mechanistically since all we can know is the successive experience of successive events. It is in the nature of the human mind, Hume asserted, to transcend the data and infer a causal relationship between the two events if we invariably experience them one before the other. . . .

Although scientists have characteristically operated in an empirical and pragmatic manner, philosophers, even philosophers of science, have tended to lag behind conceptually. Hence for many years Hume's point was regarded as undue skepticism or as mere sophistry. Most men felt bound to commit themselves metaphysically to either a rationalistic position, a mechanistic position, or some dualistic combination of the two. . . .

As far as science is concerned, its object is not to discover the ultimate nature of reality, but rather to explore empirical relationships and derive useful generalizations from them. The question of what kind of causation is involved in explanation is an unnecessary impediment, a philosophical encumbrance, to the conduct of science. It is futile for the scientist to be concerned with whether an event occurred because some other event made it occur; much more to the point is that an event occurs and its occurrence can be correlated with certain sets of conditions. Of course, we wish to refine our observations and improve our ability to control condi-

> tions until a point is reached where perfect or near perfect correlations are possible and where very powerful descriptive laws can be found. But science cannot wait for the final solution of the causation problem. We must proceed to view empirical correlations as the subject matter of science without committing ourselves to either a teleological, purposive, or materialistic philosophy. Nor do we need to go as far as Hume and say that we can never transcend empirical correlations. We may believe that, or we may take the more optimistic position that the empirical correlations we observe will ultimately be undergirded by a more profound understanding of causation. By adhering to a descriptive or correlational approach we may at least leave the way open for such a possibility. [Bolles 1975, pp. 6–8]

In these statements, Bolles summarizes what appears to be the current understanding of explanation and causality in all of the sciences. They were made in the section called "Empirical Determinism" of the first chapter of his book.

He contrasted empirical determinism with what might be called "mechanical determinism," or, as it is more often called, "mechanistic determinism." Mechanistic determinism is the rather commonly accepted view "that the world of physical events not only provides the pattern of what is natural and what is lawfully determined in nature but also provides the substance of all phenomena" (Bolles, 1975, p. 6). That is, a mechanistic determinist "is a materialist. Behavior is not only a natural phenomenon, and lawfully determined, but it is determined by precisely the same physical laws and forces that apply throughout nature. The ultimate and only reality, it is assumed, is physical in character" (Bolles, 1975, p. 6), which may be related to the fact that this world seems so easily seen; the world of events, or behavior, is not, and may require quite different principles to explain it.

Bolles (1975, p. 6) further developed this view with the statement that

> faith in the mechanistic doctrine has usually extended far beyond its usefulness in explaining the phenomena to which it has been applied. For example, most and perhaps all of our motivational concepts, such as drive and incentive, were developed and popularized during the interval between the introduction of mechanistic assumptions into psychology and the time when these concepts were put to empirical test. As a consequence, our theorizing made considerable use of drives and incentives and their postulated properties long before the usefulness of these concepts had been demonstrated by their ability to explain behavior. Indeed, virtually the entire history of motivation theory is devoted to declarations by this or that theorist that we must find the forces underlying behavior and the physiological causes of behavior if we are ever to explain it.

By contrast, the doctrine that Bolles referred to as empirical determinism "keeps the first two propositions of the mechanistic doctrine" (Bolles, 1975, p. 8). That is, it assumes that behavior is a natural phenomenon and that it is determined. However, it rejects the materialistic bias; behavior is not necessarily determined by physical causes. Behavior is determined "not because forces act on the organism to make it behave [mechanistic determinism], nor because the behavior was willed by some reasoning intellect [which has been called psychic determinism], but simply in the sense that it is intrinsically predictable. Behavior is determined in that it is lawful" (Bolles, 1975, p. 8); the discovery or demonstration that behavior is lawful may be the most significant contribution psychology has made since its inception.

According to Bolles (1975, p. 8), empirical determinism is noncommittal about physical causes.

> It provides a convenient vantage point from which we may survey other, more highly committed approaches. Psychology, particularly the area of motivation, is confused enough by the practice of

> regarding motives, or drives, or instincts, or needs, as the causes of behavior. If we are to describe behavior from a point of view that does not restrict us to any particular theoretical or philosophical position, then we should adopt a terminology that leaves these questions open. Thus the relationship that exists, for example, between a stimulus and a response will be described throughout this book, not in causal terms, but in neutral and descriptive terms. We will say that deprivation and stimulus conditions *determine* behavior or that some behavior is under the *control* of some stimulus.

But, they do not cause behavior in some physical sense of causation; they are simply related to it.

Thus, an emerging conception within psychology as the science of behavior is the doctrine of empirical determinism. It may be contrasted with mechanistic determinism and perhaps psychic determinism, although the latter may be simply a variation of the former. Psychic determinism is the view, sometimes attributed to Sigmund Freud, that behavior is determined by psychic forces, which may be another way of saying that they are internal, rather than external, to the organism. In either case, these two forms of determinism seem to require the concept of force, which, as is well known, may be a concept that was borrowed, perhaps uncritically, from physics in an effort to explain behavior; this topic will receive further discussion in the chapters on stimulus and motivation.

Empirical determinism does not require a concept of force. It accepts the proposition that behavior is determined but not necessarily in a physicalistic sense. Rather, behavior is determined only in the sense that it is lawful, that is, there are variables of which it is a function. Furthermore, behavior can be explained simply in terms of those relationships, or laws.

Bolles (1975, pp. 9–10) went on to point out that

> perhaps the most fundamental practical objection that might be raised to empirical determinism is that it fails to tell *why* an event occurs; it only describes how and when events occur. But in the last analysis, a phenomenon . . . [may be explained only] when it is put into terms with which we are familiar and shown to be an instance of a principle with which we are familiar. As P. W. Bridgman (1932) [a well-known physicist] has said, an explanation is that kind of account that puts the curiosity at rest. We may ask what is the frame of mind of a man whose curiosity is only "put at rest" by an account of why things happen. What are such men really looking for? In the case of behavior, there seem to be two different kinds of accounts that men may be seeking when they ask "why?" One is justification, and the other is an application of the mechanistic doctrine. Thus some of the time when someone is asked "why did you do that?" what is expected is a justification of the action. At other times it seems clear that what is demanded is an understanding of the physiological or neurological machinery that produced the effect.
>
> In general, a satisfactory answer to a why question is a statement involving terms with which the inquirer is familiar. The difficulty of explanation in psychology is that those who ask why of the psychologist come to him quite familiar with justifying action and quite familiar with the reality of the physical body, and they seek some explanation in these terms. On the other hand, the scientist, who is familiar with the empirical regularities in his science, does not seek the why of them. Insofar as the psychologist asks why, it is because he is curious about moral questions of justification or about the mysteries of neurology, either of which he may have legitimate reasons for wanting to relate to behavior. But the psychologist asks why only when he wants to transcend or extend the boundaries of his science and not when he is working within them.

Perhaps it cannot be emphasized too much that a science of behavior is trying to explain behavior neither in terms of its morality nor in terms of its physiology. In addition, that science is not trying to explain behavior in terms of its physics. Rather, behavioral scientists are trying to explain behavior by its laws, its empirical determinants, only a few of which are known; the topic of empirical determinism will also receive further examination in later chapters.

This discussion of causality, explanation, and empirical determinism no doubt immediately raises the question of human freedom for most of those who encounter it for the first time. This problem has been examined in some detail elsewhere (cf. Eacker, 1975) but perhaps a summary of that treatment is in order. From the perspective of the emerging science of behavior, the problem of human freedom appears to be whether human behavior occurs by chance or is determined. However, when phrased in that way, the problem is one for philosophy rather than psychology because the methods of science cannot be used to solve it. The methods of science cannot be used to solve it because conceptions of chance and determinism are inherent in those methods, at least as they are currently understood. For example, tests of hypotheses in a science, to the extent that it is a statistical science, require the use of inferential statistics. Most inferential statistics were designed to help scientists either accept or reject what is known as the null hypothesis. The null hypothesis states expectations about the outcome of some set of events if only chance factors are in operation. If we can reject the null hypothesis, we draw a positive conclusion about the operation of factors we have manipulated in our experiment. If we must accept the null hypothesis, we conclude that we have no positive evidence for the operation of the factors we have manipulated in our experiment. However, acceptance of the null hypothesis does not mean we have positive evidence for the operation of chance. It simply means that our data do not allow us to reject the hypothesis that our results are no different than those that could be expected by chance, if chance, as we conceive it, was operating. Consequently, since the methods of science are based on some conception of chance, or randomness, they cannot be used to establish that chance or randomness operates in the universe. To do so would beg the question. Thus, there may be some behaviors that occur by chance and are therefore free. However, we shall probably never know what they are with the methods of science as they are currently understood.

On the other hand, while we cannot know with the methods of science that some behaviors are free, we also cannot know with those same methods whether all behavior is determined either mechanistically or empirically. To know that all behavior is determined with the methods of science would be to know that all behavior, and all variables of which it might be a function, had been examined. However, scientific knowledge, to the extent that it is based upon observation, is probably never complete. One more observation always can be made immediately after the last one has been made, at least so long as there are people around to make observations. Thus, we cannot know with the methods of science whether all behavior is determined, or even whether some behavior is always determined, and so the freedom versus determinism issue cannot be resolved in psychology. It is a philosophical, rather than scientific, problem; the methods of science as they are currently understood cannot be used to solve it.

Perhaps enough has been said about this emerging conception of psychology as the science of behavior that some conclusions can be based on it. The first is that while this scheme of things in psychology is a dominant one there are many psychologists who disagree with it. This situation may occur when efforts are made to state the "essence" of a thing when it does not have one or, at least, when we cannot know whether or not it has one. Perhaps more importantly, however, different views represent different ways in which psychologists do psychology, and so, what finally emerges as psychology from the interplay between these different views may not be easily foreseen. Nevertheless, this view receives support from a good many psychologists at the present time.

A second conclusion based on this conception of psychology is that no one has had the last say about "the scientific method." There may be no single method but a plethora of methods, depending on the science and those who do the science. On the other hand, what has always been meant by the scientific method may be simply the peculiar way in which scientists go about solving their problems (observation) as distinct from the way in which problems are solved in the arts or the humanities (reason). A third conclusion based on this overview of psychology is that the concept of scientific law in psychology is quite different, or may be quite different, from the concept of law in the other sciences. If so, there may be those who would argue that there are no laws in psychology. To do so would suggest that the arguer knows what is the case by a different means than is available to the rest of us. There may be as many different kinds of scientific laws as there are sciences; the same may be true for principles. The law of reinforcement seems quite different than the law of gravity. To say that one is a law and the other is not suggests that one is in possession of absolute knowledge. The problem with being in possession of such knowledge is knowing the difference between it and any other kind of knowledge. The concept of scientific law is, after all, a human conception and so may not remain fixed for all time; and there may not be just one conception of scientific law.

A fourth conclusion based on this view of psychology as the science of behavior is that current popular and not so popular notions of explanation and causality attributed to contemporary science may have been discarded by contemporary scientists some time ago; they may simply have outlived their usefulness. A thing is not explained in any contemporary science by stating its "essence"; it is explained by its laws, as pointed out in the first chapter. Similarly, events are not caused, or produced, by the events that preceded or accompanied them; they are simply correlated with those events or, perhaps more simply, are contiguous and/or prior to them.

A fifth conclusion is that events, behavioral events, are nevertheless determined; they are determined in the sense that they are lawful. They are lawful in the sense that variables have been observed to be related to them; behavioral events are empirically, not mechanistically, determined. A sixth conclusion is that, while some behavior has been shown to be lawful, not all of it has. Thus, the statement that all behavior is determined has not yet been confirmed and probably cannot be confirmed with the methods of science as they are currently understood. On the other hand, this lack of confirmation does not mean that behavior is adventitious. Some of it may occur by chance, but if it does we probably will never know that it does.

The conception of psychology that emerges from a consideration of these matters is that it is the science of behavior. It uses the methods of science to develop laws and principles of behavior. Laws and principles of behavior are used to explain behavior. Behavior is explained by its laws; it is determined. However, it is not causally, or mechanistically, determined; it is empirically determined. Nevertheless, it is not known whether all of it is determined since not all of it has been examined. Furthermore, it is not known whether any of it is free since the methods of science cannot be used to show that it occurs by chance. That conception of psychology is the one that is emerging from the ashes of behaviorism.

Chapter Four

What Is Science?

Since the current consensus seems to be that psychology is the science of behavior, and since behaviorism appears to have become that science, the next question that might occur to someone who persists in their essentialist ways is the one selected as the title for this chapter. Psychologists have given different answers to this question over the years, although there is, nevertheless, considerable homogeneity among them. This homogeneity may be related to the fact that most of our views of science have come from sciences other than psychology, and it is conceivable that they may not be appropriate for psychology. That is, the sciences may not all be alike, which is a position to be examined in later chapters. A review of some of those views reveals not only their range but also how the question might be answered within psychology at the present time.

Not all psychologists and students of psychology have been concerned with the nature of science, but many of the more prominent among them have given it some special consideration. For example, Edward Bradford Titchener (1929), chief spokesman for structural psychology in the United States, devoted the entire first chapter to it in his prefatory remarks to systematic psychology. In the first few paragraphs of that chapter, he stated that "it would be strange indeed if, in an age which is proud to call itself scientific, we could not by definitely directed effort find out what science essentially is" (Titchener, 1929, p. 27). The remark quite obviously lends support to the thesis that problems, or questions, of this sort arise because of the assumption that things have essences, as in finding out "what science essentially is."

For Titchener, science is observational. It is concerned with facts. It has a special method based on observation. It uses experimentation. It is logical in the sense that it requires the use of logic. "We know roughly what science is when we regard it as a frame of mind, and we know what it is when we regard it as a mode of life, the activity of an individual in society" (Titchener, 1929, p. 55).

But science is more than a frame of mind and a mode of life. Titchener (1929, p. 55) went on to say that

> the great majority of mankind know nothing of the scientific attitude, and very little of the occupation of the scientific investigator. Science, in their eyes, is something that is laid down in books, taught in schools and colleges, embodied (so to say) in the persons of a few great men and, more generally, in the membership of certain societies, expressed in discovery, and justified by invention. The word science, so far as it conveys a meaning, means to them science in its objective and institutional form.

Thus, he apparently would support the claim that many students, if not psychologists, consider science to be a thing.

In a summary statement of what he called a working conception, rather than a definition, of science, Titchener (1929, pp. 69–72) stated that the man of science is the servant, rather than interpreter, of nature. He is "disinterested and impersonal, he makes himself one with the facts of nature; he moves in the domain of bare existence; and his intercourse with the facts is both observation and observance."

However, "scientific facts are not by any means necessarily what the layman supposes them to be, natural phenomena taken in their entirety." On the contrary, the "existential universe" is "observed always from some particular point of view, and science is therefore always a particular science, physics or biology or psychology." In somewhat different terms, facts "are rather phases or aspects than items of natural existence."

"The universal and peculiar method of science is observation," but "observation is difficult." As a result, science uses experiments which prolong the length of time phenomena may be observed, eliminate "disturbing and irrelevant phenomena," and allow "variation of circumstances." "Experiment, which is observation under favourable conditions, is in so far simply an extension of the universal method of science."

However, experimentation is complicated by logic. It is complicated at one point when "in order to plan an experiment the man of science must return to the world of meanings which, in order to observe, he must as positively renounce." It is complicated at a second point when "observation results in the immediate awareness known as 'acquaintance-with,' and if such knowledge is to be organised and socialised, it must be transformed into a 'knowledge-about.' " "That transformation is accomplished with logic," but "logic must not be permitted either to invade and colour facts or to draw conclusions that run counter to them."

Institutional science, or science as it has become institutionalized, sets "the facts of observation, transformed into knowledge-about, in their natural order of relationship" and brings "them under social control," which is a problem with two parts: analysis and synthesis. "Synthesis, in its simpler forms complementary to analysis, broadens out into the operations of classification and the formulation of scientific laws." Arrangement and reduction are the business of science, both of which may be summarized under the single rubric of "description." Description "suggests not only fidelity to fact but also restriction to fact; it bids us abstain from application as well as interpretation." Nevertheless, science may cooperate, on occasion, with technology.

Thus, for Titchener, science is disinterested and impersonal. Despite that feature of science, it proceeds from a point of view. It resorts to experimentation, or observation under favorable conditions. It is both analytic and synthetic, or descriptive. It sometimes may have application to the solution of practical problems. For Titchener, that is the nature of science, although he considered it a working conception and not a definition.

Ten years after Titchener's statements about science were published, S. S. Stevens (1939) presented a "classical position" on methodology and theory in psychology (cf. Marx and Goodson, 1976, p. 2). In the process, he said some things about the nature of science. One was that a common theme within philosophy of science was that authors who have written on the subject

> all assert essentially that *science seeks to generate confirmable propositions by fitting a formal system of symbols (language, mathematics, logic) to empirical observations, and that the propositions of science have empirical significance only when their truth can be demonstrated by a set of concrete operations.* There are thus two separate realms of discourse: the *formal* (or rational) and the *empirical.* It is the business of the philosopher to labor with the formal and discover and perfect the rules of the scientific language, and it is the business of the scientist to apply the formal symbolic model to the observable world in such a way that the concepts he generates will satisfy the rules of operational criticism. [Stevens, 1976, p. 4]

If that is an essential assertion, essentialism is once again in evidence.

Some other things he had to say about the nature of science were that, with respect to principles of operationism, "science as we find it, is a set of empirical propositions agreed upon by members of society. This agreement may be always in a state of flux, but persistent disagreement leads eventually to rejection." And "only those propositions based upon operations which are public and repeatable are admitted to the body of science" (Stevens, 1976, p. 8).

With these statements, Stevens conveys the sense of a "golden era" in psychology, especially psychological theory (Marx and Goodson, 1976, p. 2). That era was marked by an emphasis on "clarity and precision in the analysis and definition of constructs" in psychology, which probably came from the influence of pragmatism, operationism, and logical positivism; they were important elements of the Zeitgeist, or spirit of those times. The three are alike in at least one particular way but quite unlike in others. Pragmatism and logical positivism can be described as philosophical movements but operationism cannot; it is more a methodology than a philosophy. They are alike with respect to a concern for a criterion of meaning.

Pragmatism was given form by Charles Pierce and William James, although there are those who feel that it had been characteristic of the American way of life for many years, if not decades, before these men formulated it. Its major feature for this discussion is its method, which attempts to make an idea clear by examining its consequences; its consequences are what the idea is, or means. "The pragmatic method is primarily a method of settling metaphysical disputes that otherwise might be interminable." "The pragmatic method in such cases is to try to interpret each notion by tracing its respective practical consequences." "If no practical difference whatever can be traced, then the alternatives mean practically the same thing, and all dispute is idle" (James, 1948, p. 142).

Because of the emphasis on consequences, it is of some interest to point out a few similarities between pragmatism and operant conditioning. Pragmatism was developed by William James, who was educated and taught at Harvard University; operant conditioning was developed by B. F. Skinner, who did likewise. Both were psychologists, and some have referred to them both as the greatest American psychologists. Pragmatism emphasizes the practical consequences of an action or a behavior, and operant conditioning emphasizes its reinforcing consequences. In that regard, Skinner's operant conditioning may be James's pragmatism but with a scientific, rather than a philosophic, foundation.

Operationism is another way to make ideas clear. It originated in physics, with Einstein and relativity theory. According to P. W. Bridgman (1932), who promoted it as a technique, "we mean by any concept nothing more than a set of operations; the concept is synonymous with the corresponding set of operations." Bridgman did not make entirely clear what was meant by an operation, but Stevens (1976, pp. 8–9) has suggested that

> when we attempt to reduce complex operations to simpler and simpler ones, we find in the end that discrimination, or differential response, is the fundamental operation. Discrimination is prerequisite even to the operation of denoting or "pointing to," because whenever two people reduce their complex operations for the purpose of reaching agreement or understanding, they find that unless they can each discriminate the same simple objects or read the same scales they still will not agree. Agreement is usually reached in practice before these most elementary operations are appealed to.

Thus, discrimination, and perhaps that involved especially in measurement, may be the clearest and simplest example of an operation.

Logical positivism was a movement in philosophy that attempted to eliminate metaphysical concepts from scientific propositions; it was not entirely successful if, indeed, it was successful at all. It originated in what was called the "Vienna Circle," whose protagonists were Moritz Schlick, Otto Neurath, Rudolph Carnap, and Philipp Frank, among others. According to Stevens (1976, p. 15), they wanted "to replace philosophy by the systematic investigation of the logic of science."

> There are but two kinds of acceptable propositions: *formal* and *empirical.* Formal propositions concern syntax. They state the rules and procedures for combining words or symbols and have no empirical reference. Empirical propositions are assertions about the observable world and their truth or falsity can be tested by means of observational procedures. Since metaphysics consists of statements not susceptible to empirical test, it is either an array of syntactical (formal) sentences or else it is technical nonsense. Mostly it is nonsense. Philosophy must be purged of it; and, once purged, it becomes the business of philosophy, says the Circle, to investigate the rules of the language we use in formulating our scientific propositions. The goal of such philosophical research is to provide a secure foundation for the sciences.

In its early years, logical positivism touted a verifiability criterion of meaning, which, after a number of revisions, held that a statement, if it was not analytic or simply logical, was literally meaningful if it was "either directly or indirectly verifiable" in a particular sense discussed by A. J. Ayer (1946, p. 13).

Pragmatically, it appears that the meaning of a concept is its practical consequences. If two seemingly different ideas or constructs have the same practical consequences, they are not

different. Operationally, the meaning of a concept is the things we do when we use it—in most instances, the discriminations or measurements that we perform. But operations do not appear to be the same as consequences. That is, the practical consequences of an idea are not the same as the things we do when we make reference to it. Positively, a statement is meaningful if it is either directly or indirectly verifiable. But verification is not the same as practical consequences or operations. To verify something in science is to confirm it under controlled conditions of observation. Thus, during this era there were apparently three rather different approaches to the problem of meaning, or how to make ideas clear, no one of which was necessarily closer to the truth than the others. However, at the present time there is an almost constant concern with the operational definition of concepts within psychology which suggests that operationism, at least, has become an important feature of science or the science of behavior.

In the opening passages of "The Nature of Scientific Theory", the first chapter of his book *Principles of Behavior,* Clark L. Hull (1943, p. 1) stated:

> This book is the beginning of an attempt to sketch a systematic objective theory of the behavior of higher organisms. It is accordingly important at the outset to secure a clear notion of the essential nature of systematic theory in science, the relation of theory to other scientific activities, and its general scientific status and importance. . . .
>
> Here we have the two essential elements of modern science: the making of observations constitutes the empirical or factual component, and the systematic attempt to explain these facts constitutes the theoretical component. As science has developed, specialization, or division of labor has occurred; some men have devoted their time mainly to the making of observations, while a smaller number have occupied themselves largely with the problems of explanation. . . .

> Modern science has two inseparable components—the empirical and the theoretical. The empirical component is concerned primarily with observation; the theoretical component is concerned with the interpretation and explanation of observation. A natural event is explained when it can be derived as a theorem by a process of reasoning from (1) a knowledge of the relevant natural conditions antedating it, and (2) one or more relevant principles called postulates. Clusters or families of theorems are generated, and theorems are often employed in the derivation of other theorems; thus is developed a logical hierarchy resembling that found in ordinary geometry. A hierarchy of interrelated families of theorems, all derived from the same set of consistent postulates, constitutes a scientific system.

In the title for the first chapter, his opening passages, and the later summary statement, Hull not only reveals his conception of the nature of science, but also indicates how pervasive the influence of essentialism can be even among relatively modern scientists. For example, the chapter title suggests there is one thing that theory is, and in the first quotation he refers to "the essential nature of systematic theory in science." In the second quotation, he mentions "the two essential elements of modern science," as though both theory and science had essences that could be known and stated. They may have; the problem is knowing that they do and then knowing we know that they do.

His answer to the question "What is science?" appears to be that it consists of two components that cannot be separated. There is an empirical component and a theoretical component. The first is observational or related to observation, and the second is conceptual, logical, or theoretical. It is not clear whether these two components are exhaustive of the nature of science, but if they are the essential elements of science, perhaps they can be assumed to be exhaustive at least for Hull. Regardless of these considerations, both components are related to explanation, which is a topic to be discussed in greater detail later.

A view of science similar to that of both Titchener and Hull was expressed more recently by Warren Torgerson (1958, p. 2).

> Science can be thought of as consisting of theory on the one hand and data (empirical evidence) on the other. The interplay between the two makes science a going concern. The theoretical side consists of constructs and their relations to one another. The empirical side consists of the basic observable data. Connecting the two are rules of correspondence which serve the purpose of defining or partially defining certain theoretical constructs in terms of observable data. In part, these rules have to do with the process of measurement.

This perspective on science was based in large part on an analysis by Henry Margenau (1950); it, too, stresses the empirical and rational, or observational and theoretical, components of science. Margenau is a physicist who developed his scheme of science in a book entitled *The Nature of Physical Reality.* In that book, he argued that physical reality is constructed out of our sense experience; it is not discovered by means of our sense experience. His argument took the following form.

Science is based on observation and reason. Observation occurs in a P, or protocol, plane; it is the empirical component of science and consists of evidence, data, or sense experience. Reason occurs in a C, or concept, plane; it is the rational component of science and consists of logic, theory, or constructs. The two planes merge into one another but are easily distinguished at the extremes of a continuum that extends from reason at one end to observation at the other.

The two planes are explicitly related to one another at two points. One is at the point where constructs are combined with data by means of rules of correspondence, operational definitions, or measurements. The other is at the point where, by means of the logical relations among constructs, predictions are made from the C plane to the P plane. That is, the concept plane can be used to make predictions, or develop hypotheses, which then must be tested under controlled conditions of observation in the protocol plane. What emerges from this interaction between the two planes is a conception of physical reality; it is constructed.

On the other hand, according to B. F. Skinner (1953, pp. 11–14), science has some important characteristics which collectively may be what science is. Among other things, it is a set of attitudes. First, "it is a disposition to deal with the facts rather than with what someone has said about them." It "rejects even its own authorities when they interfere with the observation of nature." Second, "science is a willingness to accept facts even when they are opposed to wishes." Scientists are intellectually honest. They have found that honesty "is essential to progress." "Experiments do not always come out as one expects, but the facts must stand and the expectations fall. The subject matter, not the scientist, knows best." Third, "scientists have also discovered the value of remaining without an answer until a satisfactory one can be found." They "avoid premature conclusions"; they refrain "from making statements on insufficient evidence"; and they "avoid explanations which are pure invention."

However, science is more than a set of attitudes. "It is a search for order, for uniformities, for lawful relations among the events in nature. It begins, as we all begin, by observing single episodes, but it quickly passes on to the general rule, to scientific law." Finally, it develops systems, or theories, which not only help to integrate existing laws with one another but also enable the scientist to predict and control the events in question.

> In a later stage science advances from the collection of rules or laws to larger systematic arrangements. Not only does it make

> statements about the world, it makes statements about statements. It sets up a "model" of its subject matter, which helps to generate new rules very much as the rules themselves generate new practices in dealing with single cases. A science may not reach this stage for some time.
>
> The scientific "system," like the law, is designed to enable us to handle a subject matter more efficiently. What we call the scientific conception of a thing is not passive knowledge. Science is not concerned with contemplation. When we have discovered the laws which govern a part of the world about us, and when we have organized these laws into a system, we are then ready to deal effectively with that part of the world. By predicting the occurrence of an event we are able to prepare for it. By arranging conditions in ways specified by the laws of a system, we not only predict, we control: we "cause" an event to occur or to assume certain characteristics. [Skinner, 1953, p. 14]

Remarks of this kind may help to dispel the popular misconception that Skinner was atheoretical, since they reveal he recognized that science eventually makes statements about statements. A statement about a statement is at least one step removed from data and, in that sense, is theoretical. The quoted passages also lend support to the notion that he considered science a process rather than a thing. As a process, it is concerned with facts; it accepts facts even when they are opposed to wishes; it remains without an answer rather than offering one that is premature. It seeks order in the form of laws and integrates laws into systems which may be used for purposes of prediction and control. That conception appears to be the nature of science according to Skinner.

R. S. Peters, in his edited and abridged version of *Brett's History of Psychology* (1965, p. 37), offered a somewhat different conception of the nature of science:

> We tend to think of science as a 'body of knowledge' which began to be accumulated when men hit upon 'scientific method'. This

is a superstition. It is more in keeping with the history of thought to describe science as the myths about the world which have not yet been found to be wrong. Science had its roots partly in primitive pictures of the world and partly in primitive technology. There has been a great deal of discussion about the primacy of disinterested speculation or practical inventiveness in the early stages of science. Some maintain that those who said that the earth was made of air, or had an underlying mathematical structure, or was composed of atoms were the originators of science; others uphold the claims of those who started measuring for irrigation schemes, or mixed tin with copper in order to make bronze, or guided their ships by the stars. Both parties are surely right; yet both fail to bring out the core of what we now call 'scientific method'. This began when men began consciously to challenge the stories that they were told and to produce counter-examples to support their contentions. Men may inherit stories from their parents; they may think them up on a cold winter's night in order to pass away the time; they may evolve them while trying to make better weapons or heal their wounds. This is a matter of history —often of personal biography—and is of little methodological interest. The crucial stage for the methodologist comes when conscious attempts are made to *test* the stories provided by tradition, speculative curiosity, or practical necessity.

Showing a man that his story is wrong usually involves producing a better story oneself. In argumentation, discussion, and the production of counter-examples drawn from memory, observation, and testimony, we have the core of what we now call science. Experimentation, measurement, and all the paraphernalia of the laboratory are but more precise ways of producing confirmations or counter-examples. Science consists in conscious attempts to refute other people's stories and in the production of better stories to supplant them. The history of science is the history of stories which have been shown to be false or only partially correct.

Thus, Peters' story about the nature of science is that it consists of "attempts to refute other people's stories and in the production of better stories to supplant them." However, it is not clear how his story, or myth, about the nature of science might be refuted, which suggests that it is appropriate for a book on problems of metaphysics and psychology. Nevertheless, his emphasis on the refutation of those myths by testing them and the production of other myths to replace the refuted ones indicates that he, too, considers science a process rather than a thing.

A bit more recently, Chaplin and Krawiec (1974, p. 4) stated their views on the nature of science. Those views are, perhaps, best expressed in the following quotation:

> It has become a truism to say that science not only begins with a method but that its very essence *is* its methodology. More specifically, the essence of science is a set of rules that must be followed by anyone who aspires to be a scientist. Contrary to a widespread popular view, this statement implies that any science such as chemistry, biology, geology, or psychology is not so much a compilation of facts or a collection of impressive apparatus as it is an attitude or willingness on the part of the scientist to follow the rules of the scientific game. Facts have an annoying way of changing, and what is considered truth today may be held in error tomorrow. Therefore, facts alone are the transient characteristics and not the enduring stuff of science. Apparatus, too, however imposing it may appear, is not science but only the tool of the scientist—a tool whose application may or may not be scientific. Anyone can purchase a white coat and a laboratory full of "scientific" paraphernalia, but the possession of such equipment does not qualify him as a scientist. Rather, both his scientific status and the value of the information he is collecting are evaluated according to the manner in which he *plans* his investigations, the *procedures* he employs in collecting data, and the way in which he *interprets* his findings. It is his standing on these three fundamental steps in scientific methodology which reveals whether he is a scientist, an amateur riding a hobby-horse, or possibly a pseudoscientist. So crucial is the methodology followed in any scientific investigation that no reputable scientist will accept a fellow scientist's results as valid until he knows precisely what procedures were employed in arriving at those results.

It is clear from this quotation that psychologists still may be concerned with the essences of things or at least that essences are a rather common mode of verbal expression. For Chaplin and Krawiec, the essence of science is its methodology or, to be more specific, a set of rules followed by its aspirants. These rules are related to planning, conducting, and interpreting investigations. Science is not a set of facts, a laboratory, or equipment. Science "is an attitude or willingness on the part of the scientist to follow the rules of the scientific game." Such views indicate once more the extent to which science may be considered a process rather than a thing.

A short time before the above remarks were published, Marx and Hillix (1973, p. 3) made public their thinking on the nature of science in the following way:

> Science is a many-sided social enterprise that defies complete description. The finished product is a body of *knowledge* which has been acquired through the use of scientific *methods* applied with a scientific *attitude.* Each of these three aspects of science is complex and changes with time. As science ages, our conceptions of it change; moreover, just as the final answers about nature continue to elude us, a final conception of science eludes us.

Each of the authors mentioned in the discussion so far has stressed one or another or some combination of these three aspects of science. That is, each one of them has, in one way or another, referred to science as a body of knowledge. However, it is a special kind of knowledge, namely, that obtained by means of the methods of science. And those who use the methods attempt to display a certain impartial attitude about the outcome of that application. Thus, it may be that these three aspects of science are what science is, even though a final conception may elude us. It does not seem likely that science is simply a body of knowledge, a method, or an attitude.

These considerations aside, Marx and Hillix (1973, p. 5)

went on to say that science has several more specific and positive characteristics, as indicated in the following passage:

> Science has many characteristics, and each of these has been selected at some time as *unique* to science. However, we cannot expect to distinguish science from other human activities on the basis of a single property, any more than we would expect to be able to distinguish all dogs from all cats because they possess a black nose or a wagging tail. One characteristic of science, the use of control in observation, is most nearly unique; however, the other features of science are also usually descriptive of it and thus merit some consideration. . . . It is the combination of its characteristics that distinguishes science, not any characteristic taken alone.

The characteristics that might distinguish science for these psychologists are its purpose, subject matter, conclusions, the element of prediction and control, theory as opposed to application, terminology, precision, and control in a somewhat different sense than that related to prediction.

The purpose of science is "to provide an objective, factual, empirical account of the world." The subject matter of science "is somewhere near the transition zone between knowledge and ignorance." Scientists "recognize the tentative nature of their own statements and look upon scientific methods as simply the methods that they themselves prefer to use in the quest for knowledge." "Science is sometimes said to be distinguished by its concern with the prediction and control of events," although many others have a similar interest. "Science is not necessarily concerned with theory, as opposed to applications. A scientist may work exclusively with either, or with both." "The terminology of the scientist is not necessarily more unique or more precise in meaning than the language of others." "Exactitude and precision, especially in measurement, are often said to distinguish the scientist," but they "are not the property solely of scientists."

Thus, these authors do not contend that the foregoing characteristics are unique to science. No one of them defines its essence; they may also help to distinguish human endeavors other than science. For example, knowledge in some other human endeavor also may have both an empirical and a rational component; it simply may have less of the empirical component than science. Nevertheless, there is one characteristic which, for Marx and Hillix, is almost unique to science and serves to distinguish it from nonscience. That characteristic is the principle of control. It differs from the type of control referred to in prediction, although the two types are not always easily kept separate.

The control referred to in prediction and control has to do with the control of events through their relationship with other variables, whereas the control referred to in the principle of control has to do with control over conditions of observation:

> Control is a method used by the scientist in an attempt to identify the "reasons" for, or "causes" of, what he observes, or, to put it another way, to identify the sources of variation in his observations. An experiment is a carefully controlled situation in which there are one or more conditions whose influence the investigator wishes to determine. These conditions, or factors, are generally called *independent variables.* The conditions which are directly measured or otherwise observed are called *dependent variables* (in psychology, these are typically responses of one kind or another). Now, in order to obtain unambiguous results—that is, changes in the dependent variables that can be attributed with reasonable confidence to the independent variables—the scientist needs to eliminate—control—all other potentially effective conditions. These other conditions are called *controlled variables.* [Marx and Hillix, 1973, p. 8]

Thus, the principle of control is used to help an investigator to decide whether certain identified and independent variables affect certain other identified and dependent variables by minimizing, or holding constant, the effects of other potentially independent variables. However, since a dependent variable may also be viewed as an event, it is not always clear when the principle of control is different from prediction and control. Nevertheless, this characteristic, while not necessarily unique to science, is certainly an important aspect of it.

Still more recently, Robinson (1976, p. 12) has argued that explanation distinguishes science from nonscience. "We distinguish science from all that is not science in terms of the logical character of its explanations." The model of explanation to which Robinson referred was the hypothetico-deductive model. According to this model, every scientific explanation consists of an explanandum, or a statement of the event to be explained, and an explanans, or a statement that is the explanation. If those conditions obtain, then the following five criteria apply, at least as the model has been explicated by Carl Hempel (1965).

First, any explanation that is regarded as scientific must make reference to a general law. Second, this model of explanation requires that the explanans, or general law, must be true, although reliable empirical generalizations are acceptable since, apparently, no law of science can be known to be certain. Third, there must be a logical relationship between the explanandum and the explanans; it must be possible for the explanandum to be deduced from the explanans. Fourth, the explanandum must refer to observables. It must be empirical or have empirical content. In common parlance, it must refer to the real world. Fifth, and as a kind of summary, an observed effect or phenomenon in science is logically required by the covering law of which it is an instance, once the antecedent conditions for that effect have been made clear.

Robinson's assessment of an ongoing debate over the nature of science between Thomas Kuhn and, not too surprisingly, Karl Popper is probably at least as important as his own views on science; it is not surprising to mention Karl Popper's name in this context because he seems to have had something to say about almost everything, and controversy does not appear to be something he took pains to avoid. Robinson (1976, p. 20) stated that, according to Kuhn,

> science is an essentially cultural creation to be understood in psychological and motivational terms. The essential elements of this thesis, often called the *Kuhnian* thesis, include the following: (1) science is to be interpreted in psychosocial terms; (2) it is *not* to be understood as a set of sudden "earthquakes" but as a somewhat staid, "puzzle-oriented" process; (3) little of its research is extraordinary; rather, nearly all of it is, to use Kuhn's term, *normal* research intended to reveal how cleverly the scientist can prove what is well established; (4) it is a conservative rather than a revolutionary enterprise whose executors are judged more in terms of their ability to fit in than stand out.

Once again, and aside from Kuhn's view of science, it is interesting to note how in this case a contemporary historian of psychology can be something of an essentialist when he, Robinson, refers to science as "an essentially cultural creation" and the "essential elements" of the Kuhnian thesis.

It is also of interest to note that Kuhn, who apparently is neither a psychologist nor a sociologist, nevertheless considered it necessary to interpret science in psychosocial terms, but psychologists and sociologists, at least so far, have not dealt with it as a subject of systematic, empirical inquiry. It is a philosophical, or metaphysical, issue and not a scientific one, although the behavior of scientists certainly can be observed and, therefore, can be the subject of at least some sort of inquiry.

To contrast the positions of Kuhn and Popper, Robinson (1976, pp. 20–23) observed that Kuhn interprets science psychologically, whereas Popper interprets it logically. For Popper, science does not have a subject; it is subjectless. That is, "its nature is independent not only of the psychological dispositions of scientists but also of the particular problems to which science is addressed." It is not puzzle-oriented for Popper; it is problem-oriented, in the sense that the validity of significant theories is of major concern. "Normal" science for Kuhn is not science at all for Popper. If "a scientist is engaged in work that can only be appreciated within a given cultural or sociological context," if "he is attempting merely to reconcile his research to that which is generally accepted by the scientific community," if "the research is devoid of revolutionary potential," it is not, according to Popper, science.

For Kuhn, "science is *scientists* and the latter are *psychological* entities, not just *logical* ones." Thus, science is basically "a psychological venture."

> The successful scientific revolution, accordingly, can take place only after the theory to be replaced has failed to satisfy needs of an extralogical nature—needs that are economic, political, spiritual. The scientific theory that accommodates these needs will not be replaced by one that does not. Few scientists will search for such a theory; fewer will embrace it if it is unearthed. At a particular point in the evolution of science, the vast majority of scientists are "practitioners," performing the socially significant work of reproving, reasserting, and otherwise honoring those great scientific achievements of the past which define what science is for the practitioners. These achievements, which Kuhn calls *paradigms,* are the intellectual boundaries within which scientific inquiry can proceed. Without the paradigms there is, quite simply, no work for the practitioners! [Robinson, 1976, p. 21]

For Popper, "the validity of scientific propositions is and always could be assessed in terms" quite different than those that might be described as "sociologistic."

> In his well known "falsification" hypothesis, Popper offers a litmus test for those who wish to weigh the scientific substance of a claim: is the claim stated in such a way as to apprise the listener of those procedures that would unequivocally establish the claim as false if it is, indeed, false? And by "procedures" Popper means more than the mechanical or methodological steps involved in research. He means the logical, *syntactical* procedures employed in phrasing the claim and in tying it to the observational domain to which it refers. The rules of the syllogism are not to be affirmed or suspended as society wishes, and the logic of science does not rest on taste. A scientific theory either explains what we can observe and explains with accuracy and reliability or it does not. It is either testable or it is not. When properly tested, it either passes or fails. When we advance our theory and conduct our tests, we know more than we did before. We know about the enduring features of the real world and we can predict how it will behave. Our predictions must be confirmed or the theory must be abandoned. That which deviates from these prescriptions is not science, "normal" or otherwise. [Robinson, 1976, pp. 21–22]

Thus, according to Kuhn, science is psychological. It is scientists. Scientists develop paradigms within which they work until a variety of their needs are no longer met, at which time the paradigms begin to be replaced. According to Popper, science is logical and empirical. It involves explanation; it is accurate and reliable. It tests the predictions of a theory under controlled conditions of observation. If the predictions of the theory are not confirmed, the theory is abandoned. That summary statement is the nature of science for Kuhn and for Popper as their views have been interpreted by Robinson.

However, Shapere (1976) has remarked that two major objections have been raised about Kuhn's views as expressed in the first edition of his book. They have to do with ambiguities in the concept of paradigm and the relativism in paradigm choice to which his views seem eventually to lead. Furthermore, Kuhn's (1970) efforts to meet these objections seem to result in a retreat from his original position; his position appears to become more conventional, if that is a word that can be applied to these matters. Additional comments by Kuhn in the second edition lead Shapere (1976, p. 60) to conclude from them that

> we must study scientific communities not as one of several steps in clarifying the nature of science (in attempting, say, to separate the irrational from the rational components as a prelude to analyzing the latter); it is the *only* step. What the community says is rational, scientific, is so; beyond this, there is no answer to be found.

That conclusion is one that might be reached simply through consideration of the possibility that questions about the nature of science are very likely essentialistic, and, so far as we now know, we are never able to know that we have ever grasped the essence of a thing, even if we have. Consequently, an answer to the question "What is science?" will undoubtedly be one based on convention, or on what the community says science is. And, at the present time, it is not entirely clear what the community says science is.

For example, perhaps the most recent pronouncement (Feyerabend 1975) on the nature of science states that "science is an essentially anarchistic enterprise." "The only principle that does not inhibit its progress is: anything goes." The work of Kuhn and Popper is concerned primarily with scientific practice; the work that preceded theirs emphasized scientific method. Feyerabend argues, like Kuhn and Popper, that the most success in science has been achieved not through the use of rational methods but by anarchistic practices—practices that stress the biases, creativity, and wishes of the scientist—as opposed to method and authority. Apparently, Feyerabend is also an essentialist to the extent that "science is an essentially anarchistic enterprise."

With regard to the emphasis on method which preceded the work of Kuhn and Popper, it does seem that science has a special technique that enables it to say that it knows something; this technique is its methodology. No one has ever been able to say just what the methodology of science is, just as they have not been able to answer any other essentialist question definitively, although many have tried. However, it does appear that what distinguishes scientific methodology from, say, methodology in the arts and humanities is that the methodology of science requires, at some point, the test of a conjecture or an hypothesis under controlled conditions of observation; the same does not appear to be the case for the arts and humanities. That is, their conjectures and hypotheses are not tested under controlled conditions of observation, although they may, nevertheless, be tested against other standards, such as those of rationality or intuition. Consequently, if science has one, controlled observation might qualify as its unique, or essential, feature.

From what has been presented, it seems obvious that no one is entirely clear about the nature of science. Many of the psychologists whose views on the nature of science have been mentioned so far treat it as a thing with occasional references to it as a process. It is treated as a thing when considered a systematized body of knowledge, which many students of psychology are likely to do. It is treated as a process when the emphasis is placed on the attitudes of the scientist, methodology, or problem solution. Regardless of whether it is treated as a thing or as a process, the presumption seems to be that there is a thing or process to which the word science applies.

Aside from what appears to be an inclination toward essentialism, those who treat any matter in that way are also metaphysical realists; they assume there is a real world with real things or processes existing in it. Consequently, most of the views on the nature of science considered here are based on the metaphysics of realism.

However, science may also be treated as a human construction, which is a view of the nature of science that can be said to be based on the metaphysics of phenomenalism. From that standpoint, science is neither a thing nor a process; it is a construction. It is whatever scientists, or humanity, make of it, as in the conclusion Shapere (1976) drew from Kuhn's work: "What the community says is rational, scientific, is so; beyond this, there is no answer to be found." Another example of this kind of treatment of science is that expressed by Torgerson (1958) based on the analysis by Margenau (1950).

These considerations aside, there appears to be some agreement that science is both rational and empirical, or theoretical and observational, or conceptual and sensory. In a somewhat different context, William James (1950, p. 488) remarked that "the baby, assailed by eyes, ears, nose, skin, and entrails at once, feels it all as one great blooming, buzzing confusion." We may all feel that way, regardless of age. That is, baby or adult, scientist or nonscientist, may always be assailed by our sensory experience "as one great blooming, buzzing confusion"; the task is to make some sense of it, if we are determined not to be existentialists and remain at the level of existence, or sense experience. Whether scientist or nonscientist, we do so by representing our sensory experience with symbols; the symbols are the rational component of knowing, and sense experience is the empirical component of knowing, so far as we now know. If we didn't represent it with symbols, our sensory experience, whatever it is, would simply occur and be gone. Consequently, we structure it by means of language, or logic, or numbers. When we do, we are then able to manipulate the symbols of language or logic or numbers and, in the process, develop statements about whatever it is those symbols represent. Apparently, being able to make statements means that our confusion has been reduced, at least to some extent; the buzzing may be less intense.

The scientist may attempt to reduce his confusion in a somewhat different way than the nonscientist. The scientist assigns his symbols to the sensory events in which he is interested according to rules under controlled conditions of observation; those rules are the rules of numbers. That is, the scientist uses language as well as logic but, at some point, measures. The nonscientist does not measure to the same extent as the scientist, although he or she may still assign symbols to events according to rules, whether they are the rules of language or of logic. Thus, measurement under controlled conditions of observation may be what distinguishes science from nonscience, but that alone is not necessarily what science is.

At the present time, it does not seem possible to state what science is, especially on the basis of consensus. Furthermore, it does not even seem possible to state what it is by extrapolation from a behavioral position. Leaving the question "What is science?" unanswered may illustrate how it happens that answers to the other essentialist questions considered here are tentative rather than definitive.

Chapter Five

What Is Behavior?

Those who continue to persist in the ways of essentialism might next ask the question that serves as the title for this chapter. It seems only natural for them to do so if they have already inquired about the nature of psychology, behaviorism, and science. And, it appears to be particularly natural for them to do so if they have been told: that psychology is the science of behavior; that it became a science of behavior when psychologists took behaviorism seriously; and at least something, however unsatisfactory, about the nature of science. The next significant word after *science* in the statement "psychology is the science of behavior" is the word *behavior.*

A fairly recent introductory textbook in psychology (Smith, Sarason, and Sarason, 1978, p. 4) states that

> psychology is usually defined as the scientific study of behavior. This definition is deceptively simple, for psychologists have disagreed over the years about what should be included under the term *behavior.* Should it be restricted to externally observable or *overt* behaviors that can be seen and measured by others, or should it also include internal, or *covert,* events, such as images, thoughts,

> and feelings? Most psychologists today agree that both overt and covert behaviors are appropriate objects of study, and they use the term behavior in its broadest possible sense to include anything that an organism can do.

Their statement did not indicate, at that time, how psychology came to be what it is, and they never made clear how psychologists came to use the word *behavior* in that way, although they did hint at the historical controversy over that usage.

For present purposes, it is of some interest to point out that, if behavior is "anything that an organism can do," there presumably are organisms that, in turn, do things. A statement of that kind appears to be based upon the metaphysics of realism. It assumes that there are things that exist independently of an observer and that these things act independently of an observer. An alternative is that *behavior* is a word that is used to classify particular sense experiences of an observer, which the observer then says are what organisms do. The second kind of statement is based upon the metaphysics of phenomenalism. It assumes that sense experiences occur and can be classified in different ways but not necessarily that they are "about" anything. In either case, this apparent digression may help to illustrate how the problem of behavior can be included as a problem of metaphysics and psychology.

At least one other psychologist has acknowledged, perhaps inadvertently, that the problem of behavior may occasion a metaphysical problem for psychology. B. F. Skinner (1938, p. 6) in an almost casual remark, stated that "behavior is what an organism is *doing*—or more accurately what it is observed by another organism to be doing."

If it is more accurate to say that behavior is what one organism is observed by another organism to be doing, it may be more accurate still to say that *behavior* is a word applied to certain observed events, or observations, that are referred to as what an organism is doing. The first statement implies that there is an organism that can be observed to be doing something (realism), as does the statement by Smith et al. (1978). The second implies only that sensory events have occurred (phenomenalism), which, perhaps by convention, are referred to as behavior; it does so, of course, without saying what sensory events are, just as realism may not say what the real world is. In the first case, behavior is observed; in the second, it is constructed. Whether it is observed or constructed appears to depend upon the metaphysics, or ontology, of the observer.

William McDougall, who seems to have been the first behaviorist (Tolman, 1932, p. 4) and who some (Marx and Hillix, 1973, pp. 170, 189) claim was the first behaviorist, although he rejected that title, defined behavior as "the action or actions of some living thing" (McDougall, 1923, p. 43), but there were also "marks" of behavior. They were: "a certain spontaneity of movement"; "persistence of activity independently of the continuance of the impression which may have initiated it"; "variation of direction of persistent movements"; "coming to an end of the animal's movements as soon as they have brought about a particular kind of change in its situation"; "preparation for the new situation toward the production of which the action contributes"; and "some degree of improvement in the effectiveness of behavior, when it is repeated by the animal under similar circumstances" (McDougall, 1923, pp. 43–46). Thus, there were six "marks" of behavior for McDougall, and, if an organism exhibited the first five, its behavior was also considered purposive.

As indicated in the first chapter, John B. Watson, who, unlike McDougall, was not at all reluctant to bear the title of behaviorist, stated that behavior was what the psychologist could observe. What the psychologists could observe was "the separate systems of reactions that the individual makes to his environment" (Watson, 1929, p. 13). A reaction, or response, was "the total striped and unstriped muscular and glandular changes which follow upon a given stimulus" (Watson, 1929, p. 14). Most reactions, for Watson, fell into one or another of four categories: explicit habit responses, such as playing tennis; implicit habit responses, such as "thinking" or subvocal speech; explicit hereditary responses, such as sneezing; and implicit hereditary responses, such as endocrine or ductless gland, or hormonal, secretions.

In a later chapter, however, Watson (1929, p. 225) remarked in a footnote that "it is perfectly possible for a student of behavior entirely ignorant of the sympathetic nervous system and of the glands and smooth muscles, or even of the central nervous system as a whole, to write a thoroughly comprehensive and accurate study of the emotions—the types, their interrelations with habits, their role, etc." His remark did not go unnoticed by Tolman (1922), who expressed some mild consternation about it but agreed that a truly behavioral account need not consider muscular contractions and glandular secretions.

A year later, Watson (1930, p. 6) stated that behavior is "*what the organism does or says . . . saying* is doing—that is, *behaving.*" Consequently, it appears that he was a realist with regard to behavior. Behavior was exhibited by a subject, or it occurred. A few sentences later, he stated that anything an animal does is a response and, a few pages later (Watson, 1930, p. 14), it is clear that he used the words "behavior" and "response" interchangeably; a similar approach is taken in this account. That is, the problem of behavior is considered equivalent to the problem of response, even though there are some (e.g., Reynolds, 1975, p. 6) who consider responses to be the basic units of behavior.

For a good many psychologists and other students of psychology, a response is quite obviously and simply what an organism does or is doing. If so, it seems to be more of an event than an object, which suggests that the physical, or "thing," language of science may not be applicable to it. Those who think otherwise may be referred to as "physicalists" and in support of the doctrine of "physicalism."

The doctrine of physicalism is that "the physical language is a universal language of science and the individual languages used in any subdomain of science can be equipollently translated into the physical language" (Stevens, 1976, p. 18). However, if behavior or a response is an event, a doing, or, in the vernacular of the sixties, "a happening," it is not a physical object or a thing. And if it is not a physical object or a thing, the physical language of science may misrepresent it; that language may be inappropriate for describing or explaining behavior.

Furthermore, if physical language or the language of physics is not applicable to behavior or events, a question arises about what language is applicable. Some have suggested (cf. Stevens, 1976, p. 18) that a "psychological" language might be more appropriate. However, the problem may be not so much with the physical language per se as with the way it is used. An object language may treat events as objects and perhaps reify them (cf. Eacker, 1975, pp. 33–39). Some care must be exercised if the physical language is used to describe and explain events, when events may not be things, or objects; more will be said on this subject in later chapters.

Other prominent behavioral psychologists have had something to say about the nature of behavior or response. For example, the "purposive" or "cognitive" behaviorist, Edward C. Tolman (1932, pp. 6–7), argued that Watson "dallied with two different notions of behavior." One was behavior as defined by its "underlying physical and physiological details, i.e., in terms of receptor-process, conductor-process, and effector-process per se," which Tolman referred to as "the *molecular* definition of behavior." The other was behavior as an " 'emergent' phenomenon that has descriptive and defining properties of its own," which Tolman referred to as "the *molar* definition of behavior"; he defended the molar conception of behavior.

For him, aside from its physics and physiology, behavior exhibited emergent properties all its own. His view probably is best expressed in the following recapitulation of his position (Tolman, 1932, pp. 21–22).

> Behavior, as such, is a molar phenomenon as contrasted with the molecular phenomena which constitute its underlying physiology. And, as a molar phenomenon, behavior's immediate descriptive properties appear to be those of: getting to or from goal-objects by selecting certain means-objects-routes as against others and by exhibiting specific patterns of commerces with these selected means-objects. But these descriptions in terms of gettings to or from, selections of routes and patterns of commerces-with imply and define immediate, immanent purpose and cognition aspects in the behavior. These two aspects of behavior are, however, but objectively and functionally defined entities. They are implicit in the facts of behavior docility. They are defined neither in the last analysis, nor in the first instance, by introspection. They are envisaged as readily in the behavior-acts of the cat and of the rat as in the more refined speech reactions of man. Such purposes and cognitions, such docility, are, obviously, functions of the organism as a whole.

Thus, for Tolman, behavior is a molar phenomenon with emergent properties that cannot be found in its physics and physiology. They are purpose and cognition, and they are descriptive characteristics which, apparently, anyone can observe if they would but take the trouble to do so.

According to another not so early behaviorist, Edwin R. Guthrie (1935), movements are the primary data for a science of behavior, but movements contribute to acts, or behavior. Acts are movements or classes of movements that have certain effects or results, such as hitting a squash ball, skiing down a hill, or writing a sentence.

> What we attempt to predict in going behavior is action—response. All response is made up of movement brought about by effectors or of glandular secretion. The muscles and glands are the organs of response. Every instance of response is analyzable in terms of movement; but the classes of response on a psychological level, as distinct from the reflex movements which are in the domain of physiology, are defined and most easily observed in terms of their end results. We recognize the writing, but if there had been no ink in the pen we could not without extraordinary measures specify the response or recognize the movements of hand and arm that produced it. A description of the action of the individual muscles concerned would be hopeless confusion.
>
> There is here the ground of a separation between psychology and the natural sciences. The chains of cause and effect, the chains of connection between stimuli and responses, have an area not open to observation by known methods. End results are attainable by a variety of movement sequences, a variety that does not appear in the definition of the act, which is made in terms of outcome. Our description is on a level different from movement. What we need to know is how to predict acts. Man, viewed as a machine, learns movements, not acts. The occasion for muscular contraction is the arrival of nerve impulses at the muscle end plates of motor nerves. These impulses are transmitted from the central nervous system: their ultimate occasion is the stimulation of sense organs, though the brain and central system have complex and unexplored functions in the coordination of neural activity and may actually serve to originate, in some sense, the outgoing impulses. The chain of cause and effect therefore ends in muscular contraction. The performance of an act on any one occasion

> represents one chain of events in sequence. But successive performances of an act may involve sequences very different in nature. [Guthrie, 1959, pp. 183–184]

It seems evident that Guthrie's distinction between movements and acts corresponds to the distinction other behaviorists have made between responses and behavior, although for him "every instance of response is analyzable in terms of movement."

In his critical and detailed analysis of Clark L. Hull's theory of learning, Sigmund Koch (1954, p. 9) remarked that

> it has become a truism to observe that early behaviorists were systematically ambiguous in their definitions and applications of the concepts "stimulus" and "response." The term "stimulus" was indiscriminately applied to states of affairs ranging from the physical energy change acting on a single receptor to the behavior-evoking effect of a complex social situation, while "response" could designate anything from the contraction of a single muscle cell, to the name of a class of end results brought about by a widely varying range of movement sequences.

His criticism did not exclude Hull, but he did note that Hull "seemed sensitive to the nature and magnitude of the problems."

Hull (1943, p. 16) claimed to "consider a number of the more general characteristics of organismic behavior." He began by observing that, when an organism embarks on its own independent life, a dynamic relationship commences between it and its environment. Both it and the environment are active; "the environment acts on the organism, and the organism acts on the environment." It is this interaction between the organism and its environment that is of major concern for a science of behavior.

However, the specific objective of his work "is the elaboration of the basic molar behavioral laws underlying the 'social' sciences." This expression means "the uniformities discoverable among the grossly observable phenomena of behavior as contrasted with the laws of the behavior of the ultimate 'molecules' upon which this behavior depends, such as the constituent cells of nerve, muscle, gland, and so forth. The term *molar* thus means coarse, or macroscopic, as contrasted with molecular, or microscopic" (Hull, 1943, p. 17). Thus, his intent seems very much like that of Tolman in its emphasis on the molar aspects of behavior.

Hull (1943, p. 19) went on to say that

> it is the primary task of a molar science of behavior to isolate the basic laws or rules according to which various combinations of stimulation, arising from the state of need on the one hand and the state of the environment on the other, bring about the kind of behavior characteristic of different organisms. A closely related task is to understand why the behavior so mediated is so generally adaptive, i.e., successful in the sense of reducing needs and facilitating survival, and why it is unsuccessful on those occasions when survival is not facilitated.

However, psychology is not physiology, although "it is conceivable that the elaboration of a systematic science of behavior at a molar level may aid in the development of an adequate neurophysiology and thus lead in the end to a truly molecular theory of behavior firmly based on physiology" (Hull, 1943, p. 20).

The above excerpts from Hull's *Principles of Behavior* clearly do not treat the issue of behavior per se; the "grossly observable phenomena of behavior" are not identified. Hull simply does not confront the problem of behavior directly. Throughout his discussion on the nature of objective behavior theory, he makes frequent reference to interaction, activity, movement, and behavior somewhat interchangeably, as though they all meant the same thing. Thus, it could be that behavior was all of these things for Hull. That is, behavior was the interaction between the organism and its environment, its activity, or its movement.

On the other hand, the major dependent variable in his

theory of learning was reaction. "Briefly stated, the consequent anchoring events are reactions (R), i.e., the movements or other activities of the organism" (Hull, 1943, p. 322). Reaction is measured by means of the probability of reaction evocation (p); the latency of reaction evocation ($_{s}t_{r}$); the number of unreinforced reactions required to reach experimental extinction (n); or the amplitude, magnitude, or intensity of the reaction (A). Any one or all of these measures might be thought of as operational definitions for reaction. Consequently, if behavior for Hull is not interaction, activity, or movement, perhaps it is p, $_{s}t_{r}$, n, or A. Whatever it finally turns out to be, the early behaviorists apparently were not the only ones who were systematically ambiguous about stimulus and response.

One version of Burrhus F. Skinner's (1938, p. 6) conception of behavior has already been stated. That is, "behavior is what an organism is *doing*—or more accurately what it is observed by another organism to be doing." A somewhat different version appears in the following statement:

> By behavior, then, I mean simply the movement of an organism or of its parts in a frame of reference provided by the organism itself or by various external objects or fields of force. It is convenient to speak of this as the action of the organism upon the outside world, and it is often desirable to deal with an effect rather than with the movement itself, as in the case of the production of sounds.

Thus, where he seems inclined toward the metaphysics of phenomenalism in his first version, he reverts to the metaphysics of realism in the second. Most of the views on behavior examined so far also appear to be based on the metaphysics of realism, although it is interesting to note that none of them has made reference to the "essence" of behavior or its essential characteristics. Nevertheless, many of them have made reference to what an organism does, its activity, or movement.

As is well known, Skinner subsequently drew a distinction between respondents and operants (cf. Skinner, 1938, pp. 19–21), which did not necessarily exhaust the universe of behaviors. The organism is passive when it exhibits respondent behaviors. They are elicited very much like reflexes, although not all respondents are reflexes. The organism is active when it exhibits operant behaviors. They are emitted; they operate on the environment and have particular, usually reinforcing, consequences.

Respondents are analogous to the involuntary behaviors discussed so frequently in the past by philosophers, whereas operants are analogous to the philosophers' voluntary behaviors, except that no concept of will, or will power, is involved. Operants simply occur, although there may be unidentified stimuli that occasion them.

Some years later, Skinner (1953, pp. 257–282) apparently found it necessary to discuss public and private events and to draw another distinction among behaviors; this time it was between overt and covert behaviors.

> One important sort of stimulus to which the individual may possibly be responding when he describes unemitted behavior has no parallel among other forms of private stimulation. It arises from the fact that the behavior may actually occur but on such a reduced scale that it cannot be observed by others—at least without instrumentation. This is often expressed by saying that the behavior is "covert." Sometimes it is said that the reduced form is merely the beginning of the overt form—that the private event is incipient or inchoate behavior. A verbal repertoire which has been established with respect to the overt case might be extended to covert behavior because of similar self-stimulation. The organism is generating the same effective stimuli, albeit on a much smaller scale. [Skinner, 1953, p. 263]

In this passage, he suggests that the ancient and traditional distinction between mental and physical events be discarded. In its place, he would substitute a distinction between inner and outer, or covert and overt, behaviors. In somewhat different terms, for the tradition of psychophysical dualism as an approach to the mind-body problem in psychology (cf. Eacker, 1975, pp. 13–24), Skinner offers a monism which some have called materialistic monism.

The tradition of psychophysical dualism with regard to the mind-body problem is that the human organism in particular, and perhaps organisms in general, are composed of two quite unlike substances: mind and matter, or mind and body; in some way, mind is assumed to affect body, and body is assumed to affect mind. Materialistic monism denies this two "stuff" view; it does away with mind as a separate thing or realm and asserts that organisms are composed only of matter. But behavior does not appear to be matter; if anything, it is an event and not a thing. Consequently, the label of materialistic monism may be inappropriate for Skinner's view, as well as for that of Watson, who expressed a similar one earlier.

A more descriptive label might be "behavioristic monism," where behavior is the single "stuff" to which reference is made. If so, some behavior could be thought of as inside the organism, and some behavior could be thought of as outside of it, but, in either case, what organisms exhibit is behavior and not mind and body. One kind of behavior may be observable and the other not, as proposed by Skinner, but both, nevertheless, are behavior.

Since observables are involved, perhaps a still more accurate label is "phenomenalistic monism." This position on the mind-body problem would take seriously the metaphysics, or ontology, of phenomenalism and emphasize the seemingly obvious fact that observables are phenomena. They are, if David Hume was correct (cf. Eacker, 1975, pp. 30–31), perceptual phenomena; they are observed events; they occur. As such, a distinction has to be made between what is observed and what is not observed about what we call organismic behavior, whether that of humans or of animals. But what is observed is no different in kind than what is not observed; inferences still have to be made about inner phenomena based on conclusions reached about outer phenomena. Stated somewhat differently, the overt and covert behavior suggested by Skinner are observed and unobserved phenomena, according to this brand of monism.

However, this brand of monism seems to be linguistically cumbersome, and, until it becomes less so (if it ever does), there is perhaps some wisdom in supporting the distinctions between overt and covert behavior that have been made by Skinner. In a somewhat more recent publication, Skinner (1963) discussed seeing as one of the covert behaviors.

> If seeing does not require the presence of things seen, we need not be concerned about certain mental processes said to be involved in the construction of such things—images, memories, and dreams, for example. We may regard a dream, not as a display of things seen by the dreamer, but simply as the behavior of seeing. At no time during a daydream, for example, should we expect to find within the organism anything which corresponds to the external stimuli present when the dreamer first acquired the behavior in which he is now engaged. In simple recall we need not suppose that we wander through some storehouse of memory until we find an object which we then contemplate. Instead of assuming that we begin with a tendency to *recognize* such an object once it is found, it is simpler to assume that we begin with a tendency to *see* it. Techniques of self-management which facilitate recall—for example, the use of mnemonic devices—can be formulated as ways of strengthening behavior rather than of creating objects to be seen. Freud dramatized the issue with respect to dreaming when asleep in his concept of dreamwork—an activity in which some part of the dreamer played the role of a theatrical producer while another part sat in the audience. If a dream is, indeed,

> something seen, then we must suppose that it is wrought as such; but if it is simply the behavior of seeing, the dreamwork may be dropped from the analysis. It took man a long time to understand that when he dreamed of a wolf, no wolf was actually there. It has taken him much longer to understand that not even a representation of a wolf is there. [Skinner, 1969, pp. 233–234]

People still may not understand it and, in fact, may even refuse to consider the possibility that things seen are not represented but simply seen. That is, people still may not understand that things seen in the absence of the things seen are not necessarily hallucinations and not necessarily representations of the things seen; they are simply the behavior of seeing them. Similarly, things heard or tasted in the absence of the things heard or tasted are not necessarily representations of the things heard or tasted but simply the behavior of hearing or tasting them; it is perhaps easier to understand in the case of hearing and tasting than in that of seeing since what it is that is presumed to be represented probably is not "imaged" in the case of hearing and tasting. Seeing is behavior for Skinner; it simply occurs; it goes on inside the organism as do hearing, smelling, tasting, and touching. Each of them is apparently what eyes, ears, nose, tongue, and skin do; they are all behaviors that occur within the organism. In the long run, they may turn out to be something other than behaviors, but, for now, he invites us to consider the possibility that that is what they are. This source appears to be the one that led Smith et al. (1978), as quoted in one of the opening passages of this chapter, to mention the distinction between overt and covert behaviors in the science of behavior.

The thought is a novel one and deserves more than serious consideration. It deserves both extensive and intensive consideration because never before in the history of ideas have people believed that what goes on inside of us is the same in kind as what we are observed to do. The prevailing custom is to suppose that the things going on inside of us are a very different sort of thing than the things going on outside of us. It is now supposed that the inner events are mental whereas the outer events are physical, but there is at least a possibility that they are the same. Both may be events rather than behavior, which carries Skinner's proposal somewhat further; more is said about this subject in later chapters.

There are other prominent psychologists, behavioral and otherwise, who have had something to say about what constitutes a response, or behavior. For example, J. F. Hall (1966, p. 7) observed that "typically, responses have been defined as (a) muscular contractions or glandular secretions or (b) acts of the organism which are directed toward producing some change in the environment, either of which are occasioned by a stimulus." Similarly, Miller and Dollard (1941, p. 59) have stated that

> it is obvious that "response," as here used, is not restricted to the conventional usage, in which a response is defined as a muscular contraction or a glandular secretion. It is also obvious that "stimulation" is not restricted to the conventional usage in which a stimulus is defined as an energy change activating receptors. According to the present usage, a response is any activity by or within the individual which can become functionally connected with an antecedent event through learning; a stimulus is any event to which a response can be so connected. This definition is not circular for cases in which the events referred to have been empirically identified.

Both quotations reveal that some circularity may be encountered in the definition of a response as well as a stimulus. That is, there might be those who are tempted to assert that a response occurs to a stimulus and a stimulus occasions a response in order to define one or the other of them. However, as is well known and rather obvious, such a definition leaves both terms undefined. That is, in order to know what a response is, one must know what a stimulus is, but in order to know what a stimulus is, one must know what a response is.

The quotations also suggest, especially in the case of Hall, that other psychologists appear to assume that there is some thing that is a response to which a definition does, or can, refer. In somewhat different terms, they may approach the problem of response definition with the ontology, or metaphysics, of a realist and perhaps the inclinations of an essentialist. It is also of interest that Miller and Dollard consider a stimulus to be an event but do not consider a response to be an event, in contrast with suggestions made in the foregoing discussion.

In a paper devoted entirely to the problem of behavior and entitled "Behavior: Datum or Abstraction," R. H. Waters (1958) also displayed the metaphysics of realism in his treatment of the subject. He did so after referring, among other things, to the statement Robert S. Woodworth attributed to some "wag" that psychology first lost its soul, then its mind, and then its consciousness but that, nevertheless, it still manages to behave; at the conclusion of this discussion, if not before, there may be some who doubt that it even manages to do that. Waters (1958, p. 282) went on to contend that

> psychology's "behavior" is analogous to the physicist's heat, that the psychologist uses the term to refer to a class of activities that possess certain characteristics (spontaneity or autonomy, persistence, variability, docility, and, perhaps, purpose). . . . This means that "behavior" is an abstraction, not a datum. The data are the specific responses exhibited by the human or animal subject. Some of these specific responses can be classed as "behavior" for and by the psychologist; others presumably exist that do not belong to that class and hence are not data for psychology.

To the extent that there is "a class of activities that possess certain characteristics," and to the extent that other specific responses "presumably exist that do not belong to that class"—to that extent, his metaphysics are realistic, even though behavior is an abstraction and not a datum. If behavior were simply an abstraction but possessed no characteristics, his conception would be closer to the metaphysics of phenomenalism.

By way of contrast with Waters's statement, Logan (1960, p. 117) has acknowledged that

> although most psychologists seem to agree that behavior is the proper dependent variable in psychological research, no explicit definition of the response is generally accepted. Implicit notions about the response have been borrowed from the everyday vernacular, and relatively little attention has been paid to formalizing these or other ideas. . . . The problem of defining the response is pragmatic and cannot be solved solely by logical analysis. Analysis can help to identify the various alternatives, but the choice among them is made on the basis of how successfully any definition works. Because the body of empirical knowledge in psychology is relatively small and expanding rapidly, any propositions made at the present time must be recognized as being very tentative.

Even if the body of empirical knowledge in psychology were relatively large and expanding slowly, any propositions made about what constitutes a response, or behavior, probably still would remain tentative because of some additional considerations.

One consideration is that even if the definition of response or behavior stated by Waters (1958) were in fact true in some absolute sense, those who agreed with it might not know that it was true in that sense. This issue is another aspect of the paradoxical philosophical puzzle of how it is known that something is known. In the case of the definition of behavior, the problem becomes one of being able to state that the definition given now will still apply a year from now, or fifty years from now. The future cannot be known until it has occurred, and statements made about it are at best hypotheses to be tested. This consideration does not mean that scientific knowledge is impossible; it only means that such knowledge is never known to be certain.

A second consideration closely related to the first is that the hypotheses of a scientist are mere speculations until they have been subjected to some sort of test under controlled conditions of observation. However, even if it were possible to test the definition of behavior under such conditions, which does not seem likely, one more observation can be made immediately after the last one has been made, which suggests that the process of observation in science may never be complete. Thus, even if a scientist were in possession of absolute truth with regard to behavior or any other scientific matter, he could not know that he was, at least not with the methods of science as they are currently understood. These considerations recall the remark sometimes attributed to William James: "Absolute truth is what the last man says is true twenty seconds before he dies." Those made uneasy by such considerations may find comfort in another remark sometimes attributed to him: "It is a mark of the mature intellect to be able to live in an uncertain universe."

Turner (1967, p. 198) stated that the systematic ambiguity exhibited by the early behaviorists with regard to stimulus and response has not improved very much since that time, and he went on to develop the view that the definition of a response depends upon the conceptual predilections of those who define it.

> In its preoccupation with learning, behaviorism incorporated the reflex arc and the conditioning model into its conceptual framework. Understandably, then, response was limited to the designation of muscular contractions and glandular secretions where specific sequential tracing from stimulus to response was, at least, conceptually possible. When concern with adaptive function

> rendered the reflex concept inadequate, larger units of response description became necessary but with a concomitant loss in specificity. It was not that the facts supported the molar over the molecular point of view. It was simply that different facts emerge as intrinsic to our moving from reflexology to functionalism. Where behaviorists now take the pains to define response, it is clear that their differences of opinion are dictated by their conceptual preferences and not by discoveries or confusions about real response entities in the world apart.
>
> As it is with stimulus so it is with response. Not only does the conceptual framework determine the definition of the observation terms, it determines the type of experiment undertaken. [Turner, 1967, pp. 200–201]

This statement lends support to the phenomenalist position that behavior is constructed rather than discovered if the definition of observation terms is determined by the conceptual framework of the psychologist. Stated differently, if the conceptual preferences displayed by psychologists determine the definition of response and if the metaphysics of psychologists are included among their conceptual preferences, then the metaphysics of psychologists determine how they define behavior. What behavior is cannot be known apart from those who make assertions about it.

A view at least in part related to that of Turner was expressed by Hinde (1970, p. 10).

> In practice, there are two methods for describing behaviour. One involves reference ultimately to the strength, degree, and patterning of muscular contractions (or glandular activity, or change in some other physiological property). The other involves reference not to these changes but to their consequences. This is not a distinction between types of behaviour, as the "molecular" versus "molar" distinction is often used by learning theorists, but between criteria for describing behaviour: it is of the utmost importance since the whole character of the subsequent analysis may be influenced by which type of description is chosen.

Even though he does not distinguish between types of behavior but between criteria for describing behavior, those criteria may not be adequate if they do not enter into behavioral laws.

To explain, in a manner somewhat similar to the pragmatics of Logan, the comparative psychologists Denny and Ratner (1970, pp. 15–16) asserted that

> the approach that we will be following in the comparative analysis of behavior is that the stimulus is always an independent variable, a "cause," and that it must be fully considered in any analysis of behavior. The dependent variable, "effect," is always a response; but response, since it leads to stimulus changes (response-produced stimuli), can be either an independent or a dependent variable. In this context, all behavior can be objectively viewed and lawfully described and coordinated with a variety of theoretical positions.

Thus, a stimulus for these authors is always an independent variable, although an independent variable apparently may not always be a stimulus. Similarly, a response is always a dependent variable but may also, on occasion, be an independent variable if it produces stimuli.

To the extent that a dependent variable enters into either an S-R or an R-R law of behavior (cf. Staats and Staats, 1963, pp. 20–26), it must in some way be measured; it is a measure of behavior. If so, then it might be argued that behavior is whatever is measured as the dependent variable in a psychological or behavioral experiment, although that alone may not be enough to define it operationally.

A measurement that is not related to anything else, such as an independent variable or another dependent variable, contributes little or nothing to a science of behavior; it is the laws of behavior that are the concern of a science of behavior. If a measurement is not related to any other variables in the form of a functional or correlational relationship, it does not enter into the laws of behavior. Hence, behavior is not defined simply by how it is measured but also by how that measurement relates to other measures of behavior and/or the environment; Skinner (1931) developed an argument very similar to this one for the concept of the reflex in the description of behavior. It is these relationships that define behavior; they are what behavior is. In somewhat different terms, behavior is defined by its laws. It is in that sense that Hinde's criteria for describing behavior may not be adequate; they may not enter into laws of behavior.

Some support for this conclusion appears in a fairly recent statement by Nevin (1973, p. 6), who paused to consider the meanings of both stimulus and response for the purpose of his discussion:

> The term *stimulus* refers to that portion of the physical environment which is selected by an experimenter to be presented or withheld, or otherwise varied systematically, in order to ascertain its effects on behavior. The term *response* refers to that portion of all activities of the organism which is selected by the experimenter to be measured and related to the stimulus. Stimuli and responses can be defined operationally without reference to one another, but it is the way in which responses depend on stimuli —the relation between behavior and environment—that is of central interest.

Thus, the critical question for Nevin is not "What is behavior?" but, rather, "What are its laws?" It may be that the continued effort to answer the latter question may help to answer the former also, since, of the two, it is the latter that can be answered with the methods of science.

It may also be the case that efforts to answer the former question might lead psychologists to examine, or reexamine, their metaphysics. That examination might lead, in turn, to the realization that either realism or phenomenalism can be defended in science. And, since realism has been tried, a shift to phenomenalism might well lead to greater experimental and theoretical insights than have so far been attained by a science of behavior which really cannot be certain what behavior is.

Chapter Six

What Is a Stimulus?

The perhaps hypothetical, but nevertheless persistent, essentialists mentioned in previous chapters might next ask the question that serves as the title for this one, if they had read this far and were not only persistent but also somewhat systematic in their question-asking behavior. Based on what has already transpired, it is clear that they are not easily discouraged by their lack of success. Persistence is known to be a function of reinforcement schedules, but, then, so is extinction.

This question might arise for a systematic as well as a persistent essentialist because another prevailing custom in psychology is that a response doesn't occur without a stimulus; it is always "caused" by something. Indeed, a common dictionary definition for response is that it is any activity of an organism, or of an effector organ or part, or the inhibition of previous activity resulting from stimulation—a reaction. Since responses were discussed in the previous chapter, it seems somewhat systematic, if not just fair, to inquire about stimuli in this one.

The custom mentioned above is perhaps another instance in

psychology of an overly simplistic interpretation of a physical principle, or of a principle of physics, being extrapolated uncritically in an effort to explain matters for which it was not intended. That principle may be Newton's third law of motion, which, in a rather archaic form, states that for every action there is a reaction. In a somewhat less archaic form, the principle might be stated: for every force exerted by an object (A) on another object (B), there is an equal and opposite force on object A exerted by object B. The similarity between this principle and the principle of causality is quite remarkable, although the two are not necessarily equivalent.

Regardless of the principle involved in the case of the stimulus, neither may be very useful in attempting to understand behavior, especially if both tend to preserve the doctrine of mechanistic determinism in psychology. As pointed out in the second chapter and again in the third, that doctrine has been challenged by, if not replaced with, the doctrine of empirical determinism.

Briefly, the doctrine of mechanistic determinism is that all natural phenomena are lawfully determined by physical laws and forces. On the other hand, the doctrine of empirical determinism is that the natural phenomenon of behavior is determined but not by physical causes. Behavior is determined in the sense that it is lawful, but its laws are not the laws of physics; they are the laws of behavior, a few of which were examined in the chapter on behaviorism. In short, behavior is explained by its own laws not by the laws of physics; it is not explained by the stimulus. A response is not the "effect" of a "cause," or stimulus. Newton's principle, the principle of causality, and the doctrine of mechanistic determinism belong in physics; they may not belong in psychology.

There is another and perhaps more compelling reason to

consider this question here. S. S. Stevens (1951, pp. 31–32) has argued that

> in a sense there is only one problem of psychophysics, namely, the definition of the stimulus. In this same sense there is only one problem in all of psychology—and it is the same problem. The definition of the stimulus is thus a bigger problem than it appears to be at first sight. The reason for equating psychology to the problem of defining stimuli can be stated thus: the complete definition of the stimulus to a given response involves the specification of all the transformations of the environment, both internal and external, that leave the response invariant. This specification of the conditions of invariance would entail, of course, a complete understanding of the factors that produce and that alter responses. It is easy enough, of course, to decide upon arbitrary definitions of "stimulus objects" (e.g. a given pattern of lines, a quantity of luminous flux, an acoustic waveform, etc.), but the question is: what properties of these objects do the stimulating? Viewed in this fashion, it is evident that for no response have we yet given a complete definition of the stimulus. At best we have only partially determined the conditions and limits of invariance.

Whether he was right or wrong about the magnitude of its importance, Stevens correctly identified the problem of the stimulus as an important one, especially for what is frequently described as S-R, or stimulus-response, psychology, despite his conclusion that a general definition is probably futile.

Sigmund Koch (1954, p. 9) observed that the "early behaviorists were systematically ambiguous in their definitions" of the stimulus as well as the response. He did so without revealing how anyone could be both systematic and, at the same time, ambiguous, which might tempt some to suspect the operation of a defense mechanism in his case. But, that suspicion aside, the early behaviorists apparently were not alone in their "systematic ambiguity."

For example, W. S. Verplanck (1954, pp. 284–287) found four different ways in which the word "stimulus" is used by psychologists. Perhaps the simplest way in which it is used is as "a part, or a change in a part of environment," although that definition is often complicated by including "statements about states or changes in states, of physical energy." A second way in which it is used is for "any form of energy which elicits a response" or "an energy external to a receptor, which excites the receptor."

A third usage is as "a class of environmental events that cannot be identified independently of observations of a specified activity of the organism and that must control that activity according to a specified set of laws." The fourth use was considered somewhat similar to the second but included the qualification that "hypothetical or inferential classes of physical events (usually intraorganismic) are also referred to as stimuli."

K. W. Spence (1956, p. 41) found three different kinds of referents for the concept of stimulus: situational stimuli, effective stimuli, and intraorganic stimuli. Situational stimuli are "the realm of physical objects or events in the environment that may be specified quite independently of the responding organism and which are under the direct control of the experimenter." Effective stimuli are "the particular sample of the totality of events of the first class that are acting upon and exciting the receptors at the time of a response. These are to a considerable extent dependent upon the organism's receptor-orienting behavior." Intraorganic stimuli have properties that "are specified on the basis of known physiological laws or on the basis of hypothesized internal relations"; they "are also dependent upon the organism."

In an article devoted entirely to the concept of the stimulus in psychology, J. J. Gibson (1960) presented a short history of the experimental study of the stimulus and exposed "sources of confusion in modern usage." With respect to its experimental history, so far as he could tell, the experimental study of the stimulus began with Galvani and Volta in the eighteenth century and experiments on the twitchings of a frog leg. Gibson then traced stimulus from these men through Johannes Müller and others to S-R psychology in the United States.

With respect to sources of confusion, Gibson felt he could find eight of them. They were defined by questions. The questions were: (1) "Does a stimulus motivate the individual or does it merely trigger a response?" (2) "Can a stimulus be taken as the sufficient cause of a response, or can it not?" (3) "Must a stimulus be defined independently of the response it produces—in physical terms rather than terms of behavior or sensory process?" (4) "Do stimuli exist in the environment or only at receptors?" (5) "When is a pattern or relation to be considered a single stimulus, and when a number of separate stimuli?" (6) "When does a sequence constitute a single and when a number of separate stimuli; also, can a single enduring stimulus exist throughout a changing sequence?" (7) "How do we specify the structure of a stimulus?" (8) "Do stimuli carry information about their sources in the world, and how do they specify them?"

Aside from matters dealt with more directly by Gibson, these questions have implications here which he does not consider. For example, the first question asks whether a stimulus impels a response or simply releases one, when it may do neither; that is, it may be simply a variable of which a response is a function. In the first instance, it appears that some energy or force moves from the stimulus to the response and sustains the occurrence of the response. In the second instance, it appears that the energy or force is stored within the organism and made to flow when the stimulus is presented. In the third instance, a stimulus is simply a variable to which a response is related; more will be said about this possibility later in this chapter.

Sigmund Freud seems to have favored the first interpretation, whereas both Neal Miller and B. F. Skinner have voiced objections to it. In the first two instances, the concepts of energy and force may have been borrowed from physics, Newtonian physics, in an effort to explain behavior when no other explanations were available. As suggested by the third instance, it may be time to return the explanations to their owner.

While force and energy are very useful explanatory concepts in physics, no one has ever demonstrated how either force or energy enter into behavior. It is assumed that they do if the behavior of organisms is a natural phenomenon like the phenomena of physics. But precisely how they do has never been made clear. Both force and energy may have provided convenient and perhaps misleading analogies for relating the movements of animate objects to inanimate objects, as pointed out in the chapters on motivation and human nature.

Furthermore, this use of the concepts may reify them when neither force nor energy can be known to be things that exist in the universe which, in turn, make other things take place or move. That is, it has never been demonstrated that either concept refers to something. Elementary physics textbooks define force as equal to mass multiplied by acceleration, whereas energy is defined as the capacity to do work. Work refers to the physical displacement of objects by force. Consequently, energy and force are not defined entirely independently of one another, but, aside from that, no one has demonstrated the existence of either, except as explanations of the movements of inanimate objects; no one has ever observed either energy or force per se, and no demonstration of their effects within animate objects has been performed and probably will not be. For this and other reasons, some of which are examined here, it is becoming more and more evident that psychology is "forced" to look elsewhere for its explanations of behavior.

Gibson's second question is directly related to the philosophical problem of causality, which, as pointed out previously (cf. Eacker, 1975, pp. 55–63), may be "a relic of a bygone age." Briefly, the problem of causality is whether cause and effect operate in the universe or are a human construction imposed on our observations. Those who support the former position are metaphysical realists, and those who support the latter position are metaphysical phenomenalists. There does not appear to be any way to decide between them with the methods of science. Thus, a stimulus may or may not be the sufficient cause of a response, but it may be a variable to which a response is related.

Gibson's third question raises the problem of circularity encountered in the chapter on the nature of behavior. That is, the definition of stimulus seems to require some reference to response, and the definition of response seems to require some reference to stimulus. This problem has been recognized by a good many psychologists, including Skinner, who Gibson (1960, p. 695) says may have confessed "a sin without pointing the way to salvation."

Indeed, this question may be a somewhat different form of essentialism with respect to the stimulus. For example, Skinner (1938, p. 9) suggested that neither stimulus nor response "can be defined as to its essential properties without the other." If so, it may be that neither has essential properties, or essence.

The dilemma is further illustrated by the argument that the stimulus must be defined in objective physical terms without reference to response. However, it seems remarkably obvious that a stimulus entirely defined in objective physical terms to which an organism does not respond can in no way be regarded as a stimulus; stimuli that do not stimulate are not stimuli, no matter how precisely they are defined by objective methods. Consequently, it would seem that at least some reference must be made to the response in the definition of the stimulus, if only with respect to its effects in other experiments.

Gibson's fourth question appears to be quite obviously ontological. It asks about the existence of the stimulus, and, as pointed out in this, prior, and subsequent chapters, ontological questions, or questions of existence, of what there is, probably are not answerable with the methods of science as they currently are understood. The stimulus may exist in the environment, or it may exist only at receptors, but where it exists, really, probably cannot be known definitively because it is by means of receptors that psychologists would try to answer the question.

When they do, the question of whether the stimulus is "out there" or "in here" still remains unanswered because the location of the stimuli, wherever they are, is used to determine the location of the stimuli. It is the problem of metaphysics, or ontology, in a somewhat different form. Perhaps that explains why both "out there" and "in here" uses of the term are somehow correct (cf. Gibson, 1960, p. 697); the stimulus is both "out there" and "in here," depending upon your metaphysics. There is no way of knowing, and there may never be a way of knowing, whether a stimulus is "out there" or "in here" except by means of receptors. When receptors are used, the question still remains whether the stimulus is in the environment or only at receptors.

All of Gibson's questions obviously are related to one another, but the fifth one seems especially relevant to the third. That is, it appears to be answerable only on the basis of that to which an organism responds. If an organism responds differentially in the presence of a pattern or relation but not to the separate elements in the pattern or relation as they are identified by an experimenter, the pattern or relation is a single stimulus and not a number of separate stimuli. It appears that the answer to this question must be based on how, in fact, organisms behave;

no other basis seems appropriate, especially from a behavioral perspective, which, of course, begs the question of what basis to use.

Gibson's fifth and sixth questions may represent areas of confusion about the stimulus because definitive answers to them are expected; indeed, that statement may be true for all of these questions about the stimulus. That is, they are questions that may arise because of an essentialist orientation toward science when, as pointed out in the first chapter, modern science no longer asks what a thing is but, rather, how it functions. Thus, with regard to the fifth question, a pattern or relation is a single stimulus when it functions as one, and it is a number of separate stimuli when it functions as a number of separate stimuli. It isn't necessarily one or the other; it may be either or both, depending upon how it affects behavior.

Similarly, a sequence as defined by an experimenter is a single stimulus when it functions as a single stimulus, and it is a number of separate stimuli when it functions as a number of separate stimuli. With reference to whether a single enduring stimulus can exist throughout a changing sequence, the answer probably is that we cannot know since it is another question of existence or ontology.

The answer to Gibson's seventh question may be that we can specify the structure of a stimulus in any number of ways because a stimulus may have as many structures as there are ways of structuring it. The answer may not be quite as relative as that since there may be some ways in which an experimenter might structure a stimulus to which no one else would respond. In those instances, the conclusion would have to be that the stimulus did not have those structures. The many conceivable ways in which a stimulus might be structured would have to be tested against the various ways in which people, in fact, structure it, and the latter would have to be taken as the structure, or structures, of the stimulus; more will be said about this matter in the next few paragraphs, especially with regard to what we must and must not do.

Like the analogy with force and energy, another analogy with physical objects appears to be operating in the case of Gibson's eighth question. That is, the eighth question, despite the manner in which it is phrased, seems to assume that something called information exists which gets transferred, transmitted, or transported from the environment into our heads when we are stimulated by what is called a meaningful stimulus. The analogy is with a physical object which must be picked up and moved in order to get it from one place to another. The use of this analogy also may be inappropriate in psychology but appears to have remained unchallenged in the area of learning; it will be discussed further in that context.

Like the concept of mind, information has never been seen, heard, touched, tasted, or smelled but is assumed, nevertheless, to exist. What it is has never been resolved and probably cannot be since the question "What is information?" is like the other questions examined here. Nevertheless, no one doubts its existence. In addition, if there is such a thing as information, so the argument goes, it must somehow be conveyed from the outside of us to the inside of us if it is to find its way into our heads. The only means available for that to happen seems to be the senses. Therefore, the senses are the avenues, or the carriers, of information to the brain.

However, this account of it may not be what takes place at all. An alternative possibility is that a meaningful stimulus is one to which a response has been established. When the stimulus or one like it subsequently occurs, it occasions or evokes its particular response or a generalized response; the response may be either overt or covert. However, no information is transmitted by the stimulus. It is meaningful simply because some sort of response has already been established to it; Staats and Staats (1963, pp. 185–258) develop more fully an argument similar to this one for language function. Thus, stimuli do not carry information about their sources and, therefore, there is no need to specify those sources.

This behavioral interpretation obviously ignores what is happening at the level of physiology when a response to a stimulus is being established. However, it is not necessarily the case that a science of behavior must say what physiological changes are occurring when behavioral changes are occurring (cf. Skinner, 1950), although we may require that a behavioral account not contradict a physiological one. The confusion of these two tasks may be what has contributed to many of our current conceptual confusions, especially those that have led us to invent concepts like information. That is, early in the history of our attempts to explain ourselves, we may have tried to answer both behavioral and physiological questions at the same time when we attempted to understand our behavior. However, we may not have had adequate explanations from either physiology or psychology for us to do so.

The concept of information may have been used to fill that void and, perhaps, was subsequently retained as a scientific concept when no others were available. But it may not explain so much as name something that must be exchanged between ourselves and our environments if the doctrine of physicalism is true. The concept of information makes some sense, perhaps only to common sense, with regard to how something might get into our heads (if anything does) when we communicate, but, of course, how information enters into behavior has never been resolved, as it has never been resolved how energy and force enter into behavior. The situation is very much like that of Tolman's rat, who Guthrie claimed was left "lost in thought" in its maze; how thinking results in behavior has also not been resolved, although a behavioral analysis seems adequate to the task (cf. Staats and Staats, 1963, pp. 179–184).

To explain the way that thinking relates to behavior may require use of the distinction between overt and covert behaviors discussed in the last chapter. Most people seem to regard thinking as a cause of behavior without too much consideration for what, in turn, causes thinking. It may not be a cause of behavior at all, although it may precede or accompany behavior. Thinking, like seeing and hearing, may be one of the covert behaviors, or, at least, it might be thought of as one of them. As a behavior or an event, it cannot cause another one; according to the doctrine of mechanism discussed in this and previous chapters, only things can cause other things.

If thinking is not a cause of overt behavior, it is either an antecedent or an accompaniment of overt behavior. With respect to the first possibility, thinking may be simply a series of events that occurs between the observable aspects of overt behavior. That is, it is conceivable that an environmental event might function as a stimulus for a covert thinking response, which, in turn, might be followed by covert stimuli and they, in turn, by other covert responses and stimuli until one of them eventually would be followed by a covert stimulus that either occasions or evokes an overt behavior. In that sense, thinking might be the covert portion of a complex chain of responses (cf. Reynolds, 1975, pp. 59–62).

With respect to the second possibility, thinking may be simply a series of internal events that occurs at the same time as other external events, some of which result in reinforcement. If both kinds of events occur at the same time as reinforcement, they are both more likely to recur together on subsequent occasions; reinforcement appears to affect whatever behavior it follows, regardless of what produces it. Consequently, covert thinking behavior might be shaped in the same way as the overt behavior it accompanies. Of course, a third possibility is that thinking may be either an antecedent or an accompaniment of overt behavior or both. Whatever the case, some such account as this one is the way in which contemporary behavior theory might try to help Tolman's rat out of its quandary.

These implications of Gibson's eight questions about the stimulus obviously are based on the metaphysics of phenomenalism and extrapolations from a behavioral position. For example, statements made about the structure of a stimulus in the seventh question suggest what the structure of a stimulus might be according to both phenomenalism and an experimental analysis of behavior. The ontology, or metaphysics, expressed by Gibson in the way he presents the question is that of realism, which assumes that a stimulus has a single structure that can be precisely defined with objective methods; it may be that a stimulus has structure simply because of the methods we use to define it, that is, the methods are its structure. In addition, the areas of disagreement represented by the questions may very well have arisen because of an essentialist view in science which seeks to discover the nature of a thing, in this case the stimulus, rather than how it functions. A shift to phenomenalism and methodological nominalism might help to eliminate, or at least help to change, our perspectives on these areas of disagreement.

Gibson (1960) closed his discussion of the stimulus with a proposal which, at least for him, made sense of the senses. His proposal was that, perhaps, there is a reservoir of stimuli in the environment consisting of, for example, relevant stimuli, molar stimuli, potential stimuli, invariant stimuli, specifying stimuli, and informative stimuli, any one or all of which may function as independent variables in a psychological experiment. There isn't one stimulus; there are many of them. But, whether one or many, "the stimulus is the prime independent variable of a psychological experiment" (Gibson, 1960, p. 702), and that may be what a stimulus is. It is an independent variable in a psychological experiment, but, of course, not all independent variables are stimuli.

A few years after Gibson's article appeared, B. J. Underwood (1963, p. 33) discussed discrepancies between the nominal stimulus and the functional stimulus in verbal learning studies. The nominal stimulus is the stimulus term presented to the subject; it is like Spence's situational stimulus. The functional stimulus is the characteristic, or characteristics, of the nominal stimulus that actually cues the response; it is like Spence's effective stimulus. The difference is between what the experimenter assumes to be the stimulus and what in fact functions as the stimulus. Thus, two more kinds of stimuli might be added to the list.

In a subsection of his book *The Psychology of Learning,* J. F. Hall (1966, pp. 8–12) asked the same question that has been posed in this chapter about the stimulus. He concluded that no answer could be given to the problem of adequately defining it.

> The Miller and Dollard (1941) position provides a working approach, but it does not represent a completely satisfactory solution to the problem. Perhaps the most important gain from any discussion is that experimenters become increasingly aware that a disregard for, or inattention to, the problem of discriminating the effective stimulus from the situational stimulus can lead only to confusion and pseudo-controversies.

Thus, Hall treats the distinction made by Spence between the effective stimulus and the situational stimulus as an important one; it was given additional support by Gibson as well as Underwood.

The Miller and Dollard (1941, p. 59) position with regard to both stimulus and response was quoted in the chapter on behavior. Briefly, "a response is any activity within the individual which can become functionally connected with an antecedent event through learning; a stimulus is any event to which a response can be so connected." They went on to say that "this definition is not circular for cases in which the events referred to have been empirically identified." They followed that statement with the example of "sitting up" in dogs. " 'Sitting up' in dogs is known to be a response because it can be functionally connected by reward with the antecedent command, 'Sit up!'; the command is thereby known to be a stimulus." In their judgment, this definition of both stimulus and response is not circular because both make reference to observable events. In the case of the stimulus, it is the verbal command "sit up," and, in the case of the response, it is the dog in fact sitting up. There is, therefore, a functional, or lawful, relationship between them.

Several references have been made in this and preceding chapters to the interest of psychology in events. For example, the remarks quoted above emphasize "cases in which the events referred to have been empirically identified"; they also state that a stimulus is any antecedent event to which a response can be connected. In the chapter on behavior, it was pointed out that behavior is an occurrence, a "happening," an event, and that perhaps the physical language, the thing language, or the language of physics is not appropriate for describing it because of the problem of reification. In chapter two, on the nature of psychology, it was suggested that perhaps psychology has always been concerned with events, observed events, rather than either mental processes or, quite possibly, behavior.

Howard Rachlin (1976, p. 52) has contributed some support for this thesis in his chapter on "Environmental and Behavioral

Events" but does not develop it beyond measurement considerations.

> In a psychological experiment the environmental events that are observed and recorded are called stimuli and the behavioral events that are observed and recorded are called responses. Stimuli and responses constitute the psychologist's data. His job is to discover relations between them.
>
> Many of the disputes among psychologists center on what sort of environmental events can serve as effective stimuli and what sort of behavioral events can serve as meaningful responses. The nature of principles and laws that psychologists ultimately discover will depend on what sort of data they collect.

The thesis is obviously too complex to be fully developed here for all of psychology; that task may have to be undertaken at a later time in a larger volume. However, some attempt to develop it now for the stimulus does seem appropriate, and, in the process, it will also be further developed for the response.

Contrary to Rachlin's statement in the above quotation, stimuli and responses may not constitute the data for psychology, and he (Rachlin, 1976, p. 55) later acknowledges that by saying, "discrete events are frequently used by behavioral psychologists as stimuli and responses." Furthermore, laws and principles may not be what psychologists discover. They may develop laws and principles, but discovery implies independent existence. As pointed out in this and prior discussions, the existence of things independent of an observer probably cannot be established because the methods that thus far have been developed in science cannot be used to prove the existence of things; they can be used only to test whether scientific concepts have some validity based on observations under controlled conditions. Thus, the existence of laws and principles is an assumption based on the metaphysics of realism.

The data for psychology may be the events to which Rachlin refers rather than stimuli and responses. At perhaps a less abstract level than stimulus and response, events may be the data on which we base our statements about stimuli and behavior. And, at a still less abstract level, the data on which we base our statements may be sense experiences, which, of course, is the ontological position of phenomenalism.

Restated, the thesis is that, at the least abstract level, there is sense experience. Sense experience is what occurs, happens, or perhaps exists, but, for the reasons already advanced with regard to essentialist questions, what it is cannot be stated. At a somewhat more abstract level, we call sense experience events, occurrences, or happenings. At a more abstract level, events are called stimuli and responses. And, at a still more abstract level, stimuli and responses are called independent and dependent variables, respectively; the correlational and functional relations between them are the laws of behavior. This view is compatible with phenomenalism, Henry Margenau's (1950) conception of physical reality and an inductive approach to theory construction in psychology (cf. Marx, 1970, pp. 14–15), although precisely how will not be examined at this time.

The language of events seems less cumbersome than the language of sense experience, and it may be an improvement over the language of stimulus and response because that language is at least in part physicalistic when reference is made to stimuli. That is, the word "stimulus" is often taken to mean "things that stimulate." If so, then the language of stimulus and response may be transitional between the language of physics and the language of events. It seems quite evident that responses are events rather than things, but the same cannot be said for stimuli.

However, at the level of events, stimuli may simply be antecedent to other, consequent, events. They occur before other events, which we refer to as responses or behavior. Thus, there are at least two kinds of events in which psychologists are interested, namely, antecedent events and consequent events; the problem is how to differentiate between them other than in terms of the temporal relation.

In another section of his chapter on environmental and behavioral events, Rachlin (1976, p. 53) stated that "just as responses are classifications of the behavior of a subject by an observer, stimuli are classifications of the subject's environment by an observer." His statement can be combined with Gibson's statement that the stimulus is the prime independent variable in a psychological experiment. It can also be combined with the view expressed in the preceding chapter with regard to the response, namely, that a response is a dependent variable in a psychological, or behavioral, experiment. When that is done, what results is a statement such as the following: "A stimulus is an event, or sense experience, selected by an experimenter as an independent variable in a psychological, or behavioral, experiment; it is selected because of its possible relationship to another set of events, or sense experiences, which is also selected by the experimenter as a dependent variable, or some measure of behavior." Both are of interest because of a possible lawful relationship between them which it is the task of psychology to explicate. Thus, there is a temptation to conclude that a stimulus is the sense experience of an experimenter which is selected as an antecedent event or an independent variable for purposes of an experiment.

However, not all independent variables are stimuli. For example, food deprivation is commonly manipulated as an independent variable in behavioral studies, but it seems absurd to regard the absence of food as a stimulus, at least to a positivist. Among other things, a positivist is one who requires positive rather than negative evidence in support of concepts, and the concept of stimulus especially seems to require such evidence. Presentation operations may fulfill that requirement, and so, in addition to the temporal relation between antecedent and consequent events referred to earlier, the presentation of environmental events selected by an experimenter may help to define them as a stimulus.

There is at least one additional matter to be considered. As with response, an independent variable that is not related to anything can hardly be thought of as a variable. That is, it is the lawful relationship between it and something else that makes it a variable. That something else is a dependent variable. As stated earlier, the relationship between an independent and a dependent variable constitutes a law in psychology, and, perhaps, to the extent that the major interest is in the dependent variable, it is a law of behavior. Similarly, to the extent that the major interest is in the independent variable, it is a law of the stimulus, provided that the conditions of temporal relation and presentation operations have been met. If so, then the stimulus too may be defined by its laws, and that is what a stimulus is. A stimulus is defined by its laws.

Chapter Seven

What Is Learning?

For a good many people, and especially for our somewhat maligned essentialists, discussions of behavior and the stimulus in that order might raise the question of how they become associated or connected if, in fact, they do. Associationism and connectionism have often been thought of as theories of learning in psychology, and so the question of association or connection between stimulus and response seems to raise the question of learning and, in particular, what it is.

Many students of psychology enroll in courses on learning, and on many other subjects, with the expectation that they will find out what it is. Indeed, on the first day of the class, a good number of them may wait with pencils poised, if not bated breath, to be told what it is. Nearly all of them are disappointed. They are disappointed because, in many instances, the professor may review a dozen or so different definitions of learning and end by telling them one which may be difficult to defend against all of its critics.

Their disappointment may be heightened by the fact that

the professor who is teaching the course professes some expertise in the subject but can't tell them what it is! They may leave that first meeting of the class muttering to themselves and wondering how anyone can teach a course on something, anything, when he or she doesn't know what it is. Most of them may fail to deduce the logical absurdity from their cerebrations that, before inquiry can even begin on some subject, everything about it must be known; otherwise, no one would know what to inquire about. The discussion that follows may help to explain how a professor can be so audacious when apparently so ignorant.

The definitions of learning that might be reviewed on that first day of class could come from Kimble's revision of *Hilgard and Marquis' Conditioning and Learning* (1961). In that book, Kimble discusses two general categories of definitions for learning: factual definitions and theoretical definitions. Factual definitions attempt to relate learning phenomena to events that are observable in the physical world. Theoretical definitions attempt either to describe mechanisms that might underlie learning or to state what the "true nature" of learning is. Thus, there are essentialists among those who attempt to develop theoretical definitions of learning, as evinced by their interest in the "true nature", or essence, of learning. And there are metaphysical realists among those who attempt to develop factual definitions of learning: they attempt to relate learning phenomena to the physical, or real, world.

Nevertheless, the first category of definitions contains statements like: learning is a more or less permanent change in behavior which occurs as a result of practice; learning is any systematic change in behavior, whether or not the change is adaptive, desirable for certain purposes, or accords with any other such criteria; learning is a progressive change or trend in behavior when the same stimulating situation is repeated and when fatigue or receptor and effector changes cannot account for the change; learning is a process manifested by adaptive changes in the behavior of the individual as a result of experience; learning is any modification of behavior that is more than transient and which presumably results from past experience rather than from known organic changes.

The second category of definitions contains statements like: learning is the reorganization of a perceptual field because of an obstructed need; learning is the reorganization of the cognitive field; learning is a modification of instinctive or reflex responses; learning is the process by which relatively permanent neural circuits are formed through the simultaneous activity of the elements of the circuits-to-be; learning is a case of differential strengthening of one from among a number of responses evoked by a situation of need, or the formation of fresh receptor-effector connections.

Other definitions than these might be included in the review. For example, Brogden (1951, p. 569) felt that acquisition was the "primary phenomenon of learning" and went on to define *acquisition* as "a progressive incremental change in the proficiency of performance by an organism; the direction, rate, and extent of change in the proficiency of performance are functions of the repetitive or continuous presentation of the conditions under which measurement of the change in performance is made." Thus, if a "primary" phenomenon is an essential one, there are essentialist tendencies among this category of definitions.

Consistent with Brogden's definition is one by Sidman (1960, p. 117), who noted that workers in the area of psychology referred to as learning are interested in the acquisition of new behavior, where acquisition "commonly refers to the emergence of new forms of behavior which have not existed in the organism's repertoire prior to the experimental manipulations." Finally, Marx (1969, p. 23) stated that "organisms do acquire *new* stimulus-response relationships, and such acquisition is the focus of much research in the field of learning."

This last statement cannot be left unchallenged because it may perpetuate a misconception of what happens when organisms learn. Observation seems to support the statement that new stimulus-response relationships are established when organisms learn, but it does not seem to support the statement that new stimulus-response relationships are acquired when organisms learn. New behavior may be acquired, but a stimulus-response relationship is not a behavior; only *one* of the terms refers to behavior. A stimulus-response relationship may only be observed between a stimulus and a response. To assume that they are acquired may assume more about them than is appropriate. Of course, the same may be true for the acquisition of behavior; more will be said about acquisition later in this chapter.

The above diversity of views about learning in psychology may be a strength rather than a weakness. It may be a strength because, if phenomenalism is true, learning is what researchers make of it; it does not exist independently of their efforts to know. Consequently, a diversity of views on learning may lead, by way of experimentation and theory, to one or two that are the most exciting, fruitful, or interesting. In addition, they may lead us more rapidly to a comprehensive and integrated understanding of ourselves, or perhaps less generally, our behavior.

However, new students of learning may find nothing in the definitions of learning mentioned above that even remotely resembles what they had thought to be learning; they may still want to know what learning is, really. For these students, learning occurs and helps to explain most of the changes that they observe in human behavior. If not, what is left unexplained after they have invoked the concept of learning is accounted for by invoking the concept of motivation. A good many psychologists think the same way. That is, a substantial number of psychologists give the impression that learning and motivation exhaust the entire discipline of psychology; the latter is examined in a subsequent chapter.

Thus, for example, when a new student of learning observes someone do something that has not been observed before, the student may suppose that the individuals who exhibited the new behavior must have learned it when no one was observing them, they learned it by accident, or they learned it on the spur-of-the-moment; the student assumes at least that the new behavior has been learned. If not, then it is assumed that the individual observed already knew what to do, that is, had already learned the behavior, but prior to that time had not been motivated to perform it—like the child who had never said anything because, so the story goes, no one had asked! In other words, for most people, many psychologists, and new students of learning in particular, learning and motivation are explanatory concepts; they combine to explain most of the things we do.

Within psychology, there appear to be a number of different ways to explain what we do (cf. Eacker, 1975, pp. 41–54). Among the more common are: explanation by analogy; explanation by reason or mentalistic explanation; physiological explanation; the model as an explanation; theoretical explanation; and empirical or functional explanation. The type of explanation employed when we invoke learning or motivation, as in the example above, is explanation by reason, psychic or mentalistic explanation, or traditional rationalism. That is, the change in behavior is explained by giving the reasons for the change, whether the reasons are learning or motivation. In fact, for most people, it is absurd to suppose that something could be explained in any way other than by giving the reasons for whatever is explained.

Nevertheless, things, and especially the events of psychology, can be explained in other ways, as pointed out in the chapter on behaviorism. The method that appears to be most current in psychology is to explain events with their laws. That kind of explanation is the empirical or functional type of explanation. It explains an event by reference to the general law of which the event is an instance or by reference to the variables of which the event is a function. In other words, an event is explained when we are able to state the variables to which it is related. We do not explain it by stating what it is, as in the view of science held by the methodological essentialists discussed in the first chapter; rather, an event is explained by a description of similar events with the help of general laws, as in the methodological nominalist view of science, also discussed in the first chapter.

In a somewhat more recent and direct treatment of the question "What is learning?" Houston (1976, pp. 5–8) started where Kimble had stopped, but Houston by no means resolved the matter. Kimble (1961, p. 6) eventually came to define learning as "a relatively permanent change in behavior potentiality which occurs as a result of reinforced practice." Houston discussed several key words in that definition, including permanent as opposed to temporary, practice, behavior potentiality, learning as opposed to performance, and reinforced practice. He ended his discussion of the question with the observation that "psychologists have many different ideas about what would be an adequate definition" of learning; Kimble's is only one among many.

On the other hand, Hall (1976, p. 2) felt there was a consensus among psychologists that learning is a process that takes place within the organism, that it is inferred from changes in performance, and that it arises as a result of experience or practice. However, there was not too much agreement about the permanence of the learning process. In discussing the issue of permanence, Hall perhaps inadvertently demonstrated how psychologists may treat learning as an independent variable rather than a dependent variable or, perhaps, an intervening variable; they do so when behavior changes are thought to take place as a result of learning. That is, when behavior changes are considered functions of learning, learning is treated as an independent variable.

The differences among these three kinds of variables are known by most psychologists and students of psychology. Briefly, a variable is something that changes, such as food supply or rate of response. If it can be changed by direct manipulation, it is an independent variable. Examples are the amount of food a subject can obtain when it presses a lever and how long a subject has been deprived of food before it presses a lever. If the variable can be changed only by indirect manipulation, it is a dependent variable. More simply, a dependent variable is some measure of behavior. Examples are the number of bar presses and scores on an intelligence test. Intelligence test scores may be a dependent variable, but intelligence may be made into an independent variable to the extent that an experimenter can select from among different levels of intelligence test scores and then show how that affects, or is related to, some other measure of behavior. Consequently, the differences between independent and dependent variables are not always as clear as we might like to think they are.

A similar kind of problem arises with regard to intervening variables and how they differ from what have been referred to as hypothetical constructs. According to the distinction drawn by MacCorquodale and Meehl (1948), an intervening variable is a quantity obtained by a specific manipulation of empirical variables. It involves no hypotheses about the existence of things that are not observed. For all purposes of theory and prediction, its complete statement contains no words which are not explicitly definable in terms of the empirical variables. Finally, the validity of empirical laws that include only observables is both a necessary and sufficient condition for the validity of laws that include intervening variables.

In somewhat different terms, an intervening variable is completely defined by observables; it is merely an abstraction of an empirical relationship between observables. Thus, for example, the concept of habit is an intervening variable when it is used simply to denote the relationship between the number of reinforced responses and the resistance of the response to extinction as measured by the number of responses to experimental extinction; it cannot be used to explain the relationship between the number of reinforced responses and the resistance to extinction, since that relationship is all that is meant by the concept of habit.

On the other hand, and according to this same source, a hypothetical construct is used to designate theoretical concepts which do not, in the strict sense, fulfill the conditions of being intervening variables. That is, they are constructs that involve terms which are not completely reducible to empirical terms. They make reference to processes or things that are not directly observable. They cannot be completely expressed in a mathematical formula. And the validity of empirical laws to which they refer is a necessary but not a sufficient condition for their validity. Thus, for example, habit is a hypothetical construct when it refers not only to the relationship between number of reinforced responses and resistance to extinction but also to something that corresponds to habit, perhaps within the nervous system. A hypothetical construct has "surplus-meaning"; the use of one presupposes the existence of a process or a thing in addition to the relationship between variables.

Learning has been treated at different times by different people as an independent variable, a dependent variable, an intervening variable, or a hypothetical construct, depending on the interests and proclivities of those who have had occasion to refer to it. It is treated as an independent variable when it is used to explain a change in behavior. That is, when it is used to answer the question "Why did so-and-so do that?" and the answer is "So-and-so did that because he learned to do that," learning is treated as an independent variable.

It is treated as a dependent variable when it is the result of something else. Thus, when people learn something because they get something for doing so, learning is treated as a dependent variable.

Learning is treated as an intervening variable when it is used as a label for the relationship between how often persons do something and how often they get something for exhibiting that behavior. It is treated as a hypothetical construct when the relationship between how often people do something and how often they get something for doing so suggests to someone else that there are chemical, mental, or physiological changes taking place within their bodies at the same time.

In other words, and perhaps unfortunately, learning may be different things to different people, whether they are ordinary men and women, students of psychology, or psychologists. There is no single definitive answer to the question with which this chapter began. However, for psychologists, there does seem to be a way to resolve the problem, at least from a behavioral perspective. The means for doing so is suggested by the way in which Adams (1976) treats the subject.

For Adams (1976, p. 6), "the different laws of learning . . . all represent different definitions of learning," which might be interpreted to mean that learning is defined by its laws, as are behavior and stimuli. Aside from that, however, he seems to feel that "*learning* is a relatively stable tendency to react" (Adams

1976, p. 6) and goes on to specify how data are collected on learning.

Data collection consists of six steps. The first is to define a response that can be observed reliably as a dependent variable. The second is to define one or more operations that can be reliably manipulated and which generally are regarded as learning operations; they are independent variables. The third is to arrange a situation so that a response can be performed under the conditions specified by the independent variables. The fourth is to observe changes in the response. The fifth is to rule out changes in the response that might be related to such things as motivation and fatigue. The last step is to observe whether the response shows improvement over the training series and some persistence over time. If these steps have been followed, it apparently can be said that learning has occurred. By performing these six steps, learning data can be obtained and laws of learning established, at least according to Adams (1976).

This procedure for collecting data on learning might be considered to be an operational definition of learning. In other words, if these six operations are performed, the data collected are learning data, and something more is known about learning. To the extent that those data can be used to express some sort of relationship between the independent and dependent variables in steps one and two, to that extent we have what is known as a law of learning. Consequently, it may very well be the case that learning, too, is defined by the laws of learning.

Before that conclusion can be seriously considered, however, something more needs to be said about operational definitions, learning as a process, and the learning versus performance or acquisition versus performance distinction. With regard to operational definitions, it may not be sufficiently apparent that they only make ideas clear; they provide neither definitive solutions to problems nor explanations of behavior. An operational definition of learning proposed by one author may not be the same as that proposed by another, and the differences between them may not be resolvable. Operational analysis is simply a way to make ideas clear, and nothing more. It does not provide definitive answers to questions such as "What is learning?" since others may not agree that the operations or procedures specified by one researcher are those that would be specified by all.

In addition, there may be persisting ambiguities within a particular operational definition. For example, if the steps outlined above are an operational definition of learning, there is some question about the meaning of improvement and whether it is a critical feature of learning. Similarly, the concept of motivation, as will be seen, is not as clear and simple as some of us might suppose, and the same may be true for fatigue and persistence. Consequently, even what appears to be a rather straightforward operational analysis may not be reduced sufficiently to primitive terms; more was said about operational definitions in the chapter on science.

With regard to learning as a process, it appears to casual observation that a process occurs or happens. In keeping with the previous discussion of events, a process is an event, or perhaps a series of them, and not a thing. If the process of learning is an event, it is difficult if not impossible to comprehend how learning can determine or influence other events, especially from the perspective of mechanistic determinism, which, as may be recalled from prior discussions, requires physical objects or forces as determinants. In somewhat different terms, the statement that learning is a process that occurs when relatively permanent changes in behavior take place, may never have been a very satisfactory assessment of what was happening. It may have persisted because it seemed consistent with physicalism and mechanistic determinism and because no other assessment had been made that was more acceptable.

Perhaps the time has come to recognize that, while learning seems to have served for centuries as an explanatory concept, it does not in fact explain anything; it merely serves as a label for the thing explained. To say that people do something because they learned to do so does not explain how it happens that they are doing that something now or have done it at some other point in time. To explain that action seems to require knowledge of what variables are operating now or were acting at that other point in time, and the statement that makes reference to learning does not make reference to variables.

Statements that make reference to variables are lawlike statements. In other words, it is the laws of learning that explain learning phenomena, where once again, if phenomenalism is true, learning phenomena are those we have selected and classified as being learning phenomena; they are not necessarily learning phenomena in some absolute, certain, or final sense. Thus, once more it seems evident that a subject matter, in this case learning, is explained by its laws. It is to be explained; it does not explain except, perhaps, as a shorthand expression that can be translated directly into laws.

With regard to the distinction between learning and performance and between acquisition and performance, a very small item of recent history may be appropriate. The distinction between learning and performance appears to have been stressed, or promoted, by E. C. Tolman, although he may not have been the first to make it. Nevertheless, it has persisted since his time. According to Kimble (1961, pp. 4–5),

> *Learning* refers to long-term changes of the organism produced by practice . . . the products of learning are carried with the organism

> on a fairly permanent basis and are available as a basis for action as the occasion demands. *Performance,* on the other hand, refers to just this translation of learning into behavior. The level of performance depends upon relatively short-term factors such as motivation, the existence of appropriate environmental circumstances, and fatigue.

What the long-term changes are he leaves unspecified, as are the products that "are carried with the organism on a fairly permanent basis and are available as a basis for action as the occasion demands."

Statements such as these are physicalistic, and physicalistic statements are not altogether bad. However, they may be more a manner of speaking about learning in physical terms than they are a reasonably valid description of what is going on. In other words, they may perpetuate another physical analogy in psychology which is simply inappropriate. That analogy is one in which learning is regarded as a physical process which produces things; the things produced are products called relatively permanent changes which the organism presumably carries around like eggs in a basket. Physical analogies may have helped us all they can in our efforts to understand learning; it may be time for a different approach.

Kimble goes on to say, perhaps incorrectly, that learning is an intervening variable but that it is unobservable. If learning is unobservable, it cannot be an intervening variable in the sense discussed earlier in this chapter since, in that sense, intervening variables are completely defined by observables; he may mean that learning is a hypothetical construct in the sense discussed earlier. Nevertheless, he feels that the strength of learning is estimated "through its symptoms in performance." Stated differently, learning is inferred from performance.

The beginning student of learning who encounters this last

statement for the first time might immediately wonder why learning is inferred from performance. The answer may be that it is inferred from performance because learning, per se, does not seem to be observed in performance. That is, changes in performance appear to be what are observed. They appear to be relatively permanent; fatigue and motivation apparently can be ruled out, and so all that seems to remain that might account for the changes in performance is learning, even though there is no one thing that can be observed in performance that, in turn, can be identified as learning. Nevertheless, learning is assumed to have occurred. But it may not be observed. It may be invoked simply to explain the changes in performance.

The student may continue to be puzzled when an unobservable is used to explain an observable. This situation may occur when no other explanations are at hand. That is, in the absence of any other, and perhaps more adequate, explanations, we invent one that is at least consistent with common sense and other assumptions we may make about ourselves and the world in which we live. Psychologists refer to these inventions as theories of ourselves and, in this particular case, learning. Once they develop such an explanation, they then may set about testing it. What results when they do is another theory of learning in psychology that is then used to explain learning theoretically, that is, learning phenomena are deduced from the theory, or, at least, an attempt is made to do so. The procedure seems to confirm to a remarkable extent the myth making aspect of science discussed by Peters in his revision of *Brett's History of Psychology* (1965); to paraphrase it, scientific truths are the myths invented by scientists that have not yet been found to be wrong.

Thus, learning is used to explain performance, and variables related to performance may be used to explain learning, but learning remains an unobservable for most people; it goes on somewhere other than in behavior (cf. Skinner, 1950). However, there may be a sense in which learning can be said to occur in behavior rather than somewhere else.

Perhaps relatively permanent changes in performance are not the critical, or essential, features of what is meant by learning; the search for essences simply may have misled us to suppose that they are. If learning has no essence, or we cannot know that learning has an essence, alternative formulations are possible and may be more fruitful. One is that proposed earlier in the three definitions of learning as acquisition.

This view may be interpreted to mean that learning is not something that organisms do which explains their relatively permanent changes in performance; that is, organisms don't learn. Stated differently, learning is not a behavioral phenomenon. Rather, it is something we say that organisms do when they acquire new behaviors or when we say they acquire new behaviors. And, the statement that they learn new behaviors sounds very much like an explanation for their having acquired the new behaviors when, in fact, it isn't. It isn't an explanation of their having acquired the new behaviors because it doesn't make reference to the variables of which that acquisition is a function. It merely labels, or names, acquisition as learning; it is another form of the nominal fallacy (cf. Eacker, 1975, p. 37).

The variables related to the acquisition of behavior are not well known. They are not well known perhaps because researchers have shown so little interest in them. Most researchers have been concerned with performance variables, which seem to be related more to motivation than to learning. That is, the difference between learning and motivation may be the difference between acquisition and performance rather than between learning and performance, and not very much is known about acquisition. Furthermore, the distinction between learning and performance may be, and perhaps has always been, misleading; more will be said about the relationship between motivation and performance in the chapter on motivation.

Research on the acquisition of behavior may take the form of what Sidman (1960) refers to as research on transition states. A transition state is not static; it is dynamic. It is a behavior state in which changes are taking place which may help to explain how it happens that so little is known about them; behavior that is undergoing change is difficult to identify as a particular behavior. The situation is much like that immortalized by Heraclitus, who suggested that it might not be possible to step into the same river more than once.

> We may, for the moment, define a stable, or steady, state as one in which the behavior in question does not change its characteristics over a period of time. Behavior passes through a transition state in the process of change from one steady state to another. The two are thus not completely separate. In order to identify the beginning and end of a transition state, one must know something about the properties of the boundary stable states. [Sidman, 1960, p. 234]

In other words, transition states are those in which a behavior is undergoing change, or they are states in which a behavior is being added to an organism's behavioral repertoire. Thus, acquisition has to do with how behavior gets into an organism's repertoire; performance may have to do with what brings it out of the repertoire, or its display.

Of course, any further discussion of transition states must acknowledge at the outset that, if phenomenalism rather than realism is true, the language of transition states may be a more useful way of structuring sense experience than the current language of learning. It is also somewhat unfortunate that the term "state" is used since that term tends to suggest a condition or mode of being similar to those examined in the physical sciences. That is, it also may serve to perpetuate physicalism in psychology where, as argued earlier, it may not belong. However, with these reservations, further discussion of transition states may proceed if only to show how they may be related to the traditional topic of learning in psychology.

Several statements made by Sidman (1960) throughout his book help to reveal how the study of transition states is related to, if it does not replace, the traditional topic of learning in psychology. For example, in his (Sidman, 1960, pp. 117–18) discussion of systematic replication, he states that

> a second factor that has retarded the development of behavioral baselines is the growth of a research area in experimental psychology that is called "learning." Workers in this field are interested in the acquisition of new behavior, and presumably not in behavior that has reached an "asymptotic" or other steady level. The term "acquisition" commonly refers to the emergence of new forms of behavior which have not existed in the organism's repertoire prior to the experimental manipulations. Because the newly acquired behavior is presumed, for all practical purposes, to exist originally at a zero level, students of learning are seldom led to consider the baseline state of the subject's behavior as a parameter of acquisition. The usual contention is that a behavioral baseline with a value greater than zero would impose a special condition, so that the characteristics of acquisition could not be generalized to other situations.
>
> But is acquisition of behavior from a zero baseline, if indeed a zero baseline is available, any less a special condition than its acquisition from a more active state? Is not a change for example from one pattern of behavior to another a case of acquisition also? The adjustment of existing behavior to a new variable is an example of learning whose consideration would greatly increase the generality of learning principles.

These remarks are from the context in which Sidman defined learning as the acquisition of behavior, mentioned earlier in this chapter. They very clearly relate acquisition to learning but, by means of the two questions asked toward their close, only hint at how both may involve the study of transition states.

The relationship between the study of transition states and learning is stated more openly a few sentences later when he (Sidman, 1960, pp. 118–19) observes that

> the notion of a behavioral baseline is incomprehensible except in terms of the behaving individual. If the experimenter does not have techniques that permit the manipulation and control of individual behavior, he cannot hope to study behavioral transitions, with any high degree of precision, as a function of greater-than-zero baseline states. Many investigators, therefore, choose what is presumably the easy way out. They try to investigate transitions from a zero baseline. . . . This relieves them of the necessity of manipulating behavior before they introduce the variables that are to produce learning. In consequence, most contemporary theories of learning are based upon a circumscribed and specialized set of experiments which unnecessarily restrict their generality. The proper domain of learning includes *any* transition that results from changes in the environmental contingencies maintaining behavior. There are no rational grounds for excluding transitions from a baseline level greater than zero.

Thus, for Sidman, the study of learning is the study of any transition state, including those that do not have a zero baseline. Research on transition states is research on acquisition, or learning.

Later statements by Sidman (1960, pp. 289–90) are consistent with this view, especially in his discussion of transition states per se and where their intensive investigation might lead. However, they also suggest that the study of transition states may be the more general case of which learning is an instance.

A curious situation exists today. In terms of quantity of work, experimental psychology in this country is dominated by research on transition states. Experiments on learning in many species, under many different conditions and often with a background of ingenious theorizing occupy the bulk of our journal pages—all this with little or no attempt to solve the basic technical problems attendant upon the study of behavioral transitions. It might be an interesting historical exercise to discover whether similar situations have existed in other sciences; situations in which a given problem has occupied the experimental and theoretical attention of a majority of the workers without even lip service being paid to unsolved technical problems. Psychologists are busy studying the transition state called learning without being able to identify, with any reasonable degree of precision, either the beginning or the end of the process. They handle variability by treating a group of subjects as if it represents a single ideal subject. Reversibility is a term that has been forced upon their attention by workers concerned with steady-state behavior, but there has, as yet, been only token experimental acknowledgement of this problem. The illusion that learning and other behavioral transitions are continuous processes, a view fostered by the almost exclusive utilization of group averages and inadequate experimental control, remains almost unchallenged, in spite of a few outstanding demonstrations that discontinuous change is often to be expected.

When such difficulties are faced squarely, we may expect that the study of behavioral transitions will take its place as a solid scientific endeavor. The task is a difficult one, and demands the painstaking type of experimental labor that must accompany an unexplored problem. I have no way of predicting where such research will lead, but it is certainly possible to point out the kind of initial steps that will have to be taken. The first requirement will be a reorientation in experimental rationale. The student must no longer formulate his problem in general terms. He will not be studying learning or, even more generally, behavioral transitions. He must first select a specific example of a transition state, and, even further, he must select a specific aspect of that transition for detailed study. At this stage of the game he must study the se-

> lected property of the transition as a phenomenon of interest in its own right, and not as an example of some more general class. Generalizations will come in time, after the properties of a number of individual transition states have been studied. Similarities will begin to emerge, and connections to other phenomena will become evident to the alert observer. An area of study (perhaps to be called transition states, perhaps not) will gradually be defined. It is unlikely that the resulting science will even remotely resemble what passes today as the study of learning.

At the time this sentence is written, Sidman's comments are already almost two decades old, but the study of learning has not yet moved very far in the direction he envisaged. Perhaps he foresaw a state of affairs too far in advance of his time, and ours, for the changes to be detectable. On the other hand, he may have been too far removed from the mainstream of research on learning to be able to say what direction it would take. Regardless of which possibility is the case, research on transition states seems central to the subject of learning in psychology, if it does not, in fact, encompass the study of learning, and it may require greater consideration than it has so far received from psychologists.

This chapter has examined some traditional and some not so traditional views on learning in psychology, but, on the basis of this examination, a definitive statement still cannot be made about what learning is. This situation is very probably a consequence of the thesis that the subjects treated here do not have essences or essential characteristics, and, even if they did, we probably couldn't know that they did.

Nevertheless, the examination of these views has suggested at least two somewhat novel and defensible positions with regard to the question that may not as yet have been adequately explored. One is that, as with behavior and the stimulus, learning is defined by its laws. In other words, the laws of learning are what learning is. The second is that learning is acquisition, where acquisition is studied by means of transition states or as transition states. Both eventually may be found to be equivalent, but, until then, both apparently must stand as additional answers to the question of learning.

Since the statement that the laws of learning are what learning is has been made already in a different form for both behavior and the stimulus, it may be one that can be made for all of the major subject matter areas of psychology, such as motivation, perception, and personality; that is, the laws of motivation, perception, and personality are what each of them is. If so, there is some danger that the statement is trivial. It may be trivial because it makes no distinctions among these areas except by way of the laws specific to each one of them, although that alone may be enough to save the statement from triviality.

In addition, of course, the laws of a subject matter cannot be explicated without already knowing something, perhaps only intuitively, about it; that is, the laws may have to be consistent with our intuitions about a subject, or we may not accept them as laws of that subject no matter how wrong our intuitions might be, as suggested earlier by Adams (1976) in his second step for collecting data on learning. Consequently, the laws of a subject such as learning or motivation may simply be demonstrations of what is already known by intuition. They are demonstrated intuitions or, as has often been said of psychology, demonstrations of the obvious.

However, not all intuitions are demonstrable, as suggested in the first chapter with regard to the intellectual intuitions of Plato and Aristotle. But there are few who would argue that it is not an advance to make intuitions demonstrable. The history of psychology contains too many instances in which our intuitive insights about ourselves, and why we do what we do, have not been confirmed.

Chapter Eight

What Is Reinforcement?

Most discussions of learning almost inevitably make some reference to reinforcement or to reinforced responses. Indeed, it is rather remarkable that both were mentioned so few times in the preceding chapter. Nevertheless, learning and reinforcement are nearly inextricably linked by most contemporary psychologists; so now, right after a discussion of learning, is probably a good time to give the question of reinforcement more direct consideration.

The question of reinforcement may be equivalent to the almost heart-stopping query encountered by many professors at least once each time they have offered a course on learning. That question is "Why is a reinforcer reinforcing?" and it may be asked by a perceptive and intrepid student who feels that, by asking it, the professor will receive his comeuppance, if not for his appearance of infinite wisdom, then for his exercise of absolute authority. There is even some evidence, based of course on casual observation rather than personal classroom experience, that the question may be greeted by at least a lengthy period of silence and, perhaps, some consternation.

The period of silence may be one in which the professor is uncertain whether to attack the question or the student. In addition, he or she may wonder whether now is the time to review the different theories or hypotheses of reinforcement. Some combination or all three may happen. That is, the student may, at the least, be affixed with a baleful eye and, at the most, be made to feel that the question is not worthy of serious consideration. Alternatively, the question may be attacked and different theories of reinforcement made known.

Regardless of the alternative taken, the student may still want to know why a reinforcer is reinforcing, much as the child who, after tormenting a parent with several "Why?" questions, still persists in asking "Yes, but why, Daddy?" If the father is overheard to reply "Because I said so!" it is not just professors who exercise absolute authority.

The attack on the question may take the form of asserting that science is descriptive; it can only deal with the questions "What?" and "How?" (cf. Eacker, 1975, p. 54). The question "Why?" seems to require absolutes and perhaps essences, or essential characteristics, as in the methodological essentialist's approach to science. By contrast, the truths of science are probabilistic; they are based on observation. And, since observation in science is never known to be complete, we can never know that we have found an absolute, even if we have.

If those assertions don't terminate the why-asking behavior, the professor next may present a number of different theories of reinforcement. They may include the empirical law of effect, the hedonic hypothesis, the drive-reduction hypothesis, the optimal-level hypothesis, the central confirming response hypothesis, the contiguity hypothesis, the consummatory response hypothesis, the expectancy hypothesis, the motivational feedback hypothesis, the two-factor hypothesis, the "go mechanism" hypothesis, and several others. The others may include the stimulus-change hypothesis and the Premack principle. Each one seems to be an attempt to answer the question of why a reinforcer is reinforcing. Many have been at least mentioned by Neal Miller (1963); the discussion that follows is based largely on his efforts, if only for the names he gives to them.

His examination begins with the observation that frequency of repetition is not enough for learning to take place, which, of course, is contrary to common lore, common sense, and our intuitions about the matter. That is, most of us are convinced that things are learned simply through repetition. Nearly everyone has been told, at one time or another, that practice makes perfect. However, evidence obtained under controlled conditions, rather than casual observation, indicates that responses extinguish when they are only repeated; they do not become more firmly fixed. In somewhat different terms, the law of frequency has been repealed along with, perhaps, those of exercise and readiness; there aren't very many who have heard the news.

The empirical law of effect is that "the consequence of a response is an important determiner of whether the response will be learned" (Wilcoxon, 1969, p. 28). It is referred to as an empirical law because it attempts to describe what effect is observed when a response has certain consequences; the law is not concerned with the effects of the response on the consequences, or the environment, but, rather, with the effects of the response on the response itself.

Because it is a descriptive law, it does not offer an explanation of the effects observed in the form of reasons for them; it just says that there is a relationship between a response and certain of its consequences. For that reason, the law sometimes has been criticized as circular. That is, when interpreted in the case of reinforcement, the law has been said to assert nothing more than that a reinforcer is reinforcing because it is reinforcing.

In reply to that criticism, defenders of the law may point out that descriptive statements simply describe; they do not offer reasons for an effect, although they may be used for purposes of functional, or empirical, explanation, as discussed earlier. Effects occur or are observed, and a law describes them. No reasons for the effect are given; the law of effect is simply descriptive of the relationship between a response and some of its consequences, and the law is nothing more than that.

The criticism may come from those who expect to be given reasons for the effect and not because of any deficiencies in the law. In other words, the law is adequate as stated. The criticism may be based on considerations outside the law, namely, the expectation that a law must give the reasons for effects and not just describe them, when all that it, or any other law, may be able to do is to describe effects; more may be expected of the law than the law can provide.

A good many people may feel that description is not the same as explanation, and, since the law is descriptive, it can't explain anything, especially in the sense of giving the reasons. When pursued to its logical absurdity, the search for reasons, which probably is another form of the search for essences, may lead back to some reason for which there is no reason, except, perhaps, that of creation or the basic nature, or essence, of the thing explained, as in the statement "it's the nature of the beast." The latter may be the only way in which any of the essentialist-type questions can be answered, despite efforts to give answers for them here by consensus or by extrapolation from a behavioral position.

The hedonic hypothesis of reinforcement offers a reason for the effect; the reason is pleasure. That is, according to this hypothesis, a reinforcer is reinforcing because it is pleasant or because it is pleasurable, and that is why it reinforces. The hypothesis is hedonic, or hedonistic, because of this reference to pleasure;

the hedonists felt it was their duty to seek pleasure and to avoid pain or displeasure.

However, if pleasure explained why a reinforcer was reinforcing, the same would be true for animals and for humans, and humans probably cannot know that a reinforcer is pleasant for animals. Furthermore, if pleasure explained their effects, reinforcers might always be expected to be reinforcing; they are not. Food does not always reinforce an organism, especially if it has just eaten. Similarly, sex is not always a reinforcer for humans, especially if they have very recently engaged in sexual behavior (although some may recover quite rapidly). For these and other reasons, it probably is not the case that a reinforcer is reinforcing because it is pleasant.

As is undoubtedly self-evident, the drive-reduction hypothesis is that a reinforcer is reinforcing because it reduces a drive. Thus, food is a reinforcer because it reduces food deprivation or, perhaps, a hunger drive. Sex is a reinforcer because it reduces a sex drive, at least temporarily. Any reinforcer reinforces because of its reduction of some drive, and that is why it is reinforcing.

One of the major problems with this hypothesis is that of determining when a drive is reduced. The criterion for reduction cannot be that the reinforcer is no longer reinforcing because, in that case, drive reduction would be synonymous with the point at which a reinforcer is no longer reinforcing. And the statement that reinforcers are reinforcing because they reduce drives would be circular or tautological if reinforcers and reduced drives were synonymous; it would assert the logical or at least nonempirical law of identity, namely, that reinforcement was equal to, or the same as, drive reduction, and there are few who would accept that as an explanation.

If that criterion cannot be used, the problem of a criterion for drive reduction still remains. One might require that food, for example, be ingested. Another might require that food reach the stomach. Another might require that the stomach be fully loaded. Still another might require that the digested food reach the blood stream. But, since there are several criteria that might be used, the question of when a drive is reduced persists, not to mention the problem of drive itself, or what it is. Considerations such as these suggest that the drive-reduction hypothesis probably does not answer the question of why a reinforcer is reinforcing.

The optimal-level hypothesis is that each type of stimulation has an optimum level for a particular organism. Deviations from this optimum level motivate the organism to restore the balance, whereas shifts in the direction of the level are rewarding. Therefore, a reinforcer is reinforcing because it contributes to the restoration of this optimum level of stimulation. In that sense, the hypothesis is related to the concept of homeostasis. The major problem with it is how to determine the optimum level of stimulation for a given organism other than in terms of behaviors that increase stimulation or reduce it.

The central confirming response hypothesis of reinforcement is that there is a single central response that confirms, or strengthens, any learnable connections that have been in progress immediately prior to its occurrence. In other words, there is a single central confirming response, presumably within the nervous system, that confirms all learnable connections; there is not a separate confirming response for each connection. Thus, what makes a reinforcer reinforcing is, apparently, this confirmation of learnable connections. The major problem with this hypothesis, as with most of the others, is how to confirm or, at least, test it. The confirmation of a single central confirming response may be beyond our methodological and, perhaps, technological capabilities. And, of course, to the extent that a question about the existence of such a response arises, it may press the limits of our metaphysical capabilities as well.

The contiguity hypothesis is that the close temporal contiguity between a response and a reinforcer is what makes the latter appear to have some special effect on the former. According to this hypothesis, all that is required for a connection between a stimulus and a response to be established is that they precede or follow one another closely enough in time; we are misled if we think that the stimulus has some special effect on the response. If the hypothesis is true, the obvious next question has to do with how it happens that only certain kinds of stimuli are referred to as reinforcers. If contiguity is all that is required, any stimulus might be expected to be a reinforcer, in the sense of becoming connected with any response, but that does not appear to be the case. Therefore, it would seem that contiguity alone does not explain why a reinforcer is reinforcing.

The consummatory response hypothesis of reinforcement is also referred to as the drive-induction hypothesis. While all of the hypotheses are complex, this one may be somewhat more so than the others:

> According to this hypothesis, the consummatory response tends to be conditioned to responses immediately preceding it, but since it cannot occur in the absence of the goal object, frustrational excitement is elicited which serves as an increase in drive that energizes whatever response is occurring at that time. The cues involved in responses leading most directly to the consummatory response are conditioned most strongly to it. Hence, when the subject is oscillating at a choice point, the responses leading most directly to the goal produce the most exciting cues, are more invigorated by this excitement, and are most likely to be continued. Such responses are also conditioned by contiguity and hence are more likely than others to be elicited immediately on subsequent trials. [Miller, 1963, p. 81]

Thus, there appears to be some level of drive already present which is intensified when the consummatory response is performed both in the presence and in the absence of the goal object or reinforcer. However, since some level of drive is required before that happens, this conception may be more a drive-increment than a drive-induction hypothesis of why a reinforcer is reinforcing.

To avoid the obvious pun, as might be anticipated, the expectancy hypothesis of reinforcement is that a reinforcer is reinforcing because it signifies what leads to what, or it verifies expectations. Thus, an organism that has been deprived of food or sex expects to find food or sex in its environment, and, when it does, that tells it what leads to what or confirms its expectations.

However, since expectations are considered to be internal, cognitive processes or events, the hypothesis may not be applicable to animals, since humans can't know whether animals have expectations, except perhaps in an anthropomorphic way (cf. Eacker, 1975, pp. 93–101); indeed, humans may not be able to know whether humans have expectations, since metaphysical assumptions are obviously at work when their existence is asserted. Especially in the case of Tolman, it is not entirely clear how expectations enter into behavior, as suggested by Guthrie's criticism mentioned in an earlier chapter.

The motivational feedback hypothesis may be a still more complex interpretation of why a reinforcer is reinforcing. It states that "only motivational responses are acquired during learning, and that these are acquired by classical conditioning involving only contiguity" (Miller, 1963, p. 85). In other words, fear, for example is elicited by unconditioned stimuli in the environment that are, of course, paired with other stimuli; these other stimuli eventually come to elicit fear when the organism encounters them in its environment. The feedback from these response-produced stimuli guide the animal into certain behaviors and away from others, and that is why a reinforcer is reinforcing; it is reinforcing because of this emotional feedback.

The two-factor hypothesis of reinforcement postulates two different reinforcement mechanisms. Sometimes it uses the law of effect to explain why a reinforcer is reinforcing, and sometimes it uses contiguity. The trick, of course, is to know when an interpretation is appropriate. Because of this problem, explanations by means of the two-factor hypothesis may be largely post hoc and, in some cases perhaps, ad hoc. Those two possibilities may be true of all eclectic hypotheses, especially to the extent that they select the most powerful explanatory concepts from among a number of different hypotheses or theories; at least one additional problem with an eclectic hypothesis is that an explanation given on one occasion may be inconsistent with that given on another.

The "go mechanism" hypothesis is one proposed by Miller toward the close of his article. According to this hypothesis, there is a "go mechanism," perhaps specific to each type of reinforcer, perhaps not, that intensifies ongoing responses when it is activated; consequently, it is presumed to have some physiological or neurological existence. Since it is activated by the reinforcer, that is what makes the reinforcer reinforcing. Thus, either a reduction in noxious stimulation or the taste of food, for example, might be sufficient to activate this mechanism, which would, in turn, intensify the response that either reduced the noxious stimulation or produced the taste of food. There are some more detailed assumptions related to this hypothesis, but, once again, to the extent that the mechanism is assumed to exist, some of these assumptions are metaphysical; they are based on the metaphysics of realism.

The stimulus-change hypothesis of reinforcement is that slight or moderate changes in stimulation produced by a response increase the frequency of responses, at least for a short time. The hypothesis may also be referred to sometimes as the sensory reinforcement hypothesis. Thus, according to this view, any slight or moderate change in sensory stimulation will reinforce responses that produce it, and that is why a reinforcer is reinforcing. One problem with this hypothesis is that stimulus change always seems to accompany reinforcement. As a result, there may be some difficulty in separating stimulus-change effects from other effects of the reinforcer, if there are any.

Finally, a fairly recent hypothesis of reinforcement that has been christened with the name of its author is that responses of a higher independent rate reinforce responses of a lower independent rate, and that is why reinforcers reinforce; they are paired with responses of a higher rate. The hypothesis was named after David Premack and is, therefore, referred to as the Premack principle. Thus, if a child, for example, would rather drink milk than play ball, drinking milk can be used to increase the rate of playing ball. On the other hand, if the child would rather play ball than drink milk, then playing ball can be used to reinforce milk drinking. One difficulty with this theory is determining the hierarchy of responses since it may change from time to time, and, perhaps, from moment to moment.

As a kind of summary of the discussion so far, there are at least a dozen hypotheses for why a reinforcer is reinforcing, not all of which are independent of one another. For example, there are many intentional similarities between the "go mechanism" hypothesis and the central confirming response hypothesis, as well as the others, since it attempts to integrate them at least to some extent. There are also similarities between the empirical law of effect and the contiguity hypothesis, and, of course, the two-factor hypothesis incorporates major features of both.

Nevertheless, the sheer number of hypotheses for why a

reinforcer is reinforcing or for the nature of reinforcement suggests that efforts to resolve the question might be misdirected if those concerned with it expect a definitive answer; their efforts may not be misdirected if other results are being sought, such as fruitful and systematic research or theory development. However, if the question of reinforcement is the same as why a reinforcer is reinforcing, it may be similar to the question of why gravity attracts, if, indeed, gravity does attract.

No one seems to be particularly concerned about this latter question. Most people, and especially those of us who are laymen, seem willing to accept gravity as fact without trying to explain it, although the suggestion that it attracts hints at an explanation or a theory. However, the law of gravity may be nothing more than a descriptive statement of a relationship between objects or the manner in which they move toward one another; there may not be a thing that is gravity to which the law of gravity refers, where gravity is understood to be an attracting force. In that sense, the law of gravity is simply a statement of fact which describes the movement of objects toward one another.

The law of gravity may not require an explanation, but obviously it can be used as one; "everyone knows" what happens when an object is raised to some height and then released. It is basic fact, at least in our current conception of the physical universe. Thus, facts may not require explanation but may be used as explanations; in somewhat different terms, they may just be. Reinforcement also may be one of those facts which, in turn, may just be. It may not require an explanation or an answer for why it does what it does. If it does anything, it just does, and any statements we make about it can only be descriptive of what it does. Any attempts to say more than that about it are at least hypothetical and at most explanatory, but it does not require explanation; it just is. One statement that might reveal how it happens that the reinforcement question cannot be answered is, "It does what it does because it is what it is"; that statement obviously is circular, tautological, and vacuous, as may be true for all such answers to essentialist questions, including "it's the nature of the beast."

If reinforcement is a fact of behavior, part of the problem of reinforcement or what it is may be related to the manner in which it is formulated; the manner in which the fact is stated may be the source of the many different theories, or hypotheses, of reinforcement. Even the use of the word *it* with respect to reinforcement suggests there is a thing that is reinforcement to which the word "reinforcement" makes reference; as with so many of the other problems discussed here, physicalism may once again obtrude. In other words, the different theories of reinforcement may be related, in part at least, to the way in which the fact of reinforcement is stated.

Thus, some researchers might agree that the fact of reinforcement is accurately described in the form of the empirical law of effect; others might feel that, in that form, the law is not sufficiently descriptive. Some other researchers might contend that the fact of reinforcement is most correctly formulated as the contiguity hypothesis. Still others might argue that the correct form of the fact is the stimulus-change, or sensory reinforcement, hypothesis. In short, each different statement of the fact of reinforcement may be another hypothesis or theory of reinforcement. Thus, the proposition that response strength increases when it has certain consequences, which may seem quite descriptive, may be just another hypothesis or theory of reinforcement when analyzed more closely. Nevertheless, the consequences of a response do seem to have an effect, regardless of whether that is simply a statement of fact or another theory.

The discussion in the last several paragraphs may appear to

presuppose the metaphysics, or ontology, or realism. That is, it may seem to be based on the notion that there is such a thing, or phenomenon, as reinforcement which is at work in the behavioral universe. The problem of reinforcement is, then, the problem of how to state what that phenomenon is with some degree of accuracy. While that may appear to be the case, it is not. The fact of reinforcement may be only an orderly relationship we have observed among our sense experiences, and one that we can refuse to reify. When we do, the ontology of phenomenalism is, in principle at least, our basis for doing so.

In the final chapter to his book *Reinforcement and Behavior*, J. T. Tapp (1969) reviews all of the hypotheses discussed earlier in this chapter under the headings of motivational theories, stimulus theories, response theories, and eclectic theories. Drive-reduction and arousal are included under motivational theories. Stimulus-change, optimal level of stimulation, and hedonic properties of stimuli are included under stimulus theories. And consummatory response, prepotent response, and central confirming reaction are included under response theories. Eclectic views, as a heading, has no subcategories of theories.

The arousal hypothesis of reinforcement was not discussed earlier. According to this hypothesis, the arousal level of an animal is related to the amount of activity going on in its brain. This level of arousal can be equated with drive. Thus, the more aroused the animal, the higher the drive. When the animal is too aroused, it does things to reduce arousal to a more tolerable level, and this reduction in arousal is, apparently, what makes a reinforcer reinforcing. Consequently, the arousal hypothesis of reinforcement is very much like the drive reduction hypothesis and the optimal level of stimulation hypothesis. In that sense, it would be considered another two-factor hypothesis.

In a more recent book, with a title that suggests it answers the question of reinforcement, *The Nature of Reinforcement*, Robert Glaser (1971) points out that, regardless of its theoretical interpretation, "the operational description of reinforcing situations has remained fairly stable: Behavior is acquired and its occurrence regulated as a result of a contingent relationship between the response of an organism and a consequent event" (Glaser, 1971, p. 1). His statement is further support for the view that learning has to do with the acquisition of behavior, but there are those who might take issue with his version of the "operational description of reinforcing situations."

Their argument could take exception to the word "contingent" as opposed to the word "contiguous" since events correlated with responses also affect them, as in the case of superstitious behavior (cf. Skinner, 1948). His reference to events is also of interest because of discussions presented in earlier chapters. According to his statement, consequent events, not stimuli, affect responses, which, as suggested earlier, may also be considered events.

Regardless of these considerations, the book edited by Glaser does not answer the question of reinforcement; it does not make a clear and univocal statement about what reinforcement is or the nature of reinforcement. Instead, Glaser (1971, pp. 4–5) asserts that

> the views presented in this book provide strong evidence that in the past ten years experimentation and theory in learning have significantly influenced the analysis and status of the phenomenon of reinforcement as a fundamental concept in the psychology of learning. Two major developments in psychology that have influenced conceptions of the nature of reinforcement are apparent: (1) the extension of research into new and increasingly complex classes of behavior, and (2) analysis of the constraints and artificialities imposed by the limited range of experimental situations in which reinforcement has been studied.

He goes on to characterize these two major developments on the basis of eight issues related to them. The issues are: the distinction between operant and respondent behavior, the relation between reinforcement and cognitive processes as well as task requirements, cognitive as contrasted with operational description, the distinction between learning and performance, the phenomena of social learning, the relativity of reinforcement and its applications. In the process, he draws several explicit conclusions about the nature of reinforcement.

One is that "an adequate description of the nature of reinforcement is limited by maintaining the dichotomy between operant and respondent responses classes" (Glaser, 1971, pp. 5–6). A second explicit conclusion about the nature of reinforcement is that it "must be interpreted in terms of task factors, situational and context-setting conditions, the characteristics of learning outcomes, and the organism involved" (Glaser, 1971, p. 10).

A third conclusion is that "the context of what are called 'social learning' situations adds some new dimensions to the nature of reinforcement" (Glaser, 1971, p. 11). A fourth is that "the phenomenon of vicarious reinforcement extends our conceptions about the nature of reinforcement," where "vicarious reinforcement is defined as a change in the behavior of observers as a function of witnessing the reinforcement contingencies accompanying the performance of others" (Glaser, 1971, p. 11). However, a fifth conclusion is that "while it is agreed that the empirical facts of vicarious and self-reinforcement point to key processes in understanding the nature of reinforcement in human behavior, the ways in which these processes operate and their theoretical interpretations pose significant areas for debate" (Glaser, 1971, p. 12).

A sixth conclusion is that "the traditional reference to neutral, positive, and negative stimuli which correspond to neutral stimuli, reinforcers, and punishers may be a misinterpretation of the nature of reinforcement, if reinforcement and punishment only can be dealt with relationally" (Glaser, 1971, p. 13), that is, in relation to other kinds of behaviors that occur at different rates. A seventh conclusion is that "the extension of research into new categories of behavior and into new experimental paradigms forces the breaking away from the traditional conceptions of what is a reinforcer" (Glaser, 1971, p. 13).

An eighth conclusion is that "psychologists are beginning to come into the possession of certain general principles about the nature of reinforcement" (Glaser, 1971, p. 14). Finally, a ninth explicit conclusion is that "the exciting prospect for application is that limitations of traditional conceptions are being overcome by new investigations about the nature of reinforcement" (Glaser, 1971, p. 15).

Each of these conclusions requires further development, and they are further developed by the different authors of the various chapters in Glaser's book. What is especially important about them for present purposes is that they seem to emphasize a need to look at some old problems in new ways or to explore alternative, and imaginative, solutions to some old problems, particularly that of reinforcement. One that Glaser does not discuss and that apparently has not been seriously considered in the recent literature on the nature of reinforcement is, of course, a change in metaphysical assumptions like those discussed in previous chapters of this book.

The title to Glaser's book and the conclusions he draws about the nature of reinforcement seem to represent an admixture of older and newer views of science. That is, they seem to reflect the influence of methodological essentialism as well as methodological nominalism, as both were explicated earlier based on the works of Karl Popper. It may be recalled that the former asks what a thing is, if reinforcement can be considered a thing, as in the title *The Nature of Reinforcement;* the latter asks how a thing functions, as in the research on reinforcement. Thus, it appears that current researchers such as Glaser and others are trying to find out how reinforcement functions in order to know what it is.

Their efforts may be futile, although that possibility probably will not deter them from their quest; it hasn't so far. As indicated earlier, questions about what a thing is assume: (1) there is a thing; (2) it has an essence, essential characteristics, or a basic nature; and (3) its essence or basic nature can be known. The first is the ontological assumption of realism. The second is the view of science held by methodological essentialists. The third is a matter of epistemology or how we know. The first and third combine as metaphysics. Consequently, a change in any one or all three of them can be considered a change in metaphysical assumptions.

With respect to the first, it has already been argued that phenomenalism is an alternative to realism that is equally defensible, except, perhaps, for what may be a logical problem of solipsism (cf. Eacker, 1975, pp. 167–68). Phenomenalism takes sense experience as a basic given, whereas realism takes the world as given; neither the one nor the other can say what sense experience is or what the real world is. Consequently, either realism or phenomenalism can be adopted and defended in science; realism has been tried.

With respect to the second point enumerated above, methodological nominalism rather than methodological essentialism seems to be the prevailing view in science at the present time; it asks how a thing functions and not what it is. This conception of science is entirely consistent with phenomenalism, although things may not function so much as they are functional relationships observed between differently measured aspects of sense experience. That is, a thing is a construction from logic and sense experience. It is not discovered by means of sense experience; it is developed out of sense experience, or it is constructed.

With respect to the third point, the epistemology of science seems to be its methodology or how it knows. That methodology is based on observation, at least so far as we now know. Observation is, in principle, infinite; it could continue for as long as there are observers. However, conclusions are drawn in science before observation is complete; as a result, they are probable rather than certain. Consequently, even if we knew the basic nature, or essence, of a thing, we couldn't know that we knew it with the methodology of science as it is currently understood.

These considerations have some implications for the problem of reinforcement in particular and for the discipline of psychology in general. One is that changes in these assumptions might lead those interested in reinforcement, for example, to search no longer for its basic nature, or what it is, but to devote their energies to how it functions, or its laws; the same might be true for other major topics in psychology, such as learning, motivation, and personality. In somewhat different terms, researchers would no longer assume they were discovering the basic nature of reinforcement or, for that matter, the universe but that they were simply engaged in the task of making sense out of what they were sensing. The laws of what they sensed would not be discovered by means of sense experience; the laws would be developed out of sense experience. If that is how they understood what they were doing, they might then hold any conclusions they drew from their research more lightly.

A second implication of these considerations obviously related to the first is that researchers would no longer assume there were phenomena of reinforcement or learning or motivation or personality waiting to be discovered through their research. Rather, anything they sensed might be related to reinforcement or learning or motivation or personality, depending, perhaps, on nothing more than the questions that were asked about that sense experience.

The result might be that psychologists and other students of psychology would no longer search for a peculiar class of behaviors that were, for example, motivational as distinct from another class of behaviors that were learned; any behavior might be either motivational or learned depending upon what a researcher wanted to know about it. An illustration of this attempt to identify motivational activities as a particular class of activities can be found in Bindra (1959, p. 25) who stated that

> the phenomena called "motivational," which define the scope of this work, include activities such as eating, drinking, approaching, escaping, attacking, exploring, copulating, maternal care of the young, and the like. It is these and similar activities that are sometimes labeled "drive behaviors" and that have traditionally been interpreted in terms of "instincts," "drives," or some other "primary motives." These activities are almost always to be found in the repertoire of the normal adult mammal and in that of some infra-mammalian species too. Of course, the particular form and the degree of complexity of these activities varies considerably from species to species and individual to individual, and we shall have occasion to examine these differences. However, our primary interest here lies in those features of motivational activities that are shared by most mammalian species, including man.

Thus, according to Bindra, tradition is at least one determinant of the way in which motivational activities are classified, and, of course, tradition can change or be changed.

Some other determinants by which behaviors are classified are what Bindra (1959, p. 50) refers to as their dominant features, as though the activities existed and possessed them. There are three such features:

> First, they appear to be purposeful or goal-directed activities. By observing an animal for a certain length of time it is easy to say, for example, that it is "looking for food," for it ignores objects and events that do not fall into the category of food. Similarly, activities such as nest building, attacking, escaping, and exploring can all be recognized as such by the planned, purposeful way in which the animal executes them. Second, the various motivational activities seem to emerge from a state of high excitement, lacking goal direction. Thus, the low excitement-high excitement variable seems to be closely related to motivational activities. Third, these activities show in a dramatic fashion the control on behavior that is exercised by internal and external conditions. For example, external situation remaining the same, a female chimpanzee will typically copulate only when it is in estrus. And, equally important, the same female in estrus may receive one particular male but not another.

The "planned, purposeful way" in which an animal executes such behaviors may be as much a function of the observer as they are of the animal observed (cf. Eacker, 1975, pp. 103–16). That is, they may be characteristics we impose on behavior rather than observe in it.

Despite these assertions about the features of motivational activities, Bindra (1959, p. 50) acknowledges that

> the above features of behavior are not peculiar to the activities labeled "motivational." However, these features are undoubtedly most dramatically evident in these activities. It is perhaps this fact that has led to such activities being treated as a distinct class of phenomena and has given rise to the erroneous idea that some unique processes (instincts, drives, motives, etc.) are involved in them.

An equally erroneous idea may be that there are motivational phenomena that exist apart from an observer. Another may be that the above features are characteristic of motivational as well as many other activities. Whether they are or are not, they apparently do not distinguish the former as a special, or unique, class of activities.

It may be that the attempt to distinguish them as a separate and distinct class of activities cannot succeed. And it may not be able to succeed because there may not be a class of activities that are motivational and which are distinct from a class of activities that are learned, or perceptual, or cognitive. Any so-called activity may be motivational, or learned, or perceptual depending upon what we want to know about it as it occurs in our sense experience. In short, the type of inquiry may be what helps to define the phenomena about which we inquire, especially from the ontological position of phenomenalism. Consequently, and with respect to the problem of reinforcement in particular, what it is may depend upon what we want to know about it. We may not be able to know it in itself or as it is.

If an answer to the question of reinforcement is still required or demanded, it may be that the question can be answered only by the way in which a reinforcer is made to be reinforcing. Reinforcers are not always reinforcing; sometimes they are and sometimes they are not. When they are, an animal usually has been deprived of something it normally works to obtain or it has been presented with something it normally works to eliminate, at least according to the principles of positive and negative reinforcement presented in the third chapter. Thus, a reinforcer is reinforcing because an animal has been deprived of something it normally works to obtain or it has been presented with something it normally works to eliminate, and that is why a reinforcer is reinforcing. Those operations are what make a reinforcer reinforcing and that, if it has one, is the nature of reinforcement from a behavioral perspective.

Chapter Nine

What Is Motivation?

Reference was made in the last chapter to the inevitability of mentioning reinforcement in any discussion of learning, and the same seems to be true for motivation. It was mentioned rather frequently in the discussion of reinforcement and especially with regard to the way in which reinforcers might be made to be reinforcing, that is, by means of deprivation and presentation operations. Those operations are referred to frequently as motivational, at least in the literature on the experimental analysis of behavior. However, for most people, the question of motivation is "Why do organisms behave as they do?" and not "What makes a reinforcer reinforcing?" Consequently, the question of motivation seems to require a direct and particular treatment of its own.

For those who may not have thought seriously about it, why organisms behave as they do may appear to be the one major question for all of psychology to answer. As indicated in earlier, as well as later, chapters in this book, a good many people seem to feel that it can be answered by means of physics or through a simple extension of physical, and perhaps mechanical, principles. After all, objects move when an external force is applied to them. Organisms are objects that move and are moved. Therefore, organisms move, or behave, not only when an external force is applied to them but, apparently, when internal forces are at work within them. Organisms behave as they do because of forces that make them behave as they do. The principle of causality and a few elementary principles of physics are all that are needed to explain the behavior of organisms; it is absurd to think otherwise.

As will be seen in the following review of several motivation theories, a good many psychologists apparently have not thought otherwise; they may simply have developed the above conception in somewhat greater detail and complexity. It probably is this approach to the topic of motivation in psychology that is responsible for the origin and survival of such so-called explanatory concepts as impulses, instincts, needs, motives, and drives. Thus, the human organism in particular does things on impulse. Animals, but not humans, do things because of instincts. Organisms do things in order to meet their basic needs. We search for a motive when a crime is committed. And psychologists aren't sure whether drives are intervening variables or hypothetical constructs.

The time may have come to think otherwise, but before suggestions are made for how that might be accomplished, some alternative views on the subject deserve special consideration. Alternative views are the different theories of motivation. A review of some of them may help to reveal the breadth of our thinking about the subject within psychology.

More than a decade ago, K. B. Madsen (1968) published the fourth edition of a book he called *Theories of motivation;* it had the subtitle, *A comparative study of modern theories of motivation.* In it, he compared twenty theories of motivation which he found in the writings of that many different psychologists or those with similar credentials. Not all of them need to be summarized for present purposes. However, seven of them seem to be representative of the spectrum of views on the subject within psychology, and they have been chosen for that reason as well as for the eminence of their authors. The theories selected are those of William McDougall, Paul T. Young, Kurt Lewin, Henry A. Murray, Clark Hull, Niko Tinbergen, and David C. McClelland.

William McDougall (1871–1938) has been mentioned on several occasions in previous chapters. He obviously has had a profound impact on the development of psychology in this country; that is, his eminence seems well established. According to Madsen (1968, pp. 55–56), his theory of motivation may be summarized as follows: Since all life processes reveal a basic striving for the preservation of the individual and the species, they are purposive. In higher organisms, especially humans, this basic striving, or "hormé," becomes differentiated into a number of innate but modifiable primary motivation variables called "instincts," or, in McDougall's later works, "propensities." Instincts or propensities not only determine but also organize all mental processes, as well as behavior, toward particular goals. Thus, cognitive processes become purposive, that is, they are guided or utilized; the organism experiences a primary emotion specific to each instinct; a purposive act is initiated, or the organism at least experiences an impulse to act in a certain way. The most basic and least modifiable aspects of this process are the emotion and the impulse to act; that is, they are the least affected by learning.

However, several instincts may become centered around an object through learning. When they do, they are referred to as "sentiments." It is sentiments that most often provide the motive force for actions in humans. But since sentiments are composed of innate instincts, the latter remain the basic drive or energy for behavior. When several sentiments become organized in the mature human adult, that organization is known as "character." Thus, most organisms behave as they do because of instincts or propensities, but the latter emerge out of a more basic striving for self-preservation.

In a later work, McDougall states the presuppositions of his theory as follows. First, he presupposes that psychic activity is as real as physical process; it is a part of nature and is effective in a causal way. Second, he assumes that psychic activity always involves a forward striving toward a goal, and, in that sense, it is always teleological. Furthermore, this teleological or purposive causation is not the same as mechanistic causation or mechanistic determinism. Third, he feels there is a continuity in evolution, both physical and mental, from the simplest to the most complex organisms and that ontogeny recapitulates phylogeny, although in an abbreviated and distorted way. That is, the development of the individual reflects the development of the species, approximately. His fourth presupposition is that there is a complex organization called a creature's "mental structure" that underlies and determines the major directions and limits of its mental activity. Thus, McDougall is mentalistic and purposive in his approach to motivation; behavior is purposive and is caused by mental events. As discussed in somewhat different terms in earlier chapters, his determinism is mentalistic, or psychic, rather than mechanistic or empirical.

Paul Thomas Young (born 1892) may not be as generally well known as the other motivation theorists examined here, but his theory differs rather remarkably from that of McDougall. According to Madsen (1968, pp. 91–92), it may be summarized as follows. The subject of motivation in psychology involves the energy-release and the energy-regulation of behavior. Either internal or external stimuli may cause the release of energy, and the energy released within the organism is chemical in nature. When stimuli from internal organs determine the release of energy, the energy-release or motivation is referred to as a primary drive. When external stimuli cause the release of energy, it is usually because they have acquired some connection with internal stimuli. Frequently, the internal stimuli occur because the homeostasis of the organism and its different organs are disturbed or processes related to them are disturbed. Disturbances of this kind are called needs or appetites; they are often experienced by the individual as demands, desires, wants, or wishes.

Energy-regulation is accomplished by neural-mental structures that are partly innate and partly acquired, presumably through genetic inheritance and learning, respectively. These energy-regulating and behavior-regulating structures are of considerable importance in human beings, especially those structures that are acquired or are socially determined. A disorganization of the condition and behavior of an individual occurs when motives are blocked or when motives conflict with one another; this disorganization is called "emotion." Thus, organisms behave as they do because of the energy released by external and internal stimuli.

The presuppositions of Young's theory are not as well articulated as those of McDougall. The major one seems to be attitudinal. Apparently, he feels that no one attitude toward science is defensible but that all of them need to be synthesized into a single point of view; in that sense, his approach is eclectic. A second presupposition is that there is only one kind of motivating structure within the organism, and it is sufficient to explain all of the relevant facts of psychology. A third is that motivational psychology must describe and explain purposive behavior. A fourth is that motivation involves the biomechanics or the energetics of activity, which includes the problem of behavior regulation. Consequently, his determinism seems to be a combination of mentalism and mechanism, but it is clearly not empirical determinism in the sense discussed earlier; behavior is determined, but not simply because it is lawful.

Thus far in the discussion, a number of concepts seem to have been accepted without much question by both theorists in their respective accounts of why organisms behave as they do. One is psychic activity. For McDougall, it is as real as physical process, which could mean that physical process may not be real in the sense of being a thing. A second is purpose. Both theorists seem to have little doubt that purpose is a characteristic of behavior and not of themselves. A third is the concept of need, which may be related to the ancient, and anthropomorphic, physical notion that nature abhors a vacuum. A fourth is determinism. Both McDougall and Young appear to agree that behavior is determined by either mental or physical causes, if not both, but they do not seem to agree explicitly that behavior is lawful. A fifth is energy. Young seems to entertain few doubts about the existence of energy, but, as pointed out earlier, universal doubt is not something that belonged exclusively to the French philosopher René Descartes.

A sixth concept is force, which may be related to, or is perhaps the same as, the concept of energy. Whatever the case, many motivation theorists have an idea similar to that of force within their conceptual systems. A seventh is that behavior is to be explained by whatever is going on inside the organism; that is, behavior is to be explained at a different level than at the level of behavior itself (cf. Skinner, 1950). Any one or all of these concepts might be challenged or replaced rather than assumed to be fact. The result might be an entirely different approach to the topic of motivation in psychology—one that departs radically from the more traditional views.

The third noteworthy theorist to be considered is Kurt Lewin (1890–1947). He held that behavior is a function of an individual's total situation, or life space, which consists of its own condition and the condition of the environment. According to Madsen (1968, pp. 130–31), this situation can be expressed in a formula where: B equals behavior; F equals function; L equals life space; P equals condition of the person; and E equals condition of the environment. When those substitutions are made, the formula reads: B equals F (L) equals F (P,E). Thus, organisms behave as they do because of the condition of the individual organism and the condition of its environment.

The individual, or person, is thought of as a system that consists of an internal central region and an external perceptual and motor region, or a peripheric region. These regions, in turn, are differentiated into an increasingly greater number of other regions as the individual develops, although there may be some difficulty in identifying their boundaries. Nevertheless, when an internal region is in a state of tension, the individual is in a state of need.

The environment has a cognitive structure of its own, but it also consists of the position of the individual within a personal life space and the distribution of whatever forces there are within that space. The cognitive structure can be divided into a psychological past, present, and future, and it also consists of at least two levels of reality; there may be an activity level and a daydream level and perhaps several others as well. Orientation, learning, and insight involve changes in the cognitive structure of the individual's life space.

The position of the individual in its life space is important as a determinant of the direction behavior may take with respect to goal regions; these regions may include social groups. Goal regions determine a force field with positive valence which affects the individual and directs behavior toward the goal region; the valence of a region refers to whether an individual moves toward or away from it. Thus, some regions may have force fields with negative valence, which directs behavior away from them. The distance between an individual and the valence of a goal region is only one of many variables related to the strength of the force field.

Valences determine driving forces, but there are also repulsive forces brought about by barriers, and induced forces which, in turn, are brought about by other individuals, according to Madsen (1968, p. 131). Conflicts arise when opposed forces of almost equal strength affect the individual. They occur primarily with respect to either two positive or two negative valences, but they may also take place when a positive and a negative valence happen to be in the same goal region; conflicts may involve behaviors such as choice, punishment, reward, emotional tension, and restlessness.

"The cognitive structure and valences of the environment (E) determine the forces which cause the behavior of the individual" (Madsen, 1968, p. 131). They depend "upon the condition of the individual (P)"; they are especially dependent upon whatever tensions there are within the central regions, which correspond to the needs of the organism. The need and the tension related to it partly determine the valences, and, of course, the valences determine the force fields which cause individual behavior.

Apparently, there are real needs and quasi needs. The former are biological, and the latter are related to decisions or to other types of sets. Needs are met when the original goal is consummated or when something else is substituted for it, such as a daydream. They can be changed in a number of ways, including external restraint, satisfaction and oversatisfaction, resolutions, conversion into other needs, or induction by the social environment.

Lewin presupposes that theories are necessary in psychology; they allow psychologists to go beyond the collection and the description of facts to the prediction of new ones. He also presupposes three developmental epochs in the history of science that are of special significance for the questions examined here. In fact, it was a surprise and a delight to find at least one other psychologist aside from those discussed in the first chapter who had given the problem of essentialism some consideration, however indirect.

According to Lewin, there are three epochs in the history of science: speculative, descriptive, and constructive. These epochs correspond to the transition in physics from medieval Aristotelian to modern Galilean concepts (cf. Lewin, 1936, pp. 8–9). The goal of the speculative, or Aristotelian, epoch was to discover the essence of things and the cause behind all occurrences. The goal of the descriptive epoch was to collect as many facts as possible and to describe them exactly. The goal of the constructive, or Galilean, epoch was to discover laws and to predict individual cases. The first and last epochs seem very closely related, respectively, to methodological essentialism and methodological nominalism as described by Karl Popper, including the realistic ontological assumption that laws are discovered.

Consequently, Lewin's remarks provide further support for the thesis that modern science in general, and psychology in particular, does not say what things are but how they function. They also suggest that questions about what things are may represent a misconception of what modern science is able to do. A third suggestion to be discerned in his remarks is that the search for essences is an early and perhaps rather primitive stage in our conception of science and one beyond which psychology may already have moved. Lewin developed his assessment of this transition in greater detail in a paper entitled "The Conflict between

Aristotelian and Galilean Modes of Thought in Contemporary Psychology" (Lewin, 1931); it deserves a careful reading by all serious students of psychology.

The fourth eminent motivation theorist to be considered here is Henry A. Murray (b. 1893). According to Madsen (1968, pp. 146–149), Murray and his collaborators developed a theory of motivation in the process of developing a theory of personality. The study of individual personalities is, for Murray et al., personology. The personality of an individual consists of episodes that occur over the course of that individual's lifetime. An episode is an action which can be more or less complicated and which is most often a reaction by the individual to its environment, both physical and social. Actions are determined by integrating, or regnant, brain processes, which can be either conscious or unconscious. Regnancies are the results of external press, emotional needs, conscious intentions, accepted cultural standards, and habits.

Need and press are two important motivation concepts in his theory. The combination of a need and a press, or a theme, is present in every episode that occurs in an individual's lifetime. The most important motivation concept in his theory is need (Murray 1938, pp. 123–24).

> A need is a construct (a convenient fiction or hypothetical concept) which stands for a force (the physicochemical nature of which is unknown) in the brain region, a force which organizes perception, apperception, intellection, conation and action in such a way as to transform in a certain direction an existing, unsatisfying situation. A need is sometimes provoked directly by internal processes of a certain kind (viscerogenic, endocrinogenic, thalamicogenic) arising in the course of vital sequences, but, more frequently (when in a state of readiness) by the occurrence of one of a few commonly effective press (or by anticipatory images of

> such press). Thus, it manifests itself by leading the organism to search for or to avoid encountering or, when encountered, to attend and respond to certain kinds of press. It may even engender illusory perceptions and delusory apperceptions (projections of its imaged press into unsuitable objects). Each need is characteristically accompanied by a particular feeling or emotion and tends to use certain modes (sub-needs and actones) to further its trend. It may be weak or intense, momentary or enduring. But usually it persists and gives rise to a certain course of overt behaviour (or fantasy), which (if the organism is competent and external opposition not insurmountable) changes the initiating circumstance in such a way as to bring about an end situation which stills (appeases or satisfies) the organism.

Thus, for Murray, organisms behave as they do because of needs. However, a need is a construct which may simply be a convenient fiction and not necessarily a thing, but it apparently is not observable. It stands for a force which organizes perception and other behaviors and is presumed to have a physico-chemical nature; in that sense, it is a thing or has thing characteristics. Nevertheless, how a need can be a force is rather puzzling since the word *need* suggests an absence and not a presence, whereas the word *force* suggests just the opposite. The former is a negative concept and the latter is a positive concept. If a need is both negative and positive at the same time, it seems to be at least a contradictory concept, if not a paradoxical one; motivation theorists appear not to have dealt with this paradox.

On the other hand, a press is a stimulus situation with the potential for some influence on the life of an individual. A need and a press combine as a theme or episode, and actions related to them may be successful or unsuccessful. Regardless of whether they are successful or unsuccessful, these actions frequently have an influence that determines the further development of the personality. They do so because each episode is retained, perhaps only partially, as a trace in the brain which may then become a determinant of actions in a new episode.

There are a number of explicit presuppositions in his theory. One is that the subject matter of psychology is personalities; psychology is personology. A second is that personality psychologists divide into two groups: peripheralists and centralists. The former are described as objective, positivistic, mechanistic, atomistic, and sensationistic. The latter are subjective, rationalistic, holistic, and dynamistic.

> The peripheralists are apt to emphasize the physical patterns of overt behaviour, the combination of simple reflexes to form complex configurations, the influence of the tangible environment, sensations and the compounds, intellections, social attitudes, traits, and vocational pursuits. The centralists, on the other hand, stress the directions or ends of behaviour, underlying instinctual forces, inherited dispositions, maturation and inner transformations, distortions of perception by wish and fantasy, emotion, irrational or semi-conscious mental processes, repressed sentiments and the objects of erotic interest. [Murray 1938, p. 10]

He and his associates classified themselves as centralists. A third presupposition of his theory is that speculative thought, or theory, is both necessary and valuable for the continued development of psychology.

The fifth notable motivation theory is that of Clark L. Hull (1884–1952). According to Madsen (1968, pp. 169–71), Hull held to the position that every organism is a "completely automatic entity." Furthermore, it does not have an entelechy or disembodied mind, soul, or spirit, which for centuries has been presumed to tell the various parts of the body how to cooperate behaviorally or how to achieve successful adaptation, that is, how to survive. Rather, this biological adaptation is accomplished, in part at least, by means of eight behavior mechanisms that are automatic and adaptive. Thus, organisms behave as they do because their behavior is adaptive.

One of these mechanisms is inborn response tendencies. They are unlearned stimulus-response connections or reflexes and are determined by phylogenetic development, or evolution; they make it possible for the organism to adapt to various kinds of emergencies related to its survival. Another mechanism is the primitive capacity to learn or to profit by past experience. The conditioned reflex is the simplest form of this learning; it helps to adapt the organism to situations in which the inborn forms of behavior are not effective.

The third automatic adaptive behavior mechanism is the antedating defense reaction. This mechanism is a product of the law of learning and the law of stimulus generalization; it enables the organism to avoid dangerous, injurious, or painful stimuli. The fourth mechanism is negative response learning, which prevents an organism from performing useless acts; it does so by repressing or blocking ineffective actions with more effective actions, both innate and acquired. The fifth mechanism is trial-and-error-learning; it is a combination of negative and positive response learning occurring in the same process.

The sixth adaptive behavior mechanism is discrimination learning; another name for it is positive-negative stimulus trial learning. The seventh is another type of antedating defense reaction. It consists of a reaction that is determined by, or at least positively associated with, the trace of a stimulus; this trace may persist for some time after the physical stimulus has terminated. Because of this persistence, a stimulus trace that follows a signal stimulus, for example a danger signal, continues to exist when the dangerous, injurious, or painful situation and the flight behavior related to it commences. With a few repetitions, the flight behavior may become associated with the signal stimulus by means of its stimulus trace, with the result that flight behavior at a later time is initiated by the signal stimulus acting alone; presumably, it is initiated before the dangerous situation occurs.

The eighth, and last, automatic behavior mechanism is the fractional antedating goal reaction along with its correlated proprioceptive stimulus, that is, $r_G - s_G$. All of the goals established by a given organism tend to be antedated by r_G, which is thought of as a pure stimulus act. Since r_G antedates all goals established by a particular organism, the proprioceptive goal stimulus, symbolized as s_G, automatically precedes each of those goals, as well as the acts by which the goals have been attained in the past. As a result, each s_G is a stimulus that leads to the attainment of its particular goal. This automatic stimulus guidance of an organism's behavior to goals is presumed to be adaptive in the highest sense.

Hull presupposed that the methods of science are hypothetico-deductive insofar as hypotheses are based on empirical research and, where possible, expressed in mathematical form. These hypotheses, postulates, or axioms in turn are used to deduce statements or theorems that describe empirical and perhaps experimental data.

The sixth theory of motivation is that of Niko Tinbergen. He divided instinctive responses into appetitive behavior and consummatory act. The former is the inquiring, striving, and purposive phase of instinctive behavior. It can be more or less complex from species to species, individual to individual, and situation to situation. It also can consist of reflex movements, conditioned reflex movements, as well as other acquired actions, and intelligent behavior, such as that called insight. The consummatory act is the most simple and constant part of instinctive behavior. It has two components: taxis, or orientation movements, and the fixed pattern that is a stereotyped series of movements typical of a particular species.

Generally, external and internal factors determine instinctive behavior. External factors are exteroceptive stimuli; they may be either directive or releasing. Releasing stimuli affect the fixed pattern feature of the consummatory act. Directive stimuli affect the orientation feature of the consummatory act and the entire appetitive phase of instinctive behavior. Internal factors are the motivating factors. They include hormones, internal stimuli to the interoceptors, and perhaps automatic spontaneous nervous impulses. These factors are coordinated in the central nervous system by a superior instinct center. Impulses are sent from this center to a hierarchy of subordinated centers. Each of these latter centers, in turn, directs a series of movements which contributes to the entire instinctive response.

An innate release mechanism blocks the connection from the superior center to the subordinate centers; it can be activated only by a specific kind of releasing stimuli. The instinct centers and the release mechanism function to coordinate the instinctive response to a behavior that has some biological significance under the normal conditions of existence for a particular species. Thus, organisms behave as they do because of internal and external factors that affect instinctive responses.

The major presuppositions of Tinbergen's theory have to do with his conception of his science; it is referred to as ethology. He defines ethology as the objective study of behavior. Ethology is concerned with the causal structure underlying behavior and the biological significance of behavior. However, he is interested primarily in the causes of innate behavior.

For Tinbergen, ethology is not the same as comparative psychology. The latter as it was understood at the time by Tinbergen stresses purposive behavior, whereas ethology stresses the causality of behavior. Ethology denies the explanatory value of subjective phenomena known through introspection, but it does not deny their existence. Ethology differs from physiology because it studies the behavior of the total organism; by contrast, Tinbergen felt that physiology studies the function of individual organs rather than the total organism. Ethology studies innate behavior rather than noninnate behavior; in that regard, it differs from behavioral psychology. In addition, whereas behavioral psychology mainly uses standard laboratory experiments, ethology makes use of experiments and observations in the natural environment. Finally, ethology differs from introspective psychology in its exclusive use of objective methods rather than the subjective method of introspection.

McDougall, Hull, and Tinbergen all seem to feel that organisms behave as they do because their behavior has some sort of biological significance. For McDougall, it is self-preservation. For Hull, it is adaptation. Both may be different aspects of the same concept, namely, evolution, which of course receives considerable emphasis from Tinbergen. This biological explanation for the behavior of organisms appeals to a good many students of psychology; it is a biological explanation because it is based, either directly or indirectly, on Charles Darwin's theory of evolution in biology. That theory, as most of us know, stresses chance variation and natural selection in the origin and development of species. Both may be interpreted to result in either self-preservation or adaptation; a brief summary of the theory is presented in the chapter on human nature.

The biological account does seem to explain behavior; at least it gives a reason for behavior. It states that organisms behave as they do because a certain behavior has allowed them to survive. Their behavior is self-preservative or adaptive; Skinner (1966) has discussed factors that may select behavior as contingencies of survival as well as contingencies of reinforcement. However, to say that organisms behave as they do because that behavior allows them to survive, while it may give a reason for the behavior, makes no mention of the variables related to the behavior; it makes no reference to the laws of behavior. The laws of behavior explain behavior at least according to a behavioral orientation. Consequently, the biological explanation is not a behavioral explanation. Stated differently, the biological explanation is not an empirical, or functional, explanation; it is an explanation from traditional rationalism (cf. Eacker, 1975, pp. 41–54).

Furthermore, the biological account does not give an indication of how it happens that a particular organism is behaving in a particular way on a particular occasion. To do so would seem to require some knowledge of the environmental variables that might be related to the behavior. And to know them would be to know the laws of behavior. A general and perhaps rather vague reference to the theory of evolution is not an explanation based on the laws of behavior; it does not explain behavior.

The seventh, and final, theory of motivation to be summarized is that by David C. McClelland. He "defines a motive as an *affective association* manifesting itself as purposive behavior and determined by previous association between signals and pleasure or pain" (Madsen, 1968, p. 217). Thus, all motives are acquired and, in addition, all motivation is based upon emotions; it is not identical with emotions but with an expectation of change in the affective condition. He hypothesizes that, from birth, pleasure is determined by each moderate increase in stimulus intensity; further increase is a determinant of displeasure or pain. In this way, two kinds of motives become possible.

One is the positive or approaching motive, which is an expectation of pleasure or satisfaction. The other is the negative or avoiding motive, which is an expectation of displeasure or pain; the first is symbolized with "n" as an abbreviation for need and the second is symbolized with "f" as an abbreviation for fear. Thus, the need for achievement and the fear of failure are two different motives; the first is n Achievement and the second is f Failure.

Since all motives are acquired, McClelland makes no distinction between primary, or biogenic, and secondary, or psychogenic, motives. However, biological needs almost always are related to behaviors which, at some time, result in satisfaction and therefore pleasure; if they did not, the organism would die. As a result, expectations of increased pleasure for biological needs, or motives, are learned quite early. Other motives such as, for example, n Achievement are also nearly universal in human beings, even though they are determined by external stimuli. Such stimuli may be so common in all cultures, particularly through education, that motives related to them are learned as early and persist as intensely over the lifetime of the individual as those that are biologically determined. Thus, organisms behave as they do because of the need for achievement or the fear of failure, which may seem a bit strange when applied to rats and pigeons.

McClelland presupposes the empirical studies performed by himself and his associates. These experiments involve measurements of experimentally produced motives by means of projective tests and especially the TAT, or thematic apperception test, developed by Murray. They include the study of the hunger motive, the sex motive, the need for affiliation, and the need for achievement. On the basis of these studies, he rejected most of the prevailing theories of motivation, largely because they are based too extensively upon experiments with animals; as a result, he felt they were unsatisfactory as explanations of the more complicated nonbiological motives.

The types of motivation theories he rejected were the survival model, the stimulus intensity model, and the stimulus pattern model. The survival model explains motivation on the basis of survival or survival needs; it includes the theories of Young and

Hull. McClelland criticized it for the following reasons. The first is that not all survival needs produce motives. The second is that survival needs are difficult to define. The third is that biological needs do not provide a complete explanation for how behavior is guided and controlled. The fourth is that the unusual persistence and strength of acquired human motives suggests that they do not continue to depend upon biological needs.

The stimulus intensity model defines motivation as a strong stimulus that impels action; Neal Miller developed a theory of this type. The major criticism of this model is that strong stimulation does not always produce negative affect, although it often does produce pain or negative affect. However, when pain or negative affect is not produced, strong stimulation does not appear to be a source of motivation. Thus, it seems that negative affect and not strong stimulation is the causal motivational factor.

The stimulus pattern model states that motivation is determined by a stimulus pattern in which there is a moderate discrepancy between expectation and perception. McClelland criticizes it for the following reasons. One is that for a motive to be established, the relationship between past learning and present perception must be known. The second is that the theory is so general that it is difficult to know when a motive is in effect and how to measure its effects. Thus, aside from the arguments against them advanced here, there are other criticisms of these theories, especially against those that conform to one or another of the above models defined by McClelland.

This review of seven theories of motivation within psychology and related fields may give some sense of the breadth of views proposed to explain why organisms behave as they do. In summary, it has been proposed that organisms behave as they do to preserve themselves and their species. They behave as they do because of the energy released by internal and external stimuli.

They behave as they do because of the condition of the individual or person and the condition of the environment. They behave as they do because of needs. They behave as they do because the behavior is adaptive. They behave as they do because of internal and external factors related to instinctive responses. And they behave as they do because of the need for achievement and the fear of failure. Each of the remaining thirteen theories compared by Madsen (1968) gives a somewhat different answer to the question of why organisms behave as they do.

The plethora of answers to the question suggests that no one knows precisely why we behave as we do, and, perhaps, that it is the wrong kind of question to ask about ourselves, especially if we want an answer. If the ontological position of realism is true, organisms behave. At the present time, it appears that they behave as they do because of the laws of behavior or the variables of which behaviors are a function. But a statement of what the variables are does not appear to provide an answer to the question of why the variables affect behavior in the particular ways that they do. They just do, as in the case of gravity or sunrise; objects fall and the sun rises. To say more leads to another theory and to say "it is the nature of the beast" for them to do so is no closer to an answer than simply to say that they do. In short, the why question may be unanswerable.

Nevertheless, most people would find it ludicrous to challenge the assumption that all behavior is motivated. If it were not motivated, so the argument goes, no behavior would ever occur. Something must cause behavior; otherwise, it wouldn't take place. The problem for each one of us, including psychologists, is to find out what the causes are. The statement that all behavior is motivated appears to be equivalent to the statement that all behavior is caused. Stated differently, the assumption that all behavior is motivated may be a disguised form of the principle of causality in human affairs, which, in turn, may assume mechanistic, rather than empirical, determinism.

It has been acknowledged elsewhere (cf. Eacker, 1975, pp. 55–63) that the principle of causality, as with most human concepts, may be a construction based on sense experience rather than a positive factor at work in the universe. If so, and if our concept of motivation is based on our conception of causality, then behavior may have no causes except in the functional sense. That is, it may have no cause except in the sense that there are variables of which behavior is a function. It is caused only in the sense that it is lawful. That is, behavior is empirically, rather than mechanistically, determined.

It is rather remarkable that none of the theories reviewed by Madsen (1968), including that attributed to B. F. Skinner, develops the thesis that organisms behave as they do because of the variables of which their behavior is a function. The thesis obviously is consistent with a behavioral orientation in psychology and especially with an empirical, or functional, view of explanation. The thesis also is consistent with the methodological nominalist's view of science, which asks how things function and not what they are: the latter, of course, is the conception of science held by methodological essentialists.

Interpreted in a somewhat different way, the thesis may place the traditional problem of learning versus performance in a different perspective. That is, if the problem of motivation in psychology is the problem of why organisms behave as they do, it is a problem of performance. Organisms behave; they do things; they perform. If so, then motivation has to do with how it happens that a particular behavior occurs, or is performed, on one occasion and not on another; motivation is concerned with what brings a behavior out of a behavioral repertoire rather than with what put it there in the first place.

On the other hand, the problem of learning is the problem of acquisition, or what put the behavior there in the first place. It has to do with how a particular behavior gets into the repertoire of, or is acquired by, a particular organism; learning is concerned with what puts a behavior into a behavioral repertoire rather than with what brings the behavior out of the repertoire. Both problems would seem to be resolved by stating the variables of which performance and acquisition are a function; those variables may explain why organisms behave as they do.

This answer to the question of motivation may be a slight improvement over that proposed by Littman (1958, pp. 136–37), who, after examining several different definitional approaches to the topic, concluded in a jocular way that

> motivation refers to processes or conditions which may be physiological or psychological, innate or acquired, internal or external to the organism which determine or describe how, or in respect of what, behavior is initiated, maintained, guided, selected, or terminated; it also refers to end states which such behavior frequently achieves or is designed to achieve whether they are conditions of the organism or environment; it also refers to the behavior engaged in, or aspects of that behavior, in respect of its organization, occurrence, continuation, reorganization, or termination with regard to past or present or future organic or environmental conditions; further, it refers to the fact that an individual will learn or remember or forget certain material, as well as the rate or manner in which these processes occur and the ease or difficulty with which they are altered, as well as to some of the processes or conditions which are responsible for this behavior; similarly, it determines how and what perceptual and judgmental activities and outcomes will occur, as well as some of the conditions and determinants of such activities and outcomes; similarly, it also refers to the fact of and the determinants of the occurrence and rate of affective process; finally, it describes and accounts for various individual differences which appear in respect of the vari-

> ous behaviors, processes, conditions, and outcomes referred to above. Motivation refers to any one or more of the above behaviors, conditions, processes, or outcomes in any combinations.

Obviously, a definition of this kind, and others like it, is so inclusive that it fails to distinguish motivation from the rest of psychology. That result may be all we can expect from a definitional approach to "Why?" questions, and especially to the one that seeks to find out why organisms behave as they do.

Chapter Ten

What Is Emotion?

Each one of us knows the answer to this question. We know it directly or intuitively. We have all experienced emotion in one form or another: anger, fear, grief, hope, joy, and love; most of us have agonized over a teenage romance, and some of us have even experienced something similar to it in our middle years. However, none of us may be able to say what emotion is, and, even if we could, we probably would be uncertain about our answer for the reasons advanced in earlier chapters of this book; human knowledge always lacks certainty and is never complete, so far as we know.

The subject of emotion was touched upon several times in the previous chapter. For example, McDougall asserted that organisms experience a primary emotion specific to each instinct. Young referred to the disorganization that occurs when a motive is blocked or in conflict with others as emotion. Lewin mentioned emotional tension with respect to conflicts that involved valences. Murray wrote about emotional needs. And McClelland stated that motives were affective associations; for him, all motivation was based upon emotion. Thus, the question of emotion seems to follow naturally from a discussion of motivation.

Many psychologists have shown an interest in the question of emotion. In fact, one of the earliest American psychologists, William James (1884), dealt with it in a direct way. In an essay entitled "What is emotion?" he introduced what was later to be called the James-Lange theory of emotion. Similarly, B. F. Skinner (1953), in *Science and Human Behavior,* asked "What is an emotion?" in the first section of his chapter on the subject of emotion.

The James-Lange theory of emotion is that bodily changes in emotion follow directly from the perception of the fact that excites the emotion and, in addition, that the feeling of those changes as they occur is the emotion; the theory was hyphenated because Carl Georg Lange (1834–1900), a Danish physiologist, conceived a similar theory at about the same time James conceived his theory. In somewhat different terms, and contrary to common sense or popular opinion, we do not cry because we feel sorrow, and we do not strike because we are angry. Rather, we feel sorrow when we cry and anger when we strike. The emotion does not mediate crying, and it does not mediate anger; both occur when their respective behaviors occur. Thus, for James, the feeling of bodily changes following perception of the fact that excites them is emotion; that feeling is what emotion is.

Another hyphenated theory of what emotion is has been named after two other researchers. It is the Cannon-Bard thalamic theory of emotion. This theory states that emotion is an emergency reaction and makes the body integrate whatever resources are available to it for coping with emergencies; the control center for the reaction is the hypothalamus. The theory presupposes that the sympathetic division of the autonomic nervous system is dominant when emotions occur; furthermore, behavioral reactions during emotion are controlled primarily by subcortical centers or by the hypothalamus. The theory was developed by Walter Cannon and Philip Bard; according to them, emotions are emergency reactions.

The above two theories are classified as physiological theories of emotion because of their emphasis upon physiology. There are other types of theories. For example, early in the history of experimental psychology, Wilhelm Wundt (ca. 1902) proposed a tridimensional theory of emotion. It was tridimensional in the sense that he thought there were three dimensions along which emotions might vary: pleasantness-unpleasantness, excitement-depression, and strain-relaxation. Thus, on the basis of introspection, a particular emotion might be identified by its location in the space defined by these three dimensions. According to Wundt, emotions were, therefore, tridimensional.

On the other hand, Wundt's student Edward B. Titchener, who was discussed earlier in the chapter on the nature of psychology as the founder of structuralism, argued that the characteristic element in emotions is affective states or feelings. Affection is the elementary mental process characteristic of feeling; feeling is a simple connection, or combination, of sensation and affection. Affection or feeling has three attributes and two qualities. The three attributes are quality, intensity, and duration. The two qualities are pleasantness and unpleasantness. Thus, emotions are affective states that are either pleasant or unpleasant, more or less intense, and of short or long duration.

An examination of the other systems of psychology with regard to representative views on emotion provides a sense of the range of ideas within the discipline about this subject. William James frequently is referred to as a functionalist. However, his views already have been presented as a physiological theory of emotion, and there are other functionalists who have had something to say about emotion. For example, Chaplin and Krawiec (1974, pp. 467–94) offer the views of Harvey A. Carr (1873–1954) as representative of this system.

According to Carr, emotions are the organic readjustments that automatically take place when an organism encounters a combination of conditions appropriate for a particular behavior. The different emotions can be most easily identified and defined by the behavioral situation that gives rise to them. Anger occurs when an organism confronts an obstacle that restricts its movements. Organic readjustments, such as quickened pulse, restriction of blood flow to internal organs, and increased respiration rate, make it possible for the animal or person to respond with greater intensity and speed. Hence, emotions are organic readjustments. Otherwise stated, an emotion is an organic commotion that subsides when an organism responds.

Apparently, Gestalt psychologists had very little to say about emotion in a formal or systematic way, perhaps because of their interest in perception and cognitive processes (cf. Chaplin and Krawiec, 1974, p. 476). Consequently, not much can be said about emotion within that system of psychology.

On the other hand, the classical behaviorist, John B. Watson (1878–1958), held that affective states and specifically pleasantness-unpleasantness were simply implicit muscular, as well as glandular, reactions. Most of them were sexual in nature. That is, pleasantness and unpleasantness were related either to sexual stimulation or to recovery from it, respectively, and that formed the basis for all affection.

Emotions were hereditary patterns of reaction that involved profound bodily changes but especially those in visceral and glandular systems. There were three basic patterns of these reactions in the human infant: fear, rage, and love. Fear was evoked by either a sudden loss of support or a loud sound; rage was evoked when an infant's movements were hampered; love was evoked when erogenous zones were stroked or manipulated. Thus, emotions were inherited patterns of reactions in which profound changes in visceral and glandular systems took place according to Watson; they were what emotion is.

Psychoanalysis is not commonly regarded as one of the classical systems of psychology, although it is frequently mentioned when they are discussed. Consequently, some reference to that conception of emotion seems appropriate. As is well known, Sigmund Freud (1856–1930) founded psychoanalysis as a method of treatment for behavioral disorders; it is not, therefore, a systematic or comprehensive account of the nature of psychology. Nevertheless, Freud had something to say about emotion that made a contribution to psychology if only that he gave emotion theoretical significance. According to Chaplin and Krawiec (1974, pp. 483–85), his main interest in emotion was anxiety.

For Freud, there were three major types of anxiety: objective anxiety, neurotic anxiety, and moral anxiety; each was related to some felt inadequacy between the ego and reality, the id, or the superego. Thus, objective anxiety occurred when the ego seemed inadequate with respect to the external world; neurotic anxiety occurred when the ego apparently was not adequate to the id; and moral anxiety occurred when the superego appeared more adequate than the ego.

According to Freud, anxiety in whatever form results from excessive demands placed on the ego. Primary objective anxiety is the product of birth trauma. As a result of that trauma, subsequent traumatic events of any kind are likely to evoke objective anxiety in a way similar to those described by the principle of generalization alluded to in chapter three on behaviorism. The anxiety apparently comes from an apprehension or anticipation of danger or trauma rather than from the danger or trauma itself; in the latter case, the reaction is fear.

Neurotic anxiety, according to Freud, has its origins in objective anxiety and so may be either a secondary reaction or a special form of objective anxiety. Those who display this type of anxiety are apprehensive about the demands of the id and the libido. It may be recalled that libido is presumed to be the source of energy for each one of us and that libido is sexual in nature. Consequently, neurotic anxiety occurs when we are apprehensive about the possible social consequences of engaging in forbidden sexual behavior; we might be less anxious if no sexual behavior were forbidden.

Moral anxiety also derives from objective anxiety, and so it too may be either a secondary reaction or a special form of objective anxiety. Moral anxiety occurs when our conscience or superego gets the best of us. More specifically, it results when we are apprehensive about the loss of love or goodwill from our parents and perhaps the possibility of punishment by them. As adults, the basis for this apprehension may not be conscious but nevertheless is related to possible loss or punishment. Thus, for Freud, emotion is anxiety which results from excessive demands placed on the ego.

Another theory of what emotion is has been called activation theory. It has a forerunner in the form of the Cannon-Bard theory but has developed into something more complex than its predecessor. According to Lindsley (1951), the theory is based upon five somewhat different but related kinds of experimental evidence. First, during emotion, an electroencephalogram appears to reveal a pattern of activation that involves changes in electrical activity of the brain. Second, this pattern can be elicited by electrical stimulation of certain areas of the brain. Third, destruction of other areas of the brain eliminates the pattern of activation. Fourth, behavioral changes that occur when those areas are destroyed are the opposite of excitation or activation. Fifth, lower areas of the brain seem to be responsible for the occurrence of the activation pattern.

The theory is that emotion is a condition of heightened arousal, where arousal may extend from a state of quiescence or sleep on the one hand to agitated states of excitation such as anger or fear on the other (cf. Fantino, 1973, pp. 291–95). These states are mediated by subcortical areas of the brain which function either to activate or to deactivate cortical areas of the brain. Thus, according to this theory, emotion is a state of heightened arousal.

There are other theories of what emotion is. For example, Plutchik (1962) reviewed seven of them. Aside from the James-Lange theory, the Cannon-Bard theory, activation theory, and psychoanalytic theory, he included attitude theory, motivational theory, and behavioral theory. Attitude theory was attributed to Nina Bull (1951); it is similar in some respects to the James-Lange theory. However, according to her view, emotion is considered a sequence of neuromuscular events. The initial step in the sequence is a postural set or a preparatory motor attitude, and it is this attitude upon which emotion depends. Thus, we do not cry because we are sorry, and we are not sorry because we cry. Rather, we are sorry because we are prepared to cry, are ready to cry, or are set to cry. It is the attitude or set that is, to use her word, "essential" to emotion; the essence of emotion is attitude. According to this theory, attitude is the basic nature of emotion and, of course, a theory that is expressed in that way suggests that methodological essentialism has not yet been completely replaced by methodological nominalism in this area of inquiry.

Robert W. Leeper (1948) proposed the motivational theory of emotion. According to this theory, emotions are motives because they arouse, sustain, and direct activity; they are processes that affect activity in those ways. Consequently, emotions are organized rather than disorganized responses. Nevertheless, emotions are motives that arouse, sustain, and direct activity; they are what emotion is.

Behavioral theories were introduced with that of Watson,

referred to earlier in this chapter. However, there are at least two other versions according to Plutchik (1962); one is by Tolman and the other is by Skinner. For Tolman, the relation between a stimulus and a response is what defines an emotion. More specifically, in the case of an emotion, the response does something to affect or change the stimulus in some way. Thus, a fear response protects the organism, whereas an anger response destroys the stimulus. Emotions are, therefore, drives or tendencies for an organism to exhibit behaviors that have a particular result. The behavior is a response-as-affecting-stimulus. For fear, the result is protection; for anger, the result is destruction; for love, the result is encouragement or enticement. Emotion is response-as-affecting stimulus.

Plutchik (1962, pp. 37–38) indicates that Skinner discusses three conceptions of emotion. In an early work, he refers to emotion as a state of strength, presumably of behavior, that is comparable to drive; however, it is not a response. In a later work, he rejects the view of emotion as a cause of behavior; for him, the only valid causes of behavior are the conditions of which it is a function. The third conception is that there are as many emotions as there are operations to define them, but, according to Plutchik, Skinner still seems to favor emotion as a state of strength or weakness in one or several responses brought about by those operations. If so, then emotion is a state of behavioral strength for Skinner.

However, in perhaps his best literary effort, written at the height of his career, Skinner (1953, p. 160) stated that

> the "emotions" are excellent examples of the fictional causes to which we commonly attribute behavior. We run away because of "fear" and strike because of "anger"; we are paralyzed by "rage" and depressed by "grief." These causes are in turn attributed to events in our history or present circumstances—to the things

> which frighten or enrage us or make us angry or sad. The behavior, the emotion, and the prior external event comprise the three links of our familiar causal chain.

With these remarks, he characterizes what, for most of us, is the commonly held, or commonsense, view of emotion. For example, we see a bear, are frightened, and run; the emotion is intermediate between sight of the bear and running, and, in fact, mediates running.

But Skinner does not agree with this commonsense view as pointed out by Plutchik. Furthermore, Skinner does not seem to settle for emotion as a state of behavior strength or weakness despite that interpretation of his views by Plutchik. In a later section of his chapter on emotion in *Science and Human Behavior,* Skinner (1953, p. 167) says that

> as long as we conceive of the problem of emotion as one of inner states, we are not likely to advance a practical technology. It does not help in the solution of a practical problem to be told that some feature of a man's behavior is due to frustration or anxiety; we also need to be told how the frustration or anxiety has been induced and how it may be altered. In the end, we find ourselves dealing with two events—the emotional behavior and the manipulable conditions of which that behavior is a function—which comprise the proper subject matter of the study of emotion.

If the proper subject matter for the study of emotion is emotional behavior on the one hand and the variables of which it is a function on the other, then Skinner apparently wants to know the laws of emotion, which, of course, is quite consistent with his approach to the experimental analysis of behavior. And he may want to know the laws of emotion in order to explain it; the laws of emotion explain emotion. Hence, emotion too may be defined by its laws. The laws of emotion are what emotion is; more will be said about this view later in this chapter.

Plutchik (1962) proposes his own theory of what emotion is. It is presented in the form of six postulates. The first is that, as with primary colors in color theory, there are a few pure or primary emotions; that is, there are eight emotions, or eight primary emotion dimensions. They are destruction, protection, incorporation, reproduction, deprivation, orientation, and exploration.

The second postulate of his theory is that all other emotions are some combination of the primary emotions. They are a mixture or a synthesis of the primary emotions. Historical evidence is used in support of this postulate. The idea of a few primary emotions which may combine to form more complex ones has been proposed on several different occasions in the history of philosophy and psychology. It is apparently a persuasive hypothesis, although it may preserve the tradition of physicalism in the sense that it perpetuates the notion that emotions are things analogous to colors.

The third postulate of the theory is that the primary emotions differ from one another both physiologically and behaviorally. There appears to be ample experimental evidence in support of this postulate, although that evidence may do nothing more than allow different distinctions to be made between different reactions considered to be affective.

The fourth postulate is that, in their pure form, the primary emotions are hypothetical constructs, intervening variables, or idealized states; their properties must be inferred from evidence, and it may be evidence of different kinds. Emotions are inferences or inventions; they are not things, like tables and chairs. They cannot be defined by denotation, or pointing; they are constructions (cf. Plutchik, 1962, pp. 50–51).

The fifth postulate is that pairs of primary emotions are polar opposites. Destruction is the opposite of protection; incorporation is the opposite of rejection; reproduction is the opposite of deprivation; and orientation is the opposite of exploration. Evidence from studies that used factor analysis of the data seems to support this postulate.

The sixth, and final, postulate of his theory is that emotions vary in intensity or level of arousal. They can be more or less intense, or the organism can be more or less aroused. Once again, factor analysis of data is used to support this postulate.

The point about emotions as inventions or inferences was made and developed somewhat further by Brown and Farber (1951, p. 466), who stated that

> at the outset, we would insist that the initial step in developing a theory of emotion is the frank recognition that emotion, if it is to enter usefully into scientific thinking, must be regarded as an *invention* or *inference* on the part of the psychologist. Emotion is not a *thing* in the simple, naïve sense that a chair or table is a thing. Like numerous other terms in common use, it cannot be defined by the simple, fundamental operation of "pointing at." It is not, we would insist, a directly denotable empirical datum, as such writers as Köhler have apparently maintained. But to deny to emotion the status of an immediately given real is not to imply that the concept is robbed of all scientific meaning or scientific reality.

A few sentences later, they state that "emotion is an inference or a scientific construct. Its scientific worth depends upon the degree to which it encompasses relationships among empirical events and thus leads to the more accurate understanding and prediction of behavior."

These authors cite as support for their argument remarks by the distinguished psychologist Edwin G. Boring (1933, pp. 7–8), who, in his book *The Physical Dimensions of Consciousness,* stated that one serious difficulty that enters into all discussion of this kind (consciousness) is the two-faced meaning of the term *experience*. Experience is the ground of all scientific induction. *This* experience is prior to reality. It underlies physics and psychology and enters into neither as a reality. Nevertheless, because psychologists have thought that experience enters immediately into psychology, they have spoken of their psychic reals as if they were experience. *That* experience is something different, a product of induction. *Real* experience is derived from *actual* experience. Real experience is what the psychologist knows about, but it is mediate and not direct.

We thus arrive at the first premise which underlies the discussion of this book. *Whatever exists as reality for psychology is a product of inductive inference*—usually from experimental data. To say that these realities are hypothetical constructs is not to alter the truth. The atom is a construct and a reality. Its validity is attested by its power of physical subsumption. The realities are always tentative and have to make their way and prove their worth. They are as temporary as all truth. There is no other scientific meaning for reality. . . .

If it be objected that this premise gives license to speculation, the reply is that speculation has always been free in science. The sanction for speculation is its fruitfulness, and the great scientists are those who have speculated wisely and successfully. The ultimate abandonment of dualism leaves us the physical world as the only reality. Consciousness will ultimately be measured in physical dimensions, and it is the purpose of this book to enquire how nearly we may approximate to this goal at the present time. We shall not always avoid the implications of dualism, and in fact we shall often have to begin with a dualism in order to annihilate it subsequently by the establishment of some identifying relationship between its terms. However, the goal is always the physical reality, the conceptual system that yields the most orderly view of nature. For such an aspiration no apology is required.

Thus, Boring, like Margenau (1950), who was mentioned in the chapter on the nature of science, contends that experience precedes reality or our conceptions of reality; that contention may seem contrary to common sense. Most of us are persuaded that there is a reality which precedes our experience of it rather than that our experience precedes reality. The former is, of course, the ontology of realism, whereas the latter is that of phenomenalism. Boring appears to be a realist in the matter, especially when he asserts that "the ultimate abandonment of dualism leaves us the physical world as the only reality." He could just as easily have come to the conclusion that the abandonment of dualism, mind-body dualism, leaves us with experience as the only reality, that is, the ontology of phenomenalism. Nevertheless, his remarks support the position that emotion is an invention or an inference and not a thing; emotion is a construction.

Several pages later in their article, Brown and Farber (1951, p. 469) state that

> *emotion may be retained as a separate construct if, and only if, it is empirically useful to posit a state or process that is related to antecedent events, to other constructs, or to behavior by a different set of functions from those that characterize other constructs within the theory.* Thus, emotion and some other hypothetical state might have identical properties as behavior determinants and could not, therefore, be differentiated on the response side alone. Nevertheless, it might still be useful to conceive of their differing in respect of their antecedent conditions and (or) in respect of their relations to other constructs. From the present point of view, the problem is not whether emotion does or does not exist. It is a question, rather, of determining whether certain behavioral phenomena can be accounted for satisfactorily in terms of other well-established constructs. If such is not the case, then the introduction of additional "emotional" constructs may be worthwhile.

This line of reasoning is not, of course, restricted to emotion. It applies also to any other terms such as *S-R connection, expectancy, ego, attitude, perception, consciousness,* or *libido,* which one

> might wish to introduce into a systematic analysis of behavior. If the psychologist concerns himself with whether or not the ego, for instance, is "really there" in the organism, he is wasting his time. His proper concern is whether by introducing the term ego, by specifying that the ego varies in such and such a manner with observable antecedents, and by assuming that the ego determines behavior in specific ways, behavior can be more satisfactorily explained than if no ego is assumed.

These statements were made without developing an argument for how it happens that psychologists as well as other students of psychology might waste their time wondering whether, for example, emotion is "really there." The authors do not demonstrate, either with argument or with evidence, that emotion is not a thing; they simply assert that it is not a thing. They may have done so because negative evidence, evidence against the existence of a thing, may be as difficult to obtain as positive evidence for its existence; both may be impossible to obtain. Similarly, a negative argument which denies the existence of a thing may not be persuasive since deciding between a negative argument and a positive argument may be nothing more than a matter of internal logical consistency. Consequently, negative assertion may be all that is defensible with regard to the concept of emotion as a thing; more will be said about this point later in this chapter. For now, it may be sufficient to note that, while emotion may not be a thing, the concept of emotion still may be useful.

Stated somewhat differently, some of the confusion about what emotion is may come from our ontological assumptions. As realists, we may suppose that emotion is a thing; as phenomenalists, we might be more likely to consider it a construction. Other sources of confusion about it have been discussed by Peters (1963). One is that the word *emotion* has been used with reference to three different kinds, or levels, of behavior: the emotion as felt by the person, the visceral response, and the observable response. A second source of confusion is, in his judgment, a disregard for the cognitive-perceptual aspect of emotion, or the emotion as perceived and understood. A third is the plethora of names for seemingly different emotions.

A fourth source of confusion is the apparent relationship between emotion and the doctrine of instinct. Each instinct has been presumed to have an emotion specific to it as in the case of William McDougall mentioned earlier in this chapter and in the chapter on motivation; more will be said about the doctrine of instinct in the next chapter. A fifth source of confusion about emotion, and perhaps the most basic one for Peters (1963), is reification (cf. Eacker, 1975, pp. 33–39):

> This is the same error which has infested so many of the concepts in psychology, including that of "mind" itself. Specifically, the error consists in assuming that, because we have a single noun-word, "emotion," something in nature must correspond to it, something as independent, as unique and unchanging, and as readily capable of entering subject-predicate relations with other things. This has led to treating emotion as a separate category or part of behavior, a force and an agent—it is still at the present day spoken of in this way in psychological literature. The actual data with which we are concerned are *emotional behaviors,* which are eventful, process-like in nature; this is crucial to keep in mind. It is certainly not always evident that these emotional behaviors differ in any obvious way from other forms of behavior. [Peters 1963, pp. 437–38]

Thus, Peters seems to agree with Brown and Farber that emotion is not a thing, but he goes on to suggest that our treatment of it as a thing comes from our tendency, on occasion, to reify our concepts. That is, we treat as things, things that are not things, or we treat them as something more than constructions. On the other hand, for Brown and Farber as well as Boring perhaps, emotion is a construction.

As indicated in previous discussions of ontology in this book, the problem, of course, is to know when things are things and when they are not things. A realist assumes there are things, whereas a phenomenalist constructs them, and there does not appear to be a way to resolve their differences. It is also of some interest, in the light of previous discussions about events in psychology, that Peters refers to emotional behaviors as eventful and process-like in nature; more will be said about emotional behavior and events in this and later chapters.

The remarks by Brown and Farber also reveal that the concept of emotion is used to explain other behavioral phenomena but, in turn, seems to require explanation. That is, for some, emotion may be treated as a behavior determinant and, therefore, used to explain behavior. But it also may be considered a state or process, if only a hypothetical one, which must also be explained; there are those who might find it rather paradoxical that something explains which itself must be explained. An alternative approach might be to accept Peters' suggestion and simply regard emotion as behavior to be explained, rather than as something that explains but also must be explained.

Most psychologists and other students of psychology seem to agree that emotion goes on within organisms, although perhaps only within the human organism. Several years ago, Skinner (1963) suggested that what goes on within an organism might be treated simply as behavior. For example, with respect to the copy theory of perception, Skinner (1963, p. 954) stated that

> the search for copies of the world within the body, particularly in the nervous system, still goes on, but with discouraging results. If the retina could suddenly be developed, like a photographic plate,

> it would yield a poor picture. The nerve impulses in the optic tract must have an even more tenuous resemblance to "what is seen." The patterns of vibrations which strike our ear when we listen to music are quickly lost in transmission. The bodily reactions to substances tasted, smelled, and touched would scarcely qualify as faithful reproductions. These facts are discouraging for those who are looking for copies of the real world within the body, but they are fortunate for psychophysiology as a whole. At some point the organism must do more than create duplicates. It must see, hear, smell, and so on, as forms of *action* rather than *reproduction. It must do some of the things it is differentially reinforced for doing when it learns to respond discriminatively.* The sooner the pattern of the external world disappears after impinging on the organism, the sooner the organism may get on with these other functions.

Thus, according to Skinner, seeing, hearing, smelling, tasting, and touching might be thought of as forms of action rather than reproduction. Perhaps the same can be said for emotion. As a form of action, it may be a behavior.

In other words, it may be that emotion does not need to be thought of as an intervening variable, or a hypothetical construct, or something else which helps to explain, or determine, behavior. Rather, emotion simply may be a behavior to be explained. More accurately, at least with regard to the position developed earlier about events in psychology, emotions may not be behaviors but events that take place within an organism—to be explained in the same way as any other events to be explained by psychologists.

Emotions are behaviors, events, or phenomena explained by the variables of which they are a function; they are explained by their laws. However, since they occur within an organism and are not, therefore, directly observable, there may be two kinds of laws required to explain them. One is the laws of overt behavior, and the other is the laws of covert behavior. The former are based on observable behaviors or events, whereas the latter are based on unobservable behaviors or events. Laws of overt behavior explain covert behavior by extrapolation, whereas laws of covert behavior explain covert behavior directly.

Observable behaviors are such things, events, or phenomena as walking, talking, bar pressing, and snoring. Unobservable behaviors are such things, events, or phenomena as seeing, hearing, touching, tasting, smelling, and thinking. Each may have their observable aspects but are, for the most part, not observable; they are covert.

We don't see someone seeing, and we don't hear someone hearing. We ask a person if he or she sees a sunrise or hears the sound of the ocean, and our companion responds with a yes or a no. Similarly, we don't feel what someone feels, taste what someone tastes, or smell what someone smells. We ask people whether they feel, taste, or smell, and they tell us whether they do or don't. The same seems to be true for emotions. We don't experience someone's emotions. We ask them whether they are angry, afraid, in grief, optimistic, happy, or in love, and they tell us whether they are or aren't; we don't experience their experiences.

Emotions seem to occur within us, like seeing, hearing, touching, tasting, and smelling, and we as observers inquire about them. The person of whom we inquire tells us about his or her emotions but that may be as close as we can come to knowing that person's emotions. Emotions seem to be amenable to measurement in the sense that people can talk about them, and so they can be treated as dependent variables. And, to the extent that emotion as a dependent variable can be related to other variables, whether dependent or independent, to that extent can laws of emotion be established in the manner discussed in the chapter on behaviorism.

If laws of emotion can be established, emotion can be explained in the empirical or functional sense, but we may find that we must relinquish our claim to it as an explanatory concept; we may not, in other words, be able to explain anything with it. We may not be able to explain anything with it because it would be an explanation of a different type than that used to explain emotion. To explain emotion functionally or empirically and then to use it as an explanation would contradict functional explanation; the practice would not be consistent with the meaning of that type of explanation. There may not be anything necessarily wrong with inconsistency, so long as we are clear about it, but most of us are not, and so the results of inconsistency may be confusion. Consequently, if we agree to explain emotion functionally or in terms of its laws, we may have to give it up as an explanatory concept within a theory of emotion; we may not then be able to use it in a theoretical explanation.

Some support for this position and for the ontological thesis of this book can be found in additional remarks by Brown and Farber (1951, p. 471) who state that

> finally, the traditional problem of determining how many basically different emotions "exist" is from the present viewpoint similar to that of determining whether *any* emotion "exists." The classical approach involved attempts to determine the number of different emotions that could be accurately identified from facial expressions or teased out by painstaking microanalyses of conscious contents. All efforts to reach agreement by these methods have apparently ended in failure. More progress might have been made if it had been asked instead whether observable behavior is most satisfactorily explained by the introduction of one or more constructs carrying an emotional label. If it appears desirable to have more than one, each must be shown to have relations that are in some way distinctive with reference to the other elements of the theory and to each other. Different emotions exist as realities for psychology only if different defining operations and interrelations can be clearly specified for them. If such specifications cannot be made

> the superfluous terms are scientifically inadmissible and must be coalesced or deleted; appeals for their continuance on intuitive or phenomenological grounds must be rejected.

These authors obviously have taken a theoretical approach to the problem of explanation (cf. Eacker, 1975, pp. 41–54). The position adopted here and stressed throughout this book is the functional, or empirical, approach to explanation. In the latter instance, emotion is explained by its laws. In the former instance, emotion is part of a conceptual system that is used to make predictions. Confirmed predictions are then used to attest to the validity of emotion. But, in that instance, the concept of emotion is used to explain behavior; it is not considered a behavior to be explained.

In the past, the problem of emotion apparently was to find out, or discover, just how many emotions there were. That interpretation of the problem seems to derive from the methodological essentialist, rather than nominalist, approach to science. It may be recalled that the former attempts to find out what things are, whereas the latter seeks to determine how they function. The latter seems to favor a functional, rather than theoretical, approach to explanation. These considerations suggest that, if emotion is explained in a functional sense, it may be inconsistent and confusing to then use the concept in a theoretical sense. To do so might contribute to continued reification of the concept.

For example, in a subsequent paragraph, Brown and Farber (1951, p. 471) remark that

> from an inspection of current treatments of emotion, it is apparent that a number of writers have regarded emotion not as a scientific inference but as an existential real. It is somewhat surprising, in view of the numerous excellent papers of the recent past on operationalism, that the difficulties accompanying the adoption of such a position require reiteration. The view that "real" emotions

> exist often includes the notion that they may be only partially encompassed by the specification of all the operations involved in their definition and measurement. Thus the experiential, behavioral, or physiological manifestations in terms of which emotion is typically defined are regarded as but imperfect and blurred reflections of the underlying *ding an sich.*

The thing in itself may not be knowable; the nature of the thing may not be knowable; what it is may not be knowable. And, the same may be true, aside from emotion, for psychology, behavior, stimuli, learning, reinforcement, motivation, and the other matters treated in prior and subsequent chapters of this book; they can only be known in relation to ourselves and not in themselves, probably.

On the other hand, some years prior to the statements made by Brown and Farber (1951), Max Meyer (1933, p. 292) made the following remark in an article entitled "That Whale among the Fishes—the Theory of Emotions":

> The whale has a twofold distinction among the fishes: first, when seen from a distance, it looms large among them; and second, on close examination it is found to be no fish at all. Something like that I predict for the theory of emotions among the theories in psychological textbooks and periodicals.
>
> Psychology, the science furnishing the foundations for human engineering, so young a science, need not feel ashamed of the fact that it has to cast out some humbug which has established itself within during its infancy. Physiology in its infancy had to rid itself of the theory of the four humors. Physics had to rid itself of the theory of the four elements, each "seeking" its place, if we make allowances for such unruly representatives as cork. Chemistry had to rid itself of the humbug called phlogiston. If psychology have its humbug, let it be only for a while.

At the close of his article, Meyer (1933, p. 300) made a prediction:

> I predict: The 'will' has virtually passed out of our scientific psychology today; the 'emotion' is bound to do the same. In 1950 American psychologists will smile at both these terms as curiosities of the past.

Brown and Farber apparently were not smiling in 1951. However, the concept of emotion still may be a relic of a bygone age, or a whale among the fishes, especially if psychologists continue to use it as an explanatory concept rather than as a descriptive one. This use of concepts will receive further discussion in the chapter on instinct. For now, it may suffice to repeat that, like other subjects treated in previous chapters, emotion is defined by its laws; the laws of emotion are what emotion is.

Chapter Eleven

What Is Instinct?

The last two chapters and this one seem to follow one from the other because, of course, at different times in the history of ideas and psychology, we have thought of ourselves as motivated by emotion, by instinct, or by both. This chapter is especially relevant to the last one because of the instinct doctrine, which, as mentioned in the last chapter, and depending upon who made use of it, emphasized a connection between emotion and instinct. For example, William McDougall (1911, p. 29), who has been referred to a rather surprising number of times in this book, argued for an emotion specific to each instinct:

> We may, then, define an instinct as an inherited or innate psychophysical disposition which determines its possessor to perceive, and to pay attention to, objects of a certain class, to experience an emotional excitement of a particular quality upon perceiving such an object, and to act in regard to it in a particular manner, or, at least, to experience an impulse to such action.

A short time before McDougall pronounced on the subject, William James (ca. 1890), who has also been mentioned a surprising number of times in this book, also found it necessary to talk about instinct. James (1950, p. 383) defined it as *"the faculty of acting in such a way as to produce certain ends, without foresight of the ends, and without previous education in the performance."*

Some years before James wrote about instinct, Charles Darwin (ca. 1859) stated that he (Darwin, 1898, pp. 319–20) would "not attempt any definition of instinct." Nevertheless, he felt that

> it would be easy to show that several distinct mental actions are commonly embraced by this term; but every one understands what is meant, when it is said that instinct impels the cuckoo to migrate and to lay her eggs in other birds' nests. An action, which we ourselves require experience to enable us to perform, when performed by an animal, more especially by a very young one, without experience, and when performed by many individuals in the same way, without their knowing for what purpose it is performed, is usually said to be instinctive.

His statement is remarkably similar to the statement by James and to those that appear in many introductory textbooks of psychology at the present time.

The concept of instinct appears to extend still further backward, into antiquity. In his article entitled "The Descent of Instinct," Frank Beach (1955) traced the idea from Heraclitus, through the Stoic philosophers, Aristotle, Albertus Magnus, Thomas Aquinas, and René Descartes to its early scientific usage by Darwin and his followers. And he extended his treatment of it forward through the anti-instinct revolution to current thought in psychology at the time he wrote; a more detailed account can be found in Diamond (1971).

Beach (1955) felt that the distinction between men and animals stressed by Heraclitus (ca. 400 B.C.) provided the basis for the origin and development of the instinct concept. Heraclitus thought there were two different kinds of creation. One was for gods and men; the other was for animals. The former were created as rational beings; the latter were irrational. Gods and men had souls; animals did not.

This distinction appears to have been maintained by the Stoics (ca. 100 A.D.), who supported the claim that, since men and gods were rational, they comprised a natural community. By contrast, since animals or beasts were either irrational or behaved "without reflection," they belonged to a different natural community. Beach felt it was noteworthy that the statements by Heraclitus and those by the Stoics appeared not to have been based on any empirical evidence beyond that obtained by means of casual observation.

On the other hand, Aristotle (ca. 300 B.C.) did not support the man-brute dichotomy, but instead placed man at the apex of a natural scale of intellectual powers that extended downward to the animals. Albertus Magnus (ca. 1250 A.D.) modified Aristotle's views so that they were more compatible with Scholastic theology. Albertus considered man unique because he possessed reason as well as an immortal soul. Consequently, man was not a part of Aristotle's natural order. Animals did not possess reason; they were directed by "natural instinct," and so were not free to act.

Thomas Aquinas, who was a pupil of Albertus, supported the man-brute distinction of his mentor. Animals possessed a sensitive soul as suggested by Aristotle, but men also received a rational soul sometime before they were born. Consequently, human behavior was based on reason; animal behavior was based on instinct. Around 1650, René Descartes lent still further support to the dichotomy with his machine analogy; animals were like machines, but men, in addition, were reasonable.

Darwin's understanding of the instinct concept already has been mentioned, along with that of McDougall and that of

James. However, according to Beach, one problem that arose during the early scientific application of the instinct concept was its overuse in attempts to explain behavior, especially that of humans; for some of those who used the concept, there were almost as many instincts as there were behaviors. A second problem that arose was what Beach referred to as the nominal fallacy (cf. Beach 1955, p. 403).

As its name suggests, the nominal fallacy is the fallacy of naming. It occurs when we name something and then assume that, since we have named it, we have explained it. An example might be someone who easily masters a new skill and "explains" it by saying that it's "instinctive." Our tendency to commit the fallacy may be related to the ancient and perhaps cross-cultural belief that to give a name to something, especially one's gods, was to place restrictions or limitations on it or to control it in some way. And since gods might take umbrage with such actions, they were not given names but referred to only indirectly. Giving a name to something, particularly our observations, may enable us to deal with them and hence to control them, but the act of giving them a name is not the same as explaining them (cf. Eacker, 1975, pp. 33–54).

According to Beach, these problems with the concept of instinct led to an anti-instinct revolution (1955), although Diamond (1971) has remarked that the revolution had been in progress for some time prior to the twentieth century. Nevertheless, the modern revolution began for Beach around 1920 and still has not ended, although there now may be some who treat the concept more kindly.

The modern revolution appears to have been started by Dunlap (1919), who asked the apparently metaphysical question "Are there any instincts?" The question is metaphysical, or at least existential, because it seems to inquire about the existence of instincts. Dunlap's answer was that there are no instincts in the sense in which that term most often was used at the time he wrote. At that time, he felt it most frequently was used in a teleological sense. That is, it grouped different actions or activities together on the basis of their consequences; the practice raises questions about purpose in behavior (cf. Eacker, 1975, pp. 103–16). Thus, the "instinct of flight" referred to all actions that resulted in removing an organism from a dangerous place. The "parental instinct" was all of those activities that resulted in the care and protection of children. The "reproductive instinct" included those that propagated the species. According to Dunlap, when used in that sense there were no instincts, largely because of the overlap between different activities that were classified as instincts.

Nevertheless, Dunlap acknowledged that there might be other ways of grouping activities that would allow them to be called instinctive:

> The grouping of activities into "instincts" may be admitted to be a useful procedure, if it be clearly understood to be a device of convenience only, similar to the arrangement of documents in a well ordered filing system. Just as there may be different filing systems for different purposes, so different classifications of "instincts" are useful, if they are not misunderstood as being anything more. We may classify "instincts" under two, four, twenty, or a thousand headings, according to the particular purposes we have in view, and may then use another classification for another purpose. [Dunlap, 1919, p. 309]

The teleological classification of instincts may be simply a matter of convenience as also may be the case for any other system of classification. However, to classify instincts in that or any other way does not mean that there are any. An error may occur when we treat the ways in which they are classified as conferring existence upon them or when we treat instinct as something more than a classification; that is, after we have classified instincts, we may then reify them or consider them things (cf. Eacker, 1975, pp. 33–39).

In a footnote, Z. Y. Kuo (1921, p. 648) observed that Dunlap did not deny the existence of instincts. Rather, what Dunlap did, according to Kuo, was object to the teleological groupings of instincts. He went on to say in that same footnote that he, Kuo, denied "not only the classification of instincts, but their very existence." Apparently, he was persuaded there were none, and, consequently, it was unproductive to inquire what they were. His position may baffle those of us who find it difficult enough to demonstrate that something exists, let alone that it doesn't. Nevertheless, for Kuo, there were no instincts.

What might seem to be another metaphysical treatment of the problem was published by Tolman (1923) in an article entitled "The Nature of Instincts"; the title suggests that we might expect to find out what instinct is, and we do, but perhaps only from Tolman's perspective. Contrary to Dunlap (1919), he favored, for several reasons, what he referred to as teleological and behavioral theories of instinct. First, all four of those he examined agreed in their definitions of instinct on the basis of innate drives or sets. Second, there was some agreement on the goals of those drives, although the language differed from author to author or theory to theory. Third, there was some agreement on what initiated the drive. Fourth, all four theories allowed for secondary responses that subserved the drive. Fifth, all four theories concurred that the drives were innate and permanent. Sixth, all agreed that the secondary responses that subserved the drive were modified by external conditions; they were not fixed and invariant. Thus, since the word *drive* appeared in all six points, Tolman seems to have favored a drive interpretation of instinct. That is, instincts were drives, and, according to Tolman, that was the nature of instinct.

In his book *Instinct: A Study in Social Psychology,* the sociologist or social psychologist L. L. Bernard (1924) dedicated one chapter to "The Nature of Instinct-Analysis and Criticism." In it, he reviewed what different authors at that time had to say about the nature of instinct. His review led him to make the following generalizations. The first was that nearly all of the psychologists to whom he made reference treated instinct as inherited. The second was that most psychologists and many neurologists favored a mechanistic view of instinct. That is, they regarded it as a complicated reflex or a congenitally determined specialized adaptation of the nervous system. His third generalization was that psychologists did not agree on the relationship between instincts and reflexes. Some felt that instincts were simply complex organizations of reflexes, while others either saw no difference between them or felt there was a conscious component to instincts but not to reflexes. His fourth was that many authors argued for the element of consciousness in instincts. His fifth generalization was that psychologists were not entirely clear about what they meant by including consciousness.

His conclusion about the nature of instinct seems to have been that

> an instinct is an inborn (in the sense of inherited) activity process which has remained intact, that is, which has not been remade through the process of learning or of making new adjustments by means of the substitution of new stimuli or responses for the old which were inherited. [Bernard, 1924, p. 84]

Thus, instincts for Bernard were inherited; they were inherited activities.

Although there appears to have been a modern revolution

against the concept of instinct in psychology, the current thought at the time Beach (1955) wrote about it was that instincts were complex patterned sequences of unlearned behaviors. He raised three criticisms of that view. The first was that few American psychologists had actually observed or studied behaviors they were inclined to categorize as instinctive; those who had were less likely to use the concept. The second criticism was that, despite our ignorance, we still prematurely classify some unanalyzed patterns of behavior as instinctive.

His third and perhaps most telling criticism of the concept was related to the supposedly unlearned aspect of the behavior, and it is of some interest that Verplanck (1955, p. 140) stated a similar view in earlier pages of that same journal:

> This forces psychology to deal with a two-class system, and such systems are particularly unmanageable when one class is defined solely in negative terms, that is, in terms of the absence of certain characteristics that define the other class. It is logically indefensible to categorize any behavior as unlearned unless the characteristics of learned behavior have been thoroughly explored and are well known. Even the most optimistic "learning psychologist" would not claim that we have reached this point yet. At present, to prove that behavior is unlearned is equivalent to proving the null hypothesis. [Beach, 1955, p. 405]

The null hypothesis is well known to those who have been exposed to statistical methods in psychology. For those who haven't, a brief explanation seems in order.

Briefly, the null hypothesis is the hypothesis of no difference between obtained and expected results in an experiment; obtained results are those that come from the experiment itself, whereas expected results are those expected by chance. The hypothesis of no difference between these two kinds of results is formulated for the express purpose of being rejected; it is rejected if the difference that is found is unlikely to have occurred by chance or has a low probability associated with it. That determination is made by means of inferential statistics, and only one positive instance of difference is required to reject the hypothesis.

To prove the null hypothesis would require that no difference ever be observed between obtained and expected results. In somewhat different terms, proof of the hypothesis requires proof of a universal statement and, in this case, a universal negative statement. However, universal statements, and especially negative ones, are not made in science, and they apparently are not made because we can never know when our observations are complete. This last statement is perhaps another way of saying that there are no absolutes in science; additional discussion of the null hypothesis and instinct can be found in Eacker (1975, pp. 122–23).

With respect to the problem of instinct, Beach (1955) seems to mean that, if instincts are unlearned, we have proved the universal negative statement that no learning variables have ever been shown to affect them; we have observed all instances and they are negative. But we apparently cannot know when all instances of something have been observed, at least with the methods of science as we now understand them, and so we probably can never know whether any behavior is unlearned through the use of those methods. Similarly, we may never be able to know whether all behavior is learned, which, of course, would be a universal positive statement. These implications of Beach's statement support the conclusion that to interpret instinctive behavior as unlearned is not tenable.

Beach surmised that efforts to eliminate the concept of instinct from psychology were not successful, because those who tried to do so did not question the assumption that behavior is inherited if it isn't learned. This classificatory scheme was not satisfactory for Beach, because it is based almost entirely on negative evidence. That is, it states that, if there is no evidence for learning, the behavior is not learned; it is unlearned or inherited. There may never be a time when we can know that all attempts to demonstrate the influence of learning variables have been exhausted. Thus, if instincts are unlearned, we may never be able to know with the methods of science whether there are any instincts; the same may be true for any other concept about which we may have a question of existence.

A problem that might arise if the two-class system is eliminated would be what classificatory scheme to use in its place. In other words, "if some behavior is neither learned nor unlearned, what is it?" The answer to this question could be that it is neither learned nor unlearned and that we still don't know what it is. A second answer might be that the question is not answerable, if it were possible to know which questions are and which are not answerable. A third is that the two-class system, the learned-unlearned classification of behavior, is not now and may never have been as useful as it appears to have been; it may have given us answers to questions about behavior that we are not yet ready to give.

Lashley (1939, p. 447) presented a somewhat different interpretation of the anti-instinct movement. He felt that it was directed mainly against "the postulation of imaginary forces as explanations of behavior." For him, "the psychology of instincts was a dynamics of imaginary forces and the anti-instinct movement was primarily a crusade against such a conceptual dynamism." As with motivation, so with instincts. A good many people still may suppose that it is motives or instincts which, in the form of impulses or forces, make us do what we do; Kuo (1921) also sensed this use of the instinct concept and opposed it.

The supposition that instinct is an impulse or force may be based on yet another uncritical extrapolation of physical principles to explain organismic behavior. The particular principle in this case is, once again, the principle of force; it was discussed earlier in the chapters on the stimulus and motivation. More precisely, the principle may be a somewhat distorted interpretation of Newton's third law of motion which states that for every action, there is a reaction, or that for every force exerted by one object on another, there is an equal and opposite force exerted by the second. Thus, physics may be thought to explain the movements of inanimate objects with the concept of force; forces are what make inanimate objects move. However, the force that is supposedly exerted on an object is simply equal to the object's mass times its acceleration. An additional supposition, or reification, performed by a good many people may be that there is a thing that is force to which the word *force* corresponds. That is, the word may be treated as though it corresponds to something other than to the relationship between mass and acceleration; force may be thought to exist.

When this line of reasoning is pursued in the case of animate objects, it might be further supposed that, since they also are objects, but objects that move by themselves, the forces that make them move are inside of them. Furthermore, these forces take the form of drives, impulses, instincts, or motives, and they are what make us do what we do. Such an explanation may explain our behavior for someone entranced with a rudimentary understanding of physical principles, but, contrary to popular belief, psychology is not that, or any other, form of physics and doesn't pretend to be. Behavior is not explained by saying that it is caused by forces, and it probably isn't explained by any other physical principles. To explain it, we need to know its laws or the variables of which it is a function. Only some of those laws are known at the present time, and only a few of them pertain to instinctive behavior.

In what appears to have been a rather thorough and comprehensive analysis of the instinct concept, Arthur Ginsberg (1952) held that there were at least eight logical fallacies that have been committed by instinct theorists. He referred to them as contingent connotation, ad hoc postulation, reasoning by analogy, reductionism, simplification, misplaced concreteness, inexhaustive elimination, and false dichotomization. He claimed that the fallacy of contingent connotation occurs when it is assumed that two words connote the same thing but, in fact, may not. Thus, there has been general agreement that instincts are innate or unlearned, but no one is entirely clear about that to which each word refers.

The fallacy of ad hoc postulation describes the case where an assertion either does not follow in a deductive way from the axioms and postulates of a theory or else is formulated for only one particular set of circumstances. Ginsberg felt that this fallacy applies to the situation in which aggressive behavior is explained by appeal to an aggressive or pugnacious instinct; another is where sympathetic behavior is explained by an altruistic instinct. Reasoning of this kind he considered similar to the Aristotelian notion that "fire rose not because of complex chemical alterations involving gaseous transformations and interchanges between combustible materials and exterior circumstance, but because inherent in fire was a propensity for levity, i.e., its essential nature consisted of a 'power' to rise" (Ginsberg, 1952, p. 242); for the sake of that power, a too obvious pun is hereby reluctantly resisted. With that statement, Ginsberg provides support for the thesis that essentialism may be at least one of the factors that contribute to this fallacy and, therefore, to the problem of instinct in a more general sense.

The fallacy of reasoning by analogy occurs when resemblance is interpreted as explanation. Instinct theorists commit it when they point out similarities, for example, between bicycle-riding behavior of human beings and web-building behavior of spiders and then assume that the latter explains the former or vice versa. It may be that they are not quite certain in this case when to apply the term *habitual* and when to apply the term *instinctual;* that is, habits may appear to be instincts to some people, especially when they turn instinct theorist.

The fallacy of reductionism is the propensity to suppose that the subject matter of psychology is reducible to, or can be explained by, the laws or principles of biology. According to Ginsberg, it occurs with respect to the problem of instinct when instincts are "explained" by some perhaps rather vague reference to the inherited constitution of the animal that exhibits them. Thus, when a theorist concludes that a particular behavior is the result of an animal's innate constitution, he or she commits the fallacy of reductionism. Such an account may be very much like saying "it's the nature of the beast."

The fallacy of simplification is the supposition that the simplest explanation of something is the correct one; it is akin to but is by no means the same as the law of parsimony in science. The law of parsimony is that the simplest explanation which takes into account everything that is to be explained in a particular instance is the preferred explanation. The law does not state that the simplest explanation is the correct one; it simply asserts that the preferred explanation is the one that meets the conditions of the law. The fallacy of simplification is that the simplest explanation is the correct one. It occurs when instincts are considered innate and innate is interpreted simply as a matter of genetic inheritance; in such a case, the fallacy may include that of reductionism (cf. Eacker, 1975, pp. 45–46).

The fallacy of misplaced concreteness is the confusion of abstract and concrete categories or concepts. That is, when it is supposed that an abstract concept refers to something concrete or that what the concept denotes is a thing, the fallacy of misplaced concreteness has been committed. Thus, if the concept of instinct is an abstract concept that refers to a particular category of behaviors, it may be a fallacy to suppose that those behaviors possess some characteristic that exists or that the word denotes a thing.

This fallacy is obviously related to the problem of reification in psychology (cf. Eacker, 1975, pp. 33–39) in the sense that reification occurs when we treat as things, things that are not things, if that determination can ever be made; if, in fact, instinct is simply an abstraction, then to treat it as a thing is to reify it. However, the fallacy is also related to the problem of universals as discussed in the first chapter, and, therefore, the treatment of this fallacy here lends still further support to the thesis that essentialism as the search for essences or the problem of universals is the source of many of the questions treated in this book.

The fallacy of misplaced concreteness is related to the problem of universals in the following way. If the concept of instinct is an abstract, rather than concrete, concept, it is much like the concept of color. Color is an abstraction. No one thing is a particular color. We treat color as a characteristic of things but not itself as a thing; it may be a characteristic of many things. If so, it is a universal property of things, if there are any, and hence the problem of universals, or, essentialism. Are there any universals? There certainly seem to be. Are universals things? There certainly seems to be some doubt. No definitive answers to these questions are immediately apparent, and none are imminent, so far as can be ascertained at the present time.

The fallacy of proof by inexhaustive elimination is to assume that all but one of many possible solutions to a problem have been examined and then eliminated and, therefore, that the one remaining solution is the correct one when, in fact, all possible solutions have not even been identified, let alone examined and then eliminated. Ginsberg thought that this fallacy occurs in the case of instinct when it is argued that imitation of parents, for example, can be eliminated as the basis for nest-building behavior in birds; the offspring were not around when the nest in which they were hatched was built, and the parents are not around when the time comes for their offspring to build nests. Therefore, it has no history of learning in the lifetime of the offspring and so must be instinctive in the sense that it is a pattern of behavior maintained and controlled by inherited neuroanatomy. However, learning and inheritance may not exhaust the possibilities for explaining nest building in birds. Another possible solution is to explain it by the laws of nest-building behavior, which apparently still remain to be determined; that is, an adequate explanation of nest-building behavior may only require that we know the variables of which it is a function.

The eighth fallacy explicated by Ginsberg is the fallacy of false dichotomization, which is to classify things into what appear to be two mutually exclusive categories when, in fact, they can't be classified that way. It occurs when behavior is classified as either learned or instinctive. There may be many other ways to classify behaviors than simply as learned or instinctive. For example, some psychologists have had occasion to talk about operants, respondents, and reflexes; they could very easily include instincts in the list. Furthermore, a behavior occurs in an environment, and the environment, in turn, affects it; consequently, it cannot be simply a matter of instinct interpreted as innate behavior.

These fallacies have all been discerned by Ginsberg in his review of the literature on instinct. Whether or not they are fallacies, as he says they are, they may be subject to some rather considerable scholarly debate, especially to the extent that they are regarded as either mutually exclusive in kind or exhaustive in number; for that matter, there may be some debate over whether they are even applicable. However, Ginsberg does adduce some evidence that fallacies have been committed by instinct theorists from time to time in the history of the concept, and so there is a good chance that some of them have.

If so, a question arises about what to do with the instinct concept if fallacies in its use are to be avoided. Ginsberg tries to reconstruct it. Another solution is to throw it out; instinctivists obviously might object to that practice. Another solution has been proposed by Ross and Denenberg (1960); their solution has implications for behavioral psychology which apparently have not yet been explored.

Ross and Denenberg (1960) have proposed that the concept of instinct may have been used in at least two different ways over time. One use is explanatory; the other is descriptive. It is used in an explanatory way when it purports to answer the question of why a certain behavior takes place. Thus, birds migrate because it is instinctive for them to do so. Bears hibernate for the same reason. The answer works so long as it terminates further inquiry. If it doesn't, further inquiry may reveal that the answer is empty, circular, or a nominal fallacy.

An answer is empty if it makes no reference to observables. It is circular if it asserts the law of identity or identifies the subject of an explanatory sentence with the predicate. It is a nominal fallacy, as stated earlier, if naming a phenomenon is assumed to be the same as accounting for it. Thus, the statement that bears hibernate because it is instinctive is empty if "instinctive" does not refer to observables other than the behavior of hibernation. It is circular if "instinctive" simply refers back to the behavior of hibernation. And it is a nominal fallacy if "instinctive" simply names the behavior of hibernation. The person who gives the answer and the one who receives it may not be entirely clear about just what they are doing.

When used in a descriptive way, the word *instinct* is simply a category for certain kinds of behaviors, such as the homing of pigeons, the migration of fish and fowl, the mating behavior of estrus females, the web building of spiders, the nest building of birds, and the hibernation of bears. These behaviors are, according to Ross and Denenberg (1960) complex, unlearned, innate patterns of behavior. However, it may be that what distinguishes them from other behaviors is simply that they are discriminably different from operants, reflexes, and respondents; that is, it is more useful to place them in a category of their own.

When simply placed in their own category apart from operants, reflexes, and respondents, instinctive behaviors are not thereby explained. Rather, they are merely distinguished from the others, if only on the basis that they have always, or at least traditionally, been regarded as instinctive. An alternative basis for doing so may be that what distinguishes instinctive behaviors from other behaviors is that they are complex, patterned sequences of behavior which challenge us for an explanation. However, we cannot say whether they are either learned or innate for the reasons advanced by Beach and discussed earlier in this chapter.

What research has already been performed on instincts suggests that they are affected, or influenced, by environmental conditions or variables, and, to the extent that those conditions are considered to be learning variables, they are affected by learning. Other conditions not considered to be learning conditions may also affect them. For example, there may be some that are thought of as motivational conditions and others as perceptual conditions. Regardless of how they are classified, it is nevertheless possible to inquire about how those conditions affect the behavior placed in the category of instinct. And, to the extent that inquiry is concerned with environmental conditions related to those behaviors, to that extent is the inquiry concerned with the laws of those behaviors. In short, it is concerned with the laws of instinct.

Furthermore, if the laws of instinctive behavior explain it, then, as with other topics treated in previous chapters, the laws of instinctive behavior may answer the question of what instinct is; it is the laws of instinctive behavior. The laws of instinctive behavior are what instinct is.

In a fairly recent treatment of instinct, Herrnstein (1972) wrote about "Nature as Nurture: Behaviorism and the Instinct Doctrine." In that article, he argued that B. F. Skinner supported a hormic view of drive similar to the views of instinct held by William McDougall. His argument was based on Skinner's early use of the drive concept, which appears to have been a verbal behavior that extinguished rather quickly. In its place, Skinner is interpreted by many to have substituted a purely empirical approach to the analysis of behavior which, when extrapolated to that of instinct, might result in some such approach as that discussed in the immediately preceding paragraphs. Apparently, no one has so far adopted that position, but, on the basis of the literature on instinct examined here, it may be a type of inquiry whose time has come.

Chapter Twelve

What Is Human Nature?

"Human nature" may be one of the easiest and quickest ways we human beings have invented for answering questions we have about ourselves. Almost everyone at one time or another has asked, or will ask, "Why did so-and-so do that?" and was, or will be, told "Oh, that's just human nature!" as though "everyone knows" what human nature is, and so inquiry need go no further.

However, it is probably safe to assert that each one of us has a somewhat different conception of what human nature is, including instinct, emotion, motivation, and the other topics already discussed. Our conceptions may be alike in some of their particulars but quite unlike in many others. Consequently, the answer to the question "Why did so-and-so do that?" may not be so obvious as it at first might appear.

Although there are probably as many different conceptions of human nature as there are people who have inquired about it, several conceptions have emerged in the history of ideas that have a common theme. The distinguished and scholarly psychologist Robert Macleod presented what he referred to as five "classic" doctrines of man in his book *The Persistent Problems of Psychology* (1975). Later in that book, Macleod (1975, pp. 146–55) dealt with the nature of human nature more directly. Much of the following discussion is based on his work.

For Macleod (1975, p. 44), a doctrine of man is a self-consistent interpretation of man based on assumptions that cannot be shown to be right or wrong. Apparently, they cannot be shown to be right or wrong because the methods of science, and especially experimentation, are not relevant to them. There does not appear to be any way in which we could perform an experiment to test the hypothesis that man is, for example, the "measure of all things," which is the first of the doctrines discussed by Macleod.

To test the hypothesis, or doctrine, that "man is the measure of all things" would seem to require that some creature other than man perform the experiment. If it were otherwise, men would be the measure of themselves with their own methods. Furthermore, even if it were possible to have some other kind of creature perform the experiment, man at some point would still have to interpret the results of the experiment for himself, which, the creature might argue, confirms the hypothesis regardless of whether the results were positive or negative. In addition, the creature might not be trained in the methods of science or insist on its own methods, which we in turn might reject.

Consequently, it appears, on the basis of a rather casual logical analysis, that this first classical doctrine of man is universally true. It cannot be disconfirmed that "man is the measure of all things." Otherwise stated, the doctrine cannot be falsified and therefore seems quite properly to belong in a book concerned with problems of metaphysics and psychology (cf. Popper, 1965, p. 256).

However, if it is possible for one doctrine of man to be

universally true on a logical basis, it seems equally likely that a second doctrine or a third might also be true on such a basis. And, if more than one of them is logically true, the question immediately arises of how that can be so, especially when they might contradict one another; most of us find it difficult, if not impossible, to believe that more than one answer to a question could be true.

Regardless of our beliefs, it may be that all of the classical doctrines of man are true, contradict one another, and are wrong, especially if we acknowledge a distinction between what is true on the basis of logic and what is true on the basis of observation. Before that distinction is examined, however, more needs to be said about Macleod's classic doctrines of man.

They represented "sincere attempts to solve the persistent problems that arise when one wonders about the nature and the attributes of man" (Macleod, 1975, p. 83); that kind of wonder is another instance of the search for essences or essentialism. Nevertheless, there were five of them: the relativistic doctrine, the materialistic doctrine, the idealistic doctrine, the teleological doctrine, and the religious doctrine.

Protagoras (480–411 B.C.) appears to have had primary responsibility for the relativistic doctrine. As indicated above, it is the doctrine that "man is the measure of all things." That is, all things are relative to someone who perceives, and it is man alone, so far as we know, who perceives. Hence, everything that is known is at least in part a function of the knower. Knowledge may go beyond the knower to a real state of affairs in the universe, but it cannot be known that human knowledge is about a real state of affairs since it is man who, finally, knows or claims to know. What appears to be the case and what is the case may be quite different, but all that can be known is what appears to man to be the case. Consequently, "man is the measure of all things," and that is the nature of human nature or what it is that is essential about man, according to Protagoras.

This doctrine of man may not appear to be as pervasive as the others to be examined. However, it quite obviously is related to the metaphysics of phenomenalism since it assumes that human sense experience is, at least, what there is, and only we can know it. In addition, it is found within psychology to the extent that there are those psychologists who recognize that results of an experiment, for example, can be contaminated by "experimenter bias," or that our hypotheses may come from unexplicated theories of ourselves, or that objectivity in psychology is a matter of intersubjective testability rather than "knowing things as they are." These changes in our conception of what we do seem to come more from the influence of pragmatism, logical analysis, empiricism, and positivism than they do from the relativistic doctrine of man. However, they all appear to have the common theme that human knowledge is, finally, human; the thing as it is may not be knowable, if indeed there is a thing as it is.

The second classical doctrine of man is attributed to Democritus (ca. 460–370 B.C.). For Democritus, man is matter. The nature of all things, including man, is matter. Man is a part of physical nature to be explained by physical laws. The fundamental reality is matter, and, thus, everything, including man, can be explained by means of physical laws. There is nothing in the way man is constructed or functions that cannot eventually be restated in terms of the laws of physics. Physical science can be extended to include all of the phenomena of human behavior and experience. Man is matter and that is the "essence," the essential characteristic, of man.

This materialistic doctrine of man, or conception of human nature, appears to be quite pervasive. Psychologists and nonpsychologists have assented to this doctrine in the past, whether tacitly or otherwise, and still do so. It probably is the doctrine that has led psychologists and other students of psychology to look to the physiology of an organism for an explanation of its behavior rather than to the variables of which that behavior might be a function. In addition, this conception of human nature probably has induced us to think of behavior as motivated by some impulse to action, or a force, or a source of energy within the organism, as indicated in the chapters on motivation, emotion, and instinct. We think this way because of a rather crude analogy between this conception of human nature and physical objects.

Although that analogy has been discussed in prior chapters, a restatement of it here in a somewhat different form may help to persuade psychologists and other students of psychology that alternative formulations may prove to be more useful. The analogy may be restated in the following way. If man is matter and is to be explained by physical laws, then human movement or behavior is to be explained by physical laws or the laws of physics. Human movement occurs in at least two ways. In the first, an external force appears to be applied; in the second, there does not appear to be an external force. However, since an external force appears to be applied in the first instance but not in the second, the force in the second instance must be internal rather than external, assuming that all objects move because of force. Human beings sometimes are moved by an external force as any other object is. On the other hand, human beings sometimes move on their own. When they do, they must move because of internal forces. If it were otherwise, they would either not move or their movement would be supernatural, that is, inexplicable with natural laws.

If generalized, the analogy might take the form: inanimate objects move because of external forces; animate objects move because of external and internal forces. The former has been found to be rather useful in physics. The latter has been tried rather extensively in psychology but has not been found to be especially useful, although it has a tremendous appeal to common sense. Psychologists may eventually give it up; nonpsychologists may find it difficult to give up because it provides such easy and ready explanations for why we do what we do. It may appear to a good many people that the only reply they can make to the statement "We do what we do because of internal forces" is simply "Oh!" Similar physical analogies appear to be present in common sense explanations of learning and motivation; more has been said about them in the chapters devoted to those subjects.

Macleod's third doctrine of man is what he refers to as the idealistic doctrine. He attributes it to Plato (427–347 B.C.). According to this doctrine, man is a rational being. Reason allows man to know reality, although reason may often be influenced by irrational elements in man. The human soul has three fundamental powers: appetite, spirit, and reason. To achieve the good life, control over appetite must be accomplished by reason with the assistance of spirit. Reason is man's highest attainment; it allows him to go beyond the world of appearances to the world of ideas, which are the only things that are real.

Appetite defines man's lower nature, and, as might be expected, the appetites are located in the lower parts of the body. They are necessary for living and cannot be ignored, but they are irrational and must be controlled; they include such things as hunger and sexual desire. Man's slightly higher nature is spirit, and since it is equated with courage is located in the heart. It helps to explain ambition, perseverence, and daring, but it too must be controlled or it may get out of hand. That control is provided by reason. Reason is man's highest nature and is located in the head perhaps because it is that part of man that is most elevated. Reason allows man to conquer his appetites, control his spirit, and live in the world of ideas rather than appearances.

Thus, the essence of man is nonmaterial, or ideas. He comes into contact with the material world but is not a part of it. He is a rational being whose highest faculty is reason; reason is a feature of man that may make him different than animals. Man is to be understood on the basis of a logical, or rational, analysis of his experience since it is reason that makes it possible for him to know the essence of reality, which, of course, is ideas.

This conception of human nature is also quite pervasive. Almost everyone accepts the proposition that man is a rational being. To suggest otherwise is to flirt with the absurd. "Everyone knows" that man's actions are governed by reason, at least for the most part. When we are irrational, it is simply because reason is, for the moment at least, not in control. In addition, "everyone knows" that to solve a problem or to understand anything, especially other people and ourselves, all we have to do is reason about them. Eventually, a solution will occur to us that appears to be rational, which means that it was arrived at through reasoning.

However, as suggested by Freudian theory and by the foregoing account of the relativistic doctrine of man, what appears to us to be the case may not, in fact, be the case. To the extent that we ever seem rational, appear to solve a problem, or understand anything, we may do so for very different reasons than those that occur to us when we reason about them, if, indeed, reasons are ever relevant to what we do. It is entirely possible that our solutions may only appear to be solutions as the problems appear to us and for the reasons we give or invent to solve them. In fact, much of human behavior may be irrational rather than rational; nevertheless, it still may be lawful.

This last statement may appear to border on the absurd. It may do so because of the difficulty we may have in trying to comprehend how human behavior, for example, can be irrational or unreasonable and at the same time lawful or predictable. The absurdity may arise only if rational is equated with lawful. When they are not equated, the absurdity seems to disappear. In such a scheme of things, both irrational and rational behavior may be lawful. That is, there may be found to be variables of which those behaviors are a function to the extent that they may be considered to be behaviors.

Thus, a behavior may be rational and lawful. It may be reasonable and lawful. It may be irrational and lawful. Or it may be unreasonable and lawful. The latter may be what we mean by emotional behavior, which, as "everyone knows," may be unreasonable but nevertheless quite predictable. To be rational is not necessarily to be lawful and vice versa; the two terms may, on close analysis, be shown to refer to rather different events, observations, phenomena, processes, or things.

The fourth doctrine of man discussed by Macleod is the teleological doctrine; it is attributed to Aristotle (384–322 B.C.). According to this doctrine, man is a part of nature in the sense that he is composed of matter. His essence or soul, however, is the form that matter takes, and gradually becomes what it is as man develops. The soul, or essence, or nature of man is not independent of the body. It is the form of body, and the body operates in accord with it. Soul is the way in which the body is organized, and it has characteristics that can be determined only by means of direct and systematic observation. "In his speculation about 'essences' Aristotle was carrying on the rational tradition of Plato, a tradition that was to dominate psychological thought for many centuries" (Macleod, 1975, p. 68).

That tradition may still be with us, especially when there are psychologists and students of psychology today who express an interest in the nature of human nature or, for that matter, any of the other questions examined in this book. The search for essences displayed by rational psychologists has a long history within the discipline of psychology, as suggested in the above quotation, and it may be with us for some time to come. However, it may have given rise to at least some questions for which no answers can be found with the empirical methods of science. The nature of human nature, the essence of human nature, may be one of those things that cannot be known by means of empirical investigation except, perhaps, by way of generalization.

That is, a direct experimental analysis of human behavior very probably will not tell us what human nature is. However, we may be able to generalize across a good many analyses of human behavior and empirical investigations from other disciplines and then make such a statement. But that sort of approach is inductive. Rational methods are primarily deductive; they do not require observation. They may allow us to say what human nature is without observation, but, when they do, we may in turn find it difficult to demonstrate that what we have said corresponds to a state of affairs, whether observed, real, or imagined.

The difference between rational methods and empirical methods, or rational truth and empirical truth, is the difference between reason and observation, or logic and sense experience, or deductive and inductive logic. The method and limitations of induction have been discussed elsewhere (Eacker, 1975, pp. 141–52). Briefly, the least complex case of induction is induction by simple enumeration. Induction by simple enumeration refers to the case where a general statement is made about particular instances. Particular instances of some event are observed and enumerated by someone, and then he or she makes a more general statement about them. Thus, for example, a number of space travelers on different occasions might report the presence of little green people living on the other side of the moon but nowhere else on the moon or in the universe, and someone back at the command post might conclude that little green people live on the other side of the moon. That conclusion involves an inductive leap from particular instances to all instances, based on an assumption about the uniformity of nature. The assumption is that nature continues uniformly in the future as in the past. That assumption is the chief limitation of the method since it cannot be established that nature is uniform except, so far as we know, by induction.

Deduction is somewhat different than induction and it, too, has its limitations (see Appendix). In general, deduction refers to a conclusion drawn from a general statement; a particular statement is made based on a more general one. In addition, a deductive conclusion is considered valid if the rules of deductive inference have been followed to reach the conclusion; most of us regard a valid conclusion true, although a logician might think otherwise. To take one of the simplest examples, the following conclusion is valid or, some might say, true: Little green people live only on the other side of the moon; C3PO is a little green person; therefore, C3PO lives on the other side of the moon. The conclusion "C3PO lives on the other side of the moon" is valid, or true, because the second statement, "C3PO is a little green person," asserts the antecedent of the major premise, "Little green people live on the other side of the moon." The rules of logic were followed when the conclusion was reached. Therefore, the conclusion is true, or logically valid, whether or not there are little green people living on the other side of the moon. The conclusion is true regardless of any observations that might be made to test it. (As "everyone knows" who has seen the moving picture "Star Wars," C3PO was not a person, but an android. In addition, he/she/it was not green but gold.) Many conclusions about human nature and human behavior have been reached in the history of psychology with methods similar to this one. They are still being used.

When a conclusion of this kind, or any other, is tested under controlled conditions of observation and confirmed, it is empirically true rather than logically valid or logically true. Thus, if we wanted to know whether C3PO lived on the other side of the moon, we would have to make some observations that would confirm it lives there. When we did and confirmed that it did, our conclusion would then be both logically and empirically true, although our major and minor premises might still be in error. In summary, a logical truth requires only that the rules of logic be followed for it to be valid, or true. An empirical truth requires that some observations be made to confirm it; if they do, it is empirically true.

Aristotle's doctrine of man, like those of the others, appears to have been arrived at primarily with rational methods. Not only is his doctrine rational, it is teleological to the extent that he states what human nature is and the purpose it serves. Man is an animal, but he is more than just an animal; he is rational. He grows, reproduces, perceives, and moves. He has appetites that must be controlled. He has senses that allow him to respond to his environment. He is mobile and, thus, can escape dangerous situations and work toward distant goals. Man is a rational animal who does things, and he does things because it is his nature to do them; what he does are his purposes. It is the nature of man to do what he does. He does what he does because it is human nature to do so; he does what he does because he is what he is. Such a conception of human nature may give answers to questions we have about the subject, but it is obvious that those answers may be vacuous.

The fifth doctrine of man examined by Macleod is what he calls the religious doctrine, although it might more appropriately be called the Christian doctrine since the only religion that is mentioned is Christianity. Paul (died ca. 67 A.D.) formulated one of the first versions of this doctrine. For him and the early Christians, God is the ultimate reality, creator of the universe, and shaper of man's destiny. God is a spirit that transcends space and time—omniscient, omnipresent, and omnipotent. Man is also a spirit in the sense that contained within him is at least an element of divinity.

However, man is spirit that is encased within a mortal body. It is only as man overcomes the frailties of the body that complete communion with God is achieved. By so doing, man reaches his true goal, which is the glorification and eternal enjoyment of God. Man fell from a state of grace into a state of sin and now strives to reestablish unity with God. Christ is an intermediary between man and God; his sacrifice made man's salvation possible.

Man is an immaterial and immortal being who depends upon his God, rather than his reason, for all that he achieves. The Good Life is a matter of clear thinking and, perhaps more importantly, right willing. Those who accept the will of God as a matter of faith rather than reason will know what is true and will do what is right. There is a natural and a supernatural order to things; the latter gives direction to the former. When what is true and good has been revealed by a supernatural being, only then can man be certain of what truth and goodness are.

Another version of the Christian doctrine was expressed by Augustine (354–430). For Augustine (Macleod, 1975, pp. 76–77), only the spirit is real. God is the supreme spirit who created the universe according to plan. In the process, God made it possible for man to know what is true with certainty. To do so, one has only to observe one's own experience. Eternal truths have been implanted in us by God, and we can recognize what they are if we submit to the discipline of faith. Temporal things are known through observation of nature, or science; eternal things are known through "divine illumination," or faith. It is possible for men to learn by studying nature, but they can know with certainty only by means of divine revelation.

A third version of the Christian doctrine of man can be found in the writings of Thomas Aquinas (1225–1274). According to Macleod (1975, p. 81), Aquinas held that the human soul had three sets of faculties: organic, sensory, and rational. As with Aristotle, the organic faculties were related to generation, growth, and nutrition. There were three classes of the sensory faculty: the sensory-cognitive faculty, the sensory-orectic or appetitive faculty, and the motor faculty. The sensory-cognitive faculty was comprised of what was considered at the time to be five senses and the more general faculties of imagination, judgment, memory, and perception. Man was able to survive and reproduce because of the sensory-orectic faculties; they were the appetites of his lower nature. He was able to move about because of his motor faculty.

The organic and sensory faculties operate in and through the body and are parts of man's lower nature. By contrast, the rational faculties are not dependent upon the body, and the procedures of natural science cannot be used to understand them. Intellect and will are the two types of rational faculty. Intellect may be active or passive, and the powers of reasoning and understanding are contained within it. Will helps to guide man toward knowledge of God; it is often called the "intellectual appetite." As such, intellect and will are coordinate powers of a single rational soul. The full use of their rational powers will lead men to God.

Some version of this doctrine is also quite pervasive, especially within our culture at the present time. Its persistence is very probably related to the fact that it is based largely on faith, somewhat less on reason, and very little on observation. The first has been caricatured as an act in which "you believe something that you know ain't true." That is, those who subscribe to faith as a way of knowing may be asked to believe the Christian doctrine of man when belief in it may contradict common sense, or reason, or observation. Thus, for example, they may be asked to believe their God is omniscient, omnipresent, and omnipotent but still created man. It may seem strange to them that something which possesses those characteristics would find it necessary to create man, let alone the universe. Those who do find it strange may be asked to believe as a matter of faith that God possesses those characteristics and still engaged in that act of creation. In addition, or alternatively, they may be informed that God's works may often defy human comprehension or that, if they do not accept these matters on faith, they do not have the faith, and, therefore, may be in danger of losing their immortal souls. These may be only some of the more extreme, and less frequently used, arguments for keeping those with doubts within the fold or those with faith on the straight and narrow path of Christianity. But, regardless of these considerations, the Christian doctrine of man may be said to assert that man is divine or at least that he is in part divine, and that is the nature of human nature.

Examination of this fifth doctrine completes the review of the "classic" doctrines of man presented by Macleod. There are others. For example, when Macleod discusses human nature more directly, he (1975, pp. 146–155) mentions views of human nature expressed by Thomas Hobbes (1588–1679), Jean Jacques Rousseau (1712–1778), Adam Smith (1723–1790), and Thomas Jefferson (1743–1826). Similarly, Leslie Stevenson (1974) summarizes seven theories of human nature but includes in his analysis, aside from the Platonic and Christian theories, those of Karl Marx, Sigmund Freud, Jean-Paul Sarte, B. F. Skinner, and Konrad Lorenz. It seems evident that an entire book might be devoted to the answers notable figures in the history of ideas have given to this question. Since this book is concerned with the question of human nature as only one among many other questions of a particular kind, the discussion of it here will terminate with what could be the current consensus from a behavioral perspective in psychology.

A behavioral perspective on the nature of man or human nature must make at least some reference to B. F. Skinner since it is he who for so many years has been recognized as the leading exponent of behavioral psychology. According to Stevenson (1974, p. 94), Skinner contends that "only science can tell us the truth about nature, including human nature." Furthermore, "the scientist tries to find uniformities or lawful relations between phenomena, and to construct general theories which will successfully explain all particular cases." Thus, Stevenson (1974, p. 95) concludes that Skinner would arrive at a true theory of human nature through the empirical study of human behavior, and he surmises that Skinner's view of human nature is that we are "organisms whose behavior has identifiable and manipulable causes" (Stevenson, 1974, p. 104); another way of putting it might be that we are organisms whose behavior is lawful.

Skinner himself seems to address the question of human nature directly in a chapter entitled "What Is Man?" which can be found in *Beyond Freedom and Dignity* (1971). In that chapter, he opposes another prevalent view of human nature, namely, that man is autonomous or self-governing. He does so by considering some examples of the way "in which the environment takes over the function and role of autonomous man":

> The first, often said to involve human nature, is *aggression.* Men often act in such a way that they harm others, and they often seem to be reinforced by signs of damage to others. The ethologists have emphasized contingencies of survival which would contribute these features to the genetic endowment of the species, but the contingencies of reinforcement in the lifetime of the individual

> are also significant, since anyone who acts aggressively to harm others is likely to be reinforced in other ways—for example, by taking possession of goods. The contingencies explain the behavior quite apart from any state or feeling of aggression or any initiating act by autonomous man. [Skinner, 1971, pp. 185–86]

Thus, it is not our autonomy that explains what we do but the variables of which our behavior is a function; it also may be that they explain what we are.

To the casual observer, it may appear that most beginning and advanced students of psychology acknowledge the validity of Charles Darwin's theory of evolution; intellectually, they seem to think it's true. As is well known, his theory asserted that living organisms have changed from one form to another through a process of chance variation and natural selection. Each animal and plant species exhibits slight differences in structure among its members, and some of these variations make it more likely that some members of those species will adapt to the environmental circumstances in which they find themselves; others may not. The circumstances to which they adapt are contingencies of survival. Those that adapt to them pass on their variations in structure to the next generation. The result is that species change as environmental circumstances change; if not, they eventually become extinct.

The theory was applied to humans as well as to animals and plants. Thus, humans were treated as no different than animals in the sense that they were a species that had evolved like any other species and were like animals in other respects as well. In somewhat different terms, the theory proposed that man was an animal.

A good many people balked at that assertion, and there are a good many students of psychology at the present time who do likewise. That is, while most people accept the validity of Darwin's theory, a good many of them, including many students of psychology, do not agree that man is an animal, or, alternatively, they may not agree that man is merely an animal. Rather, they seem to feel that men, or human beings, are somehow different than animals. In other words, human beings are special animals, if they are animals, and perhaps are even the result of a divine creation; we human beings may always have had a rather elevated opinion of ourselves and may sometimes have had to work very hard to preserve it.

The research orientation of contemporary behavioral psychology seems to agree with the proposition that man is an animal. However, as with other animals, that research has shown that human beings exhibit what has come to be called learning. They learn in the sense that they adapt to environmental circumstances within the lifetime of an individual animal as well as the species. That is, contingencies of reinforcement affect them as well as contingencies of survival, and it may be this feature that eventually may distinguish human beings from the other animals. In other words, it may eventually be found that human beings learn more and faster than any of the other animals, which means that our behavioral repertoire is more complex than theirs. Furthermore, it may be this complexity that has misled us to think of ourselves as created by a divine act or as an animal that is somehow unusually different from all the rest.

Thus, to the extent that it is possible to know what the nature of human nature is, it might be concluded that man is an animal. Nevertheless, we are adaptable and therefore complex animals, and that is the nature of human nature or the "essence" of man from a behavioral perspective.

As with so many of the other questions examined in this book, however, an alternative interpretation of the nature of man from a behavioral perspective can be proposed; it is that we are known by our laws or the laws of our behavior. In other words, just as behavior is defined by its laws, the stimulus by its laws, learning and motivation by their laws, and emotion and instinct by theirs, so may the same be said of human nature. That is, the laws of human nature are what human nature is. Of course, until someone finds a way to measure it, psychology may be forced to substitute the laws of human behavior in place of those laws. When we do, we may then have something to say about human nature, if only in that rather circumscribed way.

Chapter Thirteen

Conclusion

The discussion of human nature concludes our examination of these problems. More remain. For example, many students of psychology and even some psychologists might still want to know the nature of normality, of personality, of self, of sensation, and possibly of perception, to name only a few; we might still want to know what they are. To the extent that we do, we can be said to be concerned with problems of metaphysics and psychology.

That statement is made because, as pointed out in the preface and the first chapter, the search for the nature of a thing, or the search for the essence of a thing, or the search for what it is may assume that (1) there is a thing, (2) it has an essence, and (3) its essence can be known. The first assumption is ontological; ontology has to do with what there is. The third assumption is epistemological; epistemology has to do with how we know what there is. Ontology and epistemology are what constitute metaphysics for many of those who currently profess philosophy.

The second assumption is essentialistic and may be inseparable from the first since to assume there is a thing may also assume it has an essence, an essential nature, or essential characteristics. Essentialism is the search for essences. According to Popper, it has its origins in the works of Plato and Aristotle. Whether it does or does not seems not to preclude the tendency for people to search for essences. While no experimental evidence has been provided in support of the assertion that they search for essence, people nevertheless seem to seek the essences of things, as suggested by casual observation and by more than casual acquaintance with students of psychology, including psychologists. What we may sometimes fail to acknowledge is that, even if we knew the essence of a thing, we probably wouldn't know that we knew it; human knowledge seems never to be complete. Despite that consideration, we still ask about the nature of things, and some possible answers to questions about the nature of things in psychology have been presented here. They have been offered with the full recognition that many, if not all, of these questions might very well be unanswerable.

The first question was about the nature of psychology, and, apparently, the various systems of psychology provided different answers to it. Currently the most influential system of psychology seems to be behaviorism, and behaviorists define psychology as the science of behavior. Therefore, the first conclusion might be that the answer to the question "What is Psychology?" is that psychology is the science of behavior.

However, all of the systems of psychology emphasized observation of internal or mental events, adaptive acts, gestalts, or behavior and, to that extent, they are phenomenal; the same may be true for the other sciences as well. They are phenomenal in the sense that the basis for knowing is considered to be empirical or observational; knowing is thought to be based on sense experience. In that regard, they are phenomenal in the ontological tradition of David Hume. Thus, an argument might be developed in support of the position that the subject matter for all of the sciences, but especially psychology, is phenomena interpreted as occurrences of sense experience.

System building in psychology is no longer in vogue. It may have been abandoned when it was found to be unfruitful. However, what was either fruitful or unfruitful in one era may be the opposite in another. The systematic extension of phenomenalism as a comprehensive and integrated view of psychology might, in this era, lead to theoretical and experimental insights which might otherwise not occur or else be long delayed.

A similar remark was made in a previous work (cf. Eacker, 1975, p. 32). That work was reviewed by Hendrich (1976, p. 704); his review was entitled "An Owlet of Minerva Visits Psychology." In that review he stated that the next time around he "would like to see the full-grown owl." While these efforts are probably another owlet, the next ones may be an owl in the form of phenomenalism as a system of psychology; it seems to be the next halting step to be taken in the exploration of these philosophical aspects of psychology.

The behaviorists claimed that psychology was the science of behavior, and, of course, that claim followed from the system of psychology known as behaviorism. Behaviorism was at one time thought of as a philosophy of science for psychology, but it seems to have expired in the sense that no one any longer seriously defends it. It may not need to be defended because from its ashes there appears to have emerged a science of behavior. Therefore, if psychology is the science of behavior, and if behaviorism has become the science of behavior, then the answer to the question "What is Behaviorism?" is that behaviorism is psychology.

That logic may not be impeccable, and the conclusion, if not just circular, may be trivial. Nevertheless, it seems to follow from the material examined in the chapters on the nature of psychology and behaviorism. However, most psychologists and students of psychology probably would not accept that conclusion no matter how faultless the logic; it may be another instance in the history of ideas of a conclusion arrived at by one means that is known by another means to be in error (cf. Eacker, 1975, p. 168).

Those who would reject that conclusion very likely would argue that psychology is either larger or wider than the behaviorist's view of it. And, while their conclusion may be true, they may not have a more acceptable alternative than the one advanced above. Furthermore, it also may be true that behavior has never been the subject matter of psychology, despite our assertions to the contrary, especially when the immediately preceding suggestion that phenomenalism might be developed as a system of psychology is taken into consideration.

In the evolution of the discipline, psychologists may have felt they were studying mental events, adaptive acts, gestalts, and/or behavior, when in fact they were not. The subject matter may in fact have been their phenomenal experience. The phenomena were occurrences in their experience, perhaps their sense experience, and they constructed these occurrences as mental events, adaptive acts, gestalts, and/or behavior. That conclusion may seem not only a bit strange but also a bit strained. However, it too appears to follow from prior considerations, especially if the ontological position of phenomenalism is taken seriously.

As pointed out elsewhere (cf. Eacker, 1975, pp. 167–68), one of the major defects in the ontology of phenomenalism is solipsism, which otherwise is known as the egocentric predicament. It appears to be a logical defect and may be stated somewhat as follows. If sense experience is what there is and if one can only know one's own sense experience, then objective knowledge is impossible since objective knowledge must be based on the sense experience of many people. In other words, if phenomenalism is true, then knowing anything beyond one's own skin is impossible.

However, we seem to have knowledge beyond our own skin, and so there may be something amiss with the ontology of phenomenalism, the argument, the logic used to formulate the argument, or our conception of knowledge.

It certainly appears to be indisputable that we cannot know the sense experience of someone else; we can only know our own. Similarly, if we only know our own sense experience, knowledge beyond it seems to be impossible; we can only know what we ourselves sense. Despite these considerations, the ontological position of phenomenalism still may be true. We learned long ago that logic, or reason, is not alone sufficient for helping us to solve our problems; many of us almost immediately distrust what appears to be indubitable. Reason may lead us to conclusions which we know by other means to be incorrect; examples are the antinomies of Kant and Zeno's paradox (cf. Eacker, 1975, p. 168).

There may not be anything amiss with the ontology of phenomenalism, the solipsistic argument, or the logic used to develop it. Rather, there may be something amiss with our conception of knowledge. In other words, and contrary to what the philosophers and common sense may have led us to believe, we may not know through our senses. Knowing may be a matter of learning, and what we know about learning are the laws of learning (cf. Eacker, 1975, pp. 129–39). We learn and that is how we know; we don't know through our senses. All our senses do is provide us with phenomenal experiences, or occurrences, to which we respond; they may not transmit anything from our environments, in the form of information, into our heads. The traditional and common sense notion of how we know may be incorrect, despite the fact that "everyone knows" how we know. This point of view requires further development but cannot be pursued in a systematic way at this time; where it leads is unclear. However, additional references to it will be made later in this chapter.

If psychology is the science of behavior, and if behaviorism has become that science, the next question to arise is, "What is Science?" The current consensus seems to be that science is what happens when we use the epistemology of science, where an epistemology, as stated earlier, is a theory of knowledge. The epistemology of science seems to be its methodology, although no one is at all certain what that is. Its "essence" seems to be that, at some point, the conjectures or speculations of a scientist are tested under controlled conditions of observation, which may distinguish science from other disciplines, such as the arts and the humanities.

On the other hand, a somewhat different conclusion than that presented in the chapter on the nature of science is that it may be simply a matter of learning and, more specifically, operant conditioning. In other words, if we learn and that is how we know, then scientists and the rest of us spend our lives in operant conditioning units. We behave, and our behavior sometimes has consequences. Some of our behaviors are reinforcing; others may be punishing. Those behaviors that are reinforced persist, and those that are not, extinguish. Since most of what passes for science is verbal, or at least symbolic, behavior, what persists takes that form in the books and the journals of a science.

These reflections, or ruminations, suggest a way in which the sciences might be unified that is somewhat different from the reductionism of Otto Neurath (cf. Joergensen, 1951, pp. 76–83). He proposed to unify the sciences through the physicalistic, or "thing," language of science. Apparently, he would have reduced all of the sciences to physics, or at least to the language of physics. An alternative might be to unify them with the ontology of phenomenalism and, perhaps, with some principles of operant conditioning.

Thus, all of the sciences might be thought of as phenomenal; their basic given is sense experience rather than a real world, as in the ontology of realism. The reactions of scientists to these givens appear to have consequences, phenomenal consequences, which in turn affect how the science develops, at least for individual scientists.

The unification of science may have been a hope of the logical empiricists that extinguished rather quickly. After all, there need not necessarily be anything about the sciences that unifies them except, perhaps, their epistemology. It is conceivable that the application of that epistemology might result in sciences that are quite different from one another but whose laws are nevertheless compatible. On the other hand, if the consequences of our actions shape our verbal behaviors in predictable, or lawful, ways, the laws that emerge expressed in the form of verbal statements may be consistent with, but not reducible to, one another, regardless of the sciences from which the laws may come.

It has been suggested on several occasions throughout this book that the language and concepts of physics may not be appropriate in psychology. The first was related to the concept of determinism. Determinism in physics is mechanistic; some things affect other things in the form of cause and effect. Determinism in psychology seems to have become empirical; behavior is determined in the sense that it is lawful. Mechanistic determinism in psychology may have misled us to suppose that psychology can be a science like physics when, in fact, psychology is a science that is not at all like physics. More will be said about this subject later in this chapter.

Some understanding of the nature of science may next lead to inquiry about the nature of behavior, especially if psychology is defined as the science of behavior. The answer to the question "What is Behavior?" seems to be, on the surface, that behavior is a dependent variable. However, it is not simply a dependent variable. Measures of behavior that do not enter into lawful relationships with other variables may not be dependent variables at all; they don't vary with anything. It is only when they do that we have some assurance that we have measured something. Therefore, the laws of behavior are what we know about it, and they may be what behavior is.

This answer, or one like it, is given many times to other questions throughout this book. As a result, it too is in danger of being trivial. Trivial questions may give rise to trivial answers. However, until we have tried to answer them, we may not know that they are trivial. If the answers are trivial, the fault may be the question, as suggested in the preface. Nevertheless, we do seem to ask these questions, and we seem to expect answers. It is only when we try to answer them that we find out whether we can refer to them as trivial. Until we do, we may not know. Consequently, there may be some redeeming value in our efforts to answer them, aside from the intellectual exercise.

Another instance where the language and concepts of physics may not be appropriate in psychology is related to the physicalistic treatment of behavior. The word *behavior* seems to be a perfectly good noun. Most of us have come to expect nouns to refer to persons, places, or things. However, when we inquire what person, place, or thing the word *behavior* refers to, we are at a loss for an answer. According to a good many behaviorists, who apparently have adopted the ontology of realism, behavior is what organisms do. But a "doing" does not seem to be a person, place, or thing. Consequently, a physical language may lead us to suppose that behavior and therefore psychology are physicalistic when, in fact, they are not. This point may be another argument against Neurath's efforts to unify science in the way he proposed; it may also be an argument against the ontology of realism.

A third instance where the language of physics may mislead us or be inappropriate in psychology is related to our tendency to physiologize behavior. Many students of psychology and a good many psychologists assume that physiology explains behavior rather than that behavior is explained by its variables or its laws. That is, they contend that a mechanism, a thing, underlies behavior and explains it, and the only mechanical thing around that might possibly be used for that purpose is physiology; therefore, physiology must explain behavior. What explains physiology is either ignored or left to that science (cf. Skinner, 1950). Physiology may include variables of which behavior is a function, but it is not, in itself, an explanation of behavior.

The subject of explanation has surfaced again and again throughout these pages and has been dealt with in some detail elsewhere (cf. Eacker, 1975, pp. 41–54). The view of explanation adopted here has been the functional, or empirical, type of explanation, in which behaviors, events, or phenomena are explained by their laws or by the variables of which they are a function. It seems to be the only defensible view of explanation for any of the sciences, but, of course, there are those who do not agree. Nevertheless, whenever a scientist is asked to explain something, whether falling bodies or increases in response rates, some reference is made somewhere to a scientific law.

A modicum of persistence in this type of inquiry might next lead to the question "What is a Stimulus?" especially if it is assumed that stimuli are what cause behavior. The problem of causality already has received extensive discussion (cf. Eacker, 1975, pp. 55–63) and so will not be dealt with in detail at this time. It may suffice for present purposes simply to assert that no one is entirely clear about whether causality operates in the universe or whether it is merely another way in which we structure, or construct, our observations. Nevertheless, we conceptualize events in that way and so may be led to suppose that for every response, or reaction, there is a stimulus.

This way of conceptualizing events may be another, a fourth, instance where the uncritical extrapolation of physical principles is inappropriate in psychology. Aside from the principle of causality, a second principle that might be involved is Newton's third law of motion, which states that for every action there is a reaction. The concept of force is contained within it, as is apparent when the principle is restated: for every force exerted by one object on another, there is an equal and opposite force exerted by the other. When extended to psychology, the principle also suggests that for every response there is a stimulus.

However, there may not be either a response for every stimulus or a stimulus for every response. Some responses may simply occur and have consequences, but both principles would lead us to look for antecedents in the form of stimuli and to continue to look until we had found them. Behavior, which is sometimes equated with response, may not occur in that way at all. It may simply occur in predictable ways without being caused; the word response may also mislead us into thinking that it is a reaction to something.

If a stimulus causes, elicits, evokes, impels, produces, or provokes a response, it somehow makes the response take place or occur. How it does so may not be immediately apparent except, perhaps, by invoking the concept of force. After all, forces are presumed to make objects move; therefore, forces in the form of stimuli make responses occur. Whether they do or don't is indeterminate since forces themselves apparently are not observable. The use of the concept in this way may be a fifth instance in which physical principles are inappropriately applied in psychology.

A sixth instance may be that related to the meaning of stimuli. A meaningful stimulus is assumed by many people to convey something in the form of information from itself to a recipient. The physical analogy here is one in which an object must be picked up and moved from one place to another for it to get from one place to another. The analogy may not, in fact, accurately represent how it happens that stimuli are meaningful. They may be meaningful simply because some sort of response has been established to them, even though they convey no information at all; this malapropism may occur again in the case of learning.

Along with others, these considerations with respect to the stimulus suggest that, like the answer given for behavior, the answer to the question "What is a Stimulus?" is that a stimulus is an independent variable. Not all independent variables are stimuli. Behavior is not an independent variable; it is a dependent variable. Something treated as an independent variable in psychology which does not enter into some sort of lawful, or functional, relationship with other, especially dependent, variables cannot be thought of as a variable; it doesn't vary with anything. Therefore, as with behavior, a stimulus may be defined by its laws, and that is what a stimulus is.

For a good many people, including psychologists, stimuli and responses become associated or connected. If they do so, or seem to do so, it may be taken as the simplest instance of learning. Consequently, the next question to arise, after a discussion of behavior and the stimulus, appears to be the question of learning.

It also may be supposed that, when we learn, something like information is transferred or transported from our environments into our heads on the analogy with the transportation of physical objects; this supposition may be another, the seventh, malapropism in psychology. However, information like force is not observable; no one has ever seen, heard, touched, tasted, or smelled information. For example, there are those who might contend that the prior sentence contains information. If they do, they may be at a loss to say what it is apart from the words in the sentence. Information is an inference; it does not appear to be a thing. As an inference, it may be an invention, like the little green man in the corner who disappears whenever we look in his direction. Hence, information may not adequately explain learning, especially on the analogy with physical objects.

Another supposition is that learning is something we do at a level different than at the level of behavior but which, nevertheless, accounts for changes in behavior; it is presumed to take place in our heads. However, what it is that takes place in our heads is not immediately evident, except that whatever changes occur there must account for whatever changes occur in our behavior. The concept of learning may here be used in an explanatory way, but it may not, in fact, explain; it may only name, as in the nominal fallacy.

Learning also may be considered a process the products of which are carried around in our heads much like yo-yo's might be produced on an assembly line and transported to the consumer on trucks or railroad cars; this analogy may be an eighth misapplication of physical principles in psychology. A ninth may be the use of the term *state* with respect to behavior on the analogy with states of the universe, as in "steady state." This analogy may lead us to think that behavior has states of being, when the very most we can say for it is that it is what organisms do; it may not exhibit states of being.

Considerations such as these suggest that learning, if it isn't simply a matter of behavioral acquisition, is also defined by its laws. The laws of learning are what we know about learning, and so they are what it is. Therefore, the answer to the question "What is Learning?" is that learning is defined by its laws; the laws of learning are what learning is. As with the other questions answered in this way, we have yet to find out what all of those laws are, and we will probably never know when the task has been completed.

Except in this case, discussions of learning usually mention reinforcement, and so the question of reinforcement seems naturally to follow that of learning. A number of answers have been given to this question, none of which, predictably, is definitive; the predictability may be a function of the task. However, this particular situation may arise whenever a "Why?" question is asked, and some of us might be expected to know better than to ask or to answer "Why?" questions by this time. Nevertheless, we do ask and at least attempt to answer them, and the result in the case of reinforcement is about a dozen different theories. We might have been better off if we simply had said "it's the nature of the beast" for a reinforcer to be reinforcing and then gone on to something else. But we might not have reached that conclusion without the inquiry, which again may attest to the value of our efforts to answer unanswerable questions.

Examination of the reinforcement question reveals still another instance where the use of a physical language may be inappropriate in psychology—the tenth. Like the word *behavior,* the word *reinforcement* is a perfectly good noun, which implies that it is a thing; even the word *it* implies that reinforcement is a thing. Consequently, many of us may be led to suppose there is a thing that is reinforcement to which the word *reinforcement* refers. That is, we may reify it, along with psychology, behaviorism, science, behavior, stimuli, learning, motivation, emotion, instinct, and human nature, as we reify gravity, force, and little green men. To reify a concept is to give it a name and then to treat the name as referring to a thing; reification may be what leads us to assume that there are universals and to seek their essences. Reinforcement may not be a thing but a relationship between observables, such as gravity and force; little green men may be a different matter.

This suggestion provides an opportunity to present the major thesis for this book in a somewhat different way than it was presented in the introduction. As developed there, questions about the nature of a thing seem to assume (1) there is a thing, (2) it has an essence, and (3) its essence can be known. All three of these assumptions can be thought of as metaphysical, and changes in any one or all three might enable us to view old problems in new ways.

For example, if we no longer assume there are things beyond our sense experience, or at least that we can't know there are with any certainty, we might relinquish the notion that we discover laws of behavior, phenomena of learning and motivation, emotions, and instincts; we might also stop treating as things, things that are not things. Instead, we might frankly recognize that the task for all of the sciences is to describe whatever orderliness we can observe in our sense experience without assuming that it is necessarily there before we begin observing. Nevertheless, we might still be able to grant that the observed orderliness is useful in helping us to solve human problems.

Similarly, if we no longer assume that things have essences, we might stop looking for them. Instead, we might focus on how things function rather than on what they are, as in the methodological nominalist's, rather than essentialist's, view of science. This change in the commonly accepted view of science would bring it up to date or make it more contemporary. The result might be a more accurate sense of what science can do.

Finally, if we no longer assume that we know things by means of the epistemology or methodology of science, we might have something more substantial to say about how it is that we know. The current view that we know by means of that methodology is not based on empirical evidence; if it were, it would beg the question of methodology by assuming what it was trying to prove. An alternative is that how we know is a matter of learning, and the laws and principles of learning are what we have to say about it; they are what we have learned about learning from an experimental analysis of behavior.

That analysis also seems to provide an answer to the question "What is Reinforcement?" The answer is that a reinforcer is reinforcing because an organism has been deprived of something it normally works to obtain or it has been presented with something it normally works to eliminate. And the answer to why reinforcers do that is—"Because." Those operations and how they affect behavior are what reinforcement is. Once again, the laws of a subject seem to define it or tell us what it is.

The operations that make reinforcers reinforcing are sometimes thought of as motivational, and so the next topic of inquiry seems to be the nature of motivation. The question reveals another, the eleventh, instance where either the laws or the principles of physics may be inappropriately used in psychology. In this case, the principle is once again Newton's third law of motion, especially as it has to do with the concept of force.

Many of us may uncritically assume that it is forces which make both animate and inanimate objects move. Hence, the question to be answered by motivation in psychology is about the forces that make organisms do what they do, as in drive theory. However, while that assumption may appeal to common sense, it may lead to a search for impulses, instincts, needs, motives, and drives which are no more observable than the concept of force and, in any case, are presumed to be inside the organism. Since we know less about what goes on inside an organism than outside, concepts related to force may be a hindrance rather than a help in the explanation of behavior. They may allow us to give answers to questions when, for lack of sufficient evidence, we are not yet ready to give them. Premature answers also may stifle further research or remove us too far from our data because of the concepts with which they are formulated.

A twelfth inappropriate use in psychology of concepts from other sciences is related to the theory of evolution in biology. A good many of us may suppose that behavior is explained by evolution. That is, when a question is raised about how it happens that an organism exhibits a certain behavior, any behavior, there is a rather strong temptation to reply that it exhibits that behavior because, in the past, that behavior has had survival value; it has allowed the animal to survive.

If that answer is not greeted with "Oh!" the next question in the sequence may be more difficult to answer. The next one is how it happens that a particular organism is exhibiting a particular behavior at a particular point in time and, of course, some general reference to evolution is not likely to be an answer. Laws of behavior are required to answer questions about behavior, and none are contained within the theory of evolution. Consequently, it is not appropriate to use the theory as a behavioral explanation.

With respect to the question "What is Motivation?" the answer may once again be, its laws; the laws of motivation are what motivation is. That answer may be especially cogent if motivation has to do with performance, and performance is the major item of interest in why organisms behave as they do. Performance questions about behavior, or how it happens that particular behaviors are performed on particular occasions, seem to be answerable only when we know the variables related to them, the variables of which they are a function, or their laws. Therefore, if there is an answer to this question, it appears that the laws of motivation are what motivation is.

Like learning and motivation, motivation and emotion frequently are mentioned in the same context, and so the next topic for discussion seems to be the nature of emotion. In addition, like learning and motivation, emotion also has been used to explain what we do rather than simply to describe it. Most of us are rather well acquainted with statements offered as explanations of behavior: "he did that because he learned to do it" or "she did that because she was motivated to do it" or "they did that because they felt like it" or "we do some of the things we do because of instinct."

In all such instances, the words are used to explain, when they may only name or give reasons for behavior, as in traditional rationalism (cf. Eacker, 1975, pp. 43–45). It may be amply evident by this time that naming a behavior does not explain it. Similarly, giving reasons may have only the appearance of an explanation since it is not always clear whose, or which, reasons are the correct ones. Consequently, learning, motivation, emotion, and instinct are suspect as explanations of behavior. When examined closely, they do not make reference to behavioral laws and so are pseudo-explanations, if that word even can be applied to them.

They can be used as descriptions of behavior, although there is always the danger that descriptions will become explanations or will seem like explanations (cf. Staats and Staats, 1963, pp. 13–16). As descriptions, they might simply refer to different types of behaviors or, at least, to different kinds of behavioral research. Thus, as a description, learning might refer to research concerned with behavioral acquisition. Motivation might refer to research about performance of behavior. Instinct might refer to research on, for example, the web building of spiders and the migration of salmon. When used in that way, these words could not then be offered as explanations of the behavior they describe; if all that is meant by an instinct is the web building of spiders, the word *instinct* could not then be used as an explanation of that behavior. The history of these topics in psychology suggests that we have not always been clear about this distinction; it is an important one, and students of the subject might be well advised to heed it. Learning, motivation, emotion, and instinct may be useful as descriptions but obfuscating as explanations of behavior.

They do not explain behavior. If anything, they are behaviors to be explained. For the purposes of a science of behavior, they are to be explained by their laws, and that, perhaps, is the clearest statement of how it happens that what they are has been answered so many times by making reference to their laws; their laws are what they are. Hence, the laws of emotion are what emotion is, and the same may be said for instinct.

The discussion of emotion uncovers a thirteenth instance of a malapropism in psychology. It occurs when emotions are treated as things analagous to colors which combine in different ways to give either various shades or various kinds of emotions. A corollary to this treatment of emotions is to consider them forces and, therefore, causes of behavior which, in turn, supposedly explain behavior. A more fruitful approach may be simply to treat emotions as behaviors and to find the variables of which they are a function. Emotion does not explain; it is to be explained.

Some authors have suggested that emotion is not a thing but an invention, an inference, or a construction. This suggestion obviously is consistent with the ontology of phenomenalism, although it also may be consistent with that of realism. Nevertheless, it provides some evidence for the contention that we might tinker with some of our metaphysical assumptions in psychology and, by so doing, encounter some new ways of viewing old problems; the treatment of emotion as a construction is a step in that direction.

As with learning and motivation, as well as motivation and emotion, emotion is not likely to be discussed without some reference to instinct, and so the next item for consideration is the nature of instinct. Since what we claim to know about instinct are its laws, the laws of instinct may be all that we can say about what it is. Therefore, the answer to the question "What is Instinct?" is that the laws of instinct are what instinct is.

A fourteenth malapropism seems to occur in the case of instinct; it is very much like those that occur in the case of motivation and in the case of emotion. It equates instinct with force, as motivation and emotion are sometimes equated with that concept from physics. Thus, motivation, emotion, and instinct may take the form in our thinking of impulses, needs, motives, feelings, and drives, which in turn are presumed to make us do what we do or cause our behavior, as in mechanistic determinism. Earlier discussions have revealed that psychology seems to have moved from that conception of determinism to empirical determinism; the latter holds that behavior is determined but only in the sense that it is lawful. Hence, the treatment of motivation, emotion, and instinct as forces may mislead us to seek explanations of those behaviors other than in terms of their laws or the variables of which they might be a function.

Apparently, some of these malapropisms are what Ginsberg (1952) would refer to as fallacies of reasoning by analogy, as when information is treated like a thing which must be transported from one place to another on the analogy with physical objects which must be transported from one place to another. Others are what he might refer to as fallacies of reductionism, as when it is assumed that behavior can be explained only by means of physiology. Still others may be fallacies of misplaced concreteness, or reification, or essentialism, as when psychology, behaviorism, science, behavior, stimuli, learning, reinforcement, motivation, emotion, instinct, and human nature are treated like things, with essences, whose essences can be known.

There are many who might contend that, aside from the mind-body problem, the nature of human nature is the most important question for all of psychology to answer, and discussions of instinct frequently raise it. Consequently, the last question considered is the nature of human nature, and, once again, our only way of answering it may be by reciting the laws of human nature.

However, no one has yet demonstrated how to measure human nature as a dependent variable, and, as a result, none of its laws have been explicated, if there are any. Until that time comes, if it ever does, the laws of human behavior may have to serve in their stead. Therefore, the answer to the question "What is Human Nature?" is the laws of human behavior; the laws of human behavior are what human nature is.

A fifteenth inappropriate use of concepts from other sciences, especially physics, in psychology may be the assumption that psychology is a science like physics and, therefore, requires the use of physical principles for purposes of explanation. This assumption obviously is apparent in the materialistic doctrine of human nature where, since man is considered matter, he is to be explained by physical laws. However, the law of gravity does not appear to be particularly useful in explaining persistent bar-pressing behavior by a rat, whereas the law of reinforcement schedules does. Therefore, the materialistic assumption may be inappropriate in psychology.

The relativistic doctrine of man and the materialistic doctrine of man reflect the two ontological positions emphasized throughout this book. Furthermore, they lend additional support to the contention that either one of them is defensible in science. The ontological position of phenomenalism is supported by the relativistic doctrine in the statement that "man is the measure of all things." It seems incontestable that all we know is relative to ourselves; hence, our conception of what is real may be a construction. The ontological position of realism is supported by the materialistic doctrine in the statement that "man is a part of physical nature." It also seems incontestable that we are a part of nature, whatever it may be; regardless of what it is, we are a part of it. However, to be a part of nature may not mean that we are matter, and so the ontology of phenomenalism might be considered more seriously in psychology than has been the case so far. Realism has been tried; it might be time for a change.

More than a dozen instances have been identified in which it appears that either physical principles or the language of physics and the other sciences have been used, perhaps inappropriately, in psychology. They have been referred to as malapropisms. Purists might argue that the use of the term in that way is itself one of them. However, to the extent that Mrs. Malaprop used words badly, or inappropriately, to that extent does the word seem to fit. In the absence of behavioral laws and principles, it seems only natural for us to have assumed that the language, laws, and principles of physics and the other sciences might help us to explain ourselves to ourselves, especially our behavior. Now, however, laws and principles of behavior are beginning to be developed from an experimental analysis of behavior that are strikingly different than those of physics and the other sciences; indeed, those borrowed from the other sciences may interfere with that process because they come from sources other than psychological data. We may have reached that point in time where psychologists can, and must, give up physical principles.

Some psychologists have a lucite paperweight on their desks in which is embedded a bronze medallion with a likeness of Wilhelm Wundt and commemorating one hundred years of scientific psychology. The science we practiced for that length of time was based on a conception of science bequeathed to us by the older, more established, sciences. If we were less bound by those traditional conceptions, psychology might become a more exciting science than so far seems to have been the case. May the next hundred years of psychology allow us to develop a conception of science appropriate to our subject matter, whatever that may turn out to be, and regardless of what the other sciences tell us we must do in order to be one; there seems to be some doubt about what a science is.

Appendix

One of the major limitations of the deductive method is revealed by its use in science. Students in an elementary logic course ordinarily learn that there are two basic forms of valid deductive inference: modus ponens and modus tollens. Before they can be discussed, however, something must be said about the form of a logical statement.

A logical statement may take the form: If A, then C. In that form, A is the antecedent, and C is the consequent. Thus, in the statement, "If it snows, I can go skiing," the antecedent is "If it snows," and the consequent is "I can go skiing."

If the antecedent is affirmed, a conclusion from this statement is considered valid and is otherwise known as modus ponens; its validity can be established by means of what are known as truth tables, which need not concern us here. Thus, a logical argument and conclusion based on the above statement might be expressed in the following way on the perhaps arguable assumption that I am at least capable of skiing.

If it snows, I can go skiing.
It is snowing.
Therefore, I can go skiing.

Another argument and conclusion based on a similar kind of statement is modus tollens and is also considered valid on the perhaps arguable assumption that I am at least capable of playing tennis.

If the sun shines, I can play tennis.
I cannot play tennis.
Therefore, the sun is not shining.

This argument denies the consequent, which distinguishes it from modus ponens.

Arguments that deny the antecedent or that affirm the consequent are not considered valid; their validity cannot be established with truth tables. Thus, an argument that takes the following form is invalid.

If it snows, I can go skiing.
It is not snowing.
Therefore, I cannot go skiing.

Similarly, an argument that takes the following form is also considered invalid.

If the sun shines, I can play tennis.
I can play tennis.
Therefore, the sun is shining.

The first argument denies the antecedent, and the second argument affirms the consequent; both are invalid.

The last argument and conclusion are important for this discussion because affirming the consequent or denying the antecedent are also frequently referred to as fallacies, logical fallacies. At the same time, affirming the consequent seems to represent the basic procedure that is followed when a hypothesis is tested in science. That is, an investigator may begin his investigation with an assumption like that expressed in the antecedent, an implication of which is expressed in the consequent. An experiment might then be performed to test the implication, and, if it is confirmed, the investigator then asserts the antecedent to be, if not true, at least worth serious consideration.

An example of this sort of procedure in psychology might be: "If a change in illumination from dark to light is reinforcing, behavior that brings it about will increase in frequency." An experiment might then be performed (and has been) to test whether behavior that changes illumination from dark to light increases in frequency (it does). Therefore, the conclusion is (and was) that such changes are reinforcing. Apparently, such response-produced changes in illumination are still regarded as reinforcing at the present time, but that "fact" was arrived at by way of a logical fallacy. Under such circumstances, there are those who might be tempted to say, "so much the worse for logic." An alternative view is simply to recognize that rational methods and empirical methods do not always complement one another.

References

Adams, J. A. *Learning and memory: An introduction.* Homewood, Ill.: Dorsey Press, 1976.

Ayer, A. J. *Language, truth and logic.* New York: Dover, 1946.

Beach, F. A. The descent of instinct. *Psychological Review,* 1955, *62,* 401–410.

Bernard, L. L. *Instinct: A study in social psychology.* New York: Holt, 1924.

Bindra, D. B. *Motivation: A systematic reinterpretation.* New York: Ronald Press, 1959.

Bolles, R. C. *Theory of motivation* (2nd ed.). New York: Harper & Row, 1975.

Boring, E. G. *The physical dimensions of consciousness.* New York: Century, 1933.

Bridgman, P. W. *The logic of modern physics* (2nd. ed.). New York: Macmillan, 1932.

Brogden, W. J. Animal studies of learning. In S. S. Stevens (ed.), *Handbook of experimental psychology.* New York: Wiley, 1951.

Brown, J. S., and Farber, I. E. Emotions conceptualized as intervening variables with suggestions toward a theory of frustration. *Psychological Bulletin*, 1951, *48,* 465–495.

Bull, N. The attitude theory of emotion. *Nervous and Mental Disease,* 1951, *81.* (Monograph)

Chaplin, J. P., and Krawiec, T. S. *Systems and theories of psychology* (3rd ed.). New York: Holt, Rinehart, & Winston, 1974.

Darwin, C. *The origin of species by means of natural selection: Or the preservation of favored races in the struggle for life* (2 vols.). New York: Appleton, 1898.

Denny, M. R., and Ratner, S. C. *Comparative psychology: Research in animal behavior* (rev. ed.). Homewood, Ill.: Dorsey Press, 1970.

Dewey, J. *Experience and nature.* Chicago: Open Court, 1925.

Diamond, S. Gestation of the instinct doctrine. *Journal of the History of the Behavioral Sciences,* 1971, *4,* 323–336.

Dunlap, K. Are there any instincts? *Journal of Abnormal Psychology,* 1919, *14,* 35–50.

Eacker, J. N. *Problems of philosophy and psychology.* Chicago: Nelson-Hall, 1975.

Fantino, E. Emotion. In J. A. Nevin (ed.), *The study of behavior: Learning, motivation, emotion, and instinct.* Glenview, Ill.: Scott, Foresman, 1973.

Feyerabend, P. *Against method: Outline of an anarchistic theory of knowledge.* London: NLB, 1975.

Gibson, J. J. The concept of the stimulus in psychology. *American Psychologist,* 1960, *15,* 694–703.

Ginsberg, A. A reconstructive analysis of the concept "instinct." *Journal of Psychology,* 1952, *33,* 235–277.

Glaser, R. *The nature of reinforcement.* New York: Academic Press, 1971.

Guthrie, E. R. Association by contiguity. In S. Koch (ed.) *Psychology: A study of a science* (Vol. 2). New York: McGraw-Hill, 1959.

Guthrie, E. R. *The psychology of learning.* New York: Harper & Row, 1935.

Hall, J. F. *The psychology of learning.* New York: Lippincott, 1966.

Heidbreder, E. *Seven psychologies.* New York: Appleton-Century, 1933.

Hempl. C. *Aspects of scientific explanation and other essays in the philosophy of science.* New York: Free Press, 1965.

Hendrick, C. An owlet of Minerva visits psychology. *Contemporary Psychology,* 1976, *21,* 703–704.

Herrnstein, R. J. Nature as nature: Behaviorism and the instinct doctrine. *Behaviorism,* 1972, *21,* 23–52.

Hinde, R. A. *Animal behaviour: A synthesis of ethology and comparative psychology* (2nd. ed.). New York: McGraw-Hill, 1970.

Houston, J. P. *Fundamentals of learning.* New York: Academic Press, 1976.

Hull, C. L. *Principles of behavior: An introduction to behavior theory.* New York: Appleton-Century-Crofts, 1943.

Hume, D. *A treatise of human nature,* 1739.

James, W. *The principles of psychology* (2 vols.). New York: Dover, 1950.

James, W. *Essays in pragmatism.* New York: Hafner, 1948.

James, W. *The varieties of religious experience: A study in human nature.* London: Longmans Green, 1902.

James, W. What is emotion? *Mind,* 1884, *10,* 188–204.

Joergensen, J. *The development of logical empiricism.* Chicago: Univ. of Chicago Press, 1951.

Keller, F. S. *The definition of psychology* (2nd ed.). New York: Appleton-Century-Crofts, 1973.

Keller, F. S. *The definition of psychology: An introduction to psychological systems.* New York: Appleton-Century-Crofts, 1937.

Kimble, G. A. *Hilgard and Marquis' conditioning and learning.* New York: Appleton-Century-Crofts, 1961.

Koch, S. Psychology and emerging conceptions of psychology as unitary. In T. W. Wann (ed.), *Behaviorism and phenomenology: Contrasting bases for modern psychology.* Chicago: Univ. of Chicago Press, 1964.

Koch, S. Clark L. Hull. In W. K. Estes, et al. (eds.), *Modern learning theory: A critical analysis of five examples.* New York: Appleton-Century-Crofts, 1954.

Kuhn, T. S. *The structure of scientific revolutions* (2nd ed.). Chicago: Univ. of Chicago Press, 1970.

Kuhn, T. S. *The structure of scientific revolutions.* Chicago: Univ. of Chicago Press, 1962.

Kuo, Z. Y. Giving up instincts in psychology. *Journal of Philosophy,* 1921, *18,* 645–666.

Lashley, K. S. Experimental analysis of instinctive behavior. *Psychological Review,* 1938, *45,* 445–471.

Leeper, R. W. A motivational theory of emotion to replace "emotion as disorganized response." *Psychological Review,* 1948, *55,* 5–21.

Lewin, K. *Principles of topological psychology.* New York: McGraw-Hill, 1936.

Lewin, K. The conflict between Aristotelian and Galilean modes of thought in contemporary psychology. *Journal of General Psychology,* 1931, *5,* 141–177.

Lindsley, D. G. Emotion. In S. S. Stevens (ed.), *Handbook of experimental psychology.* New York: Wiley, 1951.

Littman, R. A. Motives, history and causes. In M. R. Jones (ed.), *Nebraska Symposium on Motivation.* Lincoln: Univ. of Nebraska Press, 1958.

Logan, F. *Incentive: How the conditions of reinforcement affect the performance of rats.* New Haven: Yale Univ. Press, 1960.

MacCorquodale, K., and Meehl, P. E. On a distinction between hypothetical constructs and intervening variables. *Psychological Review,* 1948, *55,* 95–107.

MacLeod, R. B. *The persistent problems of psychology.* Pittsburgh: Duquesne Univ. Press, 1975.

Madsen, K. B. *Theories of motivation: A comparative study of modern theories of motivation* (4th ed.). Kent, Ohio: Kent State Univ. Press, 1968.

Margenau, H. *The nature of physical reality.* New York: McGraw-Hill, 1950.

Marx, M. H. *Learning: Theories.* London: Macmillan, 1970.

Marx, M. H. *Learning: Processes.* London: Macmillan, 1969.

Marx, M. H., and Goodson, F. E. *Theories in contemporary psychology.* (2nd ed.). New York: Macmillan, 1976.

Marx, M. H., and Hillix, W. A. *Systems and theories in psychology.* (2nd ed.). New York: McGraw-Hill, 1973.

McDougall, W. *Outline of psychology.* New York: Charles Scribner's Sons, 1923.

McDougall, W. *An introduction to social psychology* (4th ed.). Boston: Luce, 1911.

Meyer, M. F. That whale among the fishes—the theory of emotions. *Psychological Review,* 1933, *40,* 292–300.

Miller, N. E. Some reflections on the law of effect produce a new alternative to drive theory. In M. R. Jones (ed.), *Nebraska Symposium on Motivation.* Lincoln: Univ. of Nebraska Press, 1963.

Miller, N. E., and Dollard, J. *Social learning and imitation.* New Haven: Yale Univ. Press, 1941.

Murray, H. A. *Explorations in personality: A clinical and experimental study of fifty men of college age.* New York: Oxford Univ. Press, 1938.

Nevin, J. A. Problems and methods. In J. A. Nevin (ed.), *The study of behavior: Learning, motivation, emotion, and instinct.* Glenview, Ill.: Scott, Foresman, 1973.

Peters, H. N. Affect and emotion. In M. H. Marx (ed.), *Theories in contemporary psychology.* New York: Macmillan, 1963.

Peters, R. S. *Brett's history of psychology.* Cambridge, Mass.: MIT Press, 1965.

Pitcher, G. *The philosophy of Wittgenstein.* Englewood Cliffs: Prentice-Hall, 1964.

Plutchik, R., *The emotions: Facts, theories and a new model.* New York: Random House, 1962.

Popper, K. R. *Conjectures and refutations: The growth of scientific knowledge* (2nd ed.). New York: Basic Books, 1965.

Popper, K. R. *Conjectures and refutations: The growth of scientific knowledge.* New York: Basic Books, 1963.

Popper, K. R. *The logic of scientific discovery.* New York: Basic Books, 1959.

Popper, K. R. *The poverty of historicism.* Boston: Beacon Press, 1957.

Popper, K. R. *The open society and its enemies* (Vol. 1). London: Routledge and Kegan Paul, 1952a.

Popper, K. R. *The open society and its enemies* (Vol. 2). London: Routledge and Kegan Paul, 1952b.

Rachlin, H. *Behavior and learning.* San Francisco: Freeman, 1976.

Reynolds, G. S. *A primer of operant conditioning* (rev. ed.). Glenview, Ill.: Scott, Foresman, 1975.

Robinson, D. N. *An intellectual history of psychology.* New York: Macmillan, 1976.

Ross, S., and Denenberg, V. H. Innate behavior: The organism in its environment. In R. H. Waters et al. (eds.), *Principles of Comparative Psychology.* New York: McGraw-Hill, 1960.

Shapere, D. Critique of the paradigm concept. In M. H. Marx and F. E. Goodson (eds.), *Theories in contemporary psychology* (2nd ed.). New York: Macmillan, 1976.

Sidman, M. *Tactics of scientific research: Evaluating experimental data in psychology.* New York: Basic Books, 1960.

Skinner, B. F. *Beyond freedom and dignity.* New York: Knopf, 1971.

Skinner, B. F. *Contingencies of reinforcement: A theoretical analysis.* New York: Appleton-Century-Crofts, 1969.

Skinner, B. F. The phylogeny and ontogeny of behavior. *Science*, 1966, *153*, 1205–1213.

Skinner, B. F. Behaviorism at fifty. *Science*, 1963, *140*, 951–58.

Skinner, B. F. *Cumulative record* (enl. ed.). New York: Appleton-Century-Crofts, 1961.

Skinner, B. F. The flight from the laboratory. In *Current Trends in Psychological Theory.* Pittsburgh: Univ. of Pittsburgh Press, 1961.

Skinner, B. F. *Science and human behavior.* New York: Free Press, 1953.

Skinner, B. F. Are theories of learning necessary? *Psychological Review*, 1950, *57*, 193–216.

Skinner, B. F. "Superstition" in the pigeon. *Journal of Experimental Psychology*, 1948, *38*, 168–172.

Skinner, B. F. *The behavior of organisms: An experimental analysis.* New York: Appleton-Century-Crofts, 1938.

Skinner, B. F. The concept of the reflex in the description of behavior. *Journal of General Psychology*, 1931, *5*, 427–458.

Smith, R. E., Sarason, I. G., and Sarason, B. R. *Psychology: The frontiers of behavior.* New York: Harper & Row, 1978.

Spence, K. W. *Behavior theory and conditioning.* New Haven: Yale Univ. Press, 1956.

Staats, A. W., and Staats, C. K. *Complex human behavior: A systematic extension of learning principles.* New York: Holt, Rinehart, & Winston, 1963.

Stevens, S. S. Operationism and logical positivism. In M. H. Marx and F. E. Goodson (eds.), *Theories in contemporary psychology* (2nd ed.). New York: Macmillan, 1976.

Stevens, S. S. Mathematics, measurement, and psychophysics. In S. S. Stevens (ed.), *Handbook of experimental psychology.* New York: Wiley, 1951.

Stevens, S. S. Psychology and the science of science. *Psychological Bulletin,* 1939, *36,* 221–263.

Stevenson, L. *Seven theories of human nature.* New York: Oxford Univ. Press, 1974.

Tapp, J. T. Current status and future directions. In J. T. Tapp (ed.) *Reinforcement and behavior.* New York: Academic Press, 1969.

Titchener, E. B. *Systematic psychology: Prolegomena.* New York: Macmillan, 1929.

Titchener, E. B. *A primer of psychology.* New York: Macmillan, 1898.

Tolman, E. C. *Purposive behavior in animals and men.* New York: Appleton-Century-Crofts, 1932.

Tolman, E. C. The nature of instinct. *Psychological Bulletin,* 1923, *20,* 200–218.

Tolman, E. C. A new formula for behaviorism. *Psychological Review,* 1922, *29,* 44–53.

Torgerson, W. S. *Theory and methods of scaling.* New York: Wiley, 1958.

Turner, M. B. *Philosophy and the science of behavior.* New York: Appleton-Century-Crofts, 1967.

Underwood, B. J. Stimulus selection in verbal learning. In C. N. Cofer and B. S. Musgrave (eds.), *Verbal behavior and learning.* New York: McGraw-Hill, 1963.

Verplanck, W. S. Since learned behavior is innate and vice versa, what now? *Psychological Review,* 1955, *62,* 139–144.

Verplanck, W. S. Burrhus F. Skinner. In W. K. Estes, et al. (eds.) *Modern learning theory: A critical analysis of five examples.* New York: Appleton-Century-Crofts, 1954.

Wann, T. W. *Behaviorism and phenomenology: Contrasting bases for modern psychology.* Chicago: Univ. of Chicago Press, 1964.

Waters, R. H. Behavior: Datum or abstraction. *American Psychologist,* 1958, *13,* 278–282.

Watson, J. B. *Behaviorism.* Chicago: Univ. of Chicago Press, 1930.

Watson, J. B. *Psychology: From the standpoint of a behaviorist* (3rd ed. rev.). Philadelphia: Lippincott, 1929.

Watson, J. B. Psychology as the behaviorist views it. *Psychological Review,* 1913, *20,* 158–177.

Wilcoxon, H. C. Historical introduction to the problem of reinforcement. In J. T. Tapp (ed.), *Reinforcement and Behavior.* New York: Academic Press, 1969.

Wittgenstein, L. *Philosophical investigations.* New York: Macmillan, 1953.

Index